Marriage and Parenting Boosters

Marriage and Parenting Boosters

Helps to Keep Families Safe and Strong

By
Frank R. Shivers

LIGHTNING SOURCE
1246 Heil Quaker Blvd.
La Vergne, TN

Unless otherwise noted, Scripture quotations are from
The Holy Bible *King James Version*

Library of Congress Cataloging-in-Publication Data

Shivers, Frank R., 1949-
Marriage and Parenting Boosters / Frank Shivers
ISBN 978-1-878127-25-9

Library of Congress Control Number:
2016907865

Cover design by
Tim King of Click Graphics, Inc.

For Information:
Frank Shivers Evangelistic Association
P. O. Box 9991
Columbia, South Carolina 29290
www.frankshivers.com

Presented to

_____

By

_____

Date

_____

"Except the LORD build the house, they labour in vain that build it."
—Psalm 127:1.

To

My daughter and son-in-law

Stephanie and Richard McLawhorn

And their three wonderful children

Madison Clark, Jude, and Hudson

Contents

Preface

The battle against traditional/biblical marriage and family is growing intensely more aggressive. This is evidenced by the legal and cultural acceptance of gay marriage, increase in divorce, cohabitation without marriage, abortion, the dysfunctional family, and parental neglect with regard to the moral and spiritual foundation in the rearing of their children.

Marriage and Parenting Boosters is written to combat these enemies of the home by providing biblically based helps on how to have a healthy, happy marriage and success in parenting.

Each entry includes a *marriage or parenting booster, Scripture texts to read together, questions to answer together* about the entry that will enhance your understanding and implementation of it, and a *prayer* which serves as a springboard for joint prayer together. It is designed for both husband and wife to read together daily for six months for maximum benefit. If, however, only one reads the book, it is so written that it will yet strengthen and enhance the marriage and help with parenting issues.

It is my sincerest prayer that our great and gracious God may use this volume to minister to the needs in your marriage and family so that they will ever be happy, harmonious, holy, and honoring unto Him both now and forevermore.

God created marriage. No government subcommittee envisioned it. No social organization developed it. Marriage was conceived and born in the mind of God.[1]—Max Lucado

As God by creation made two of one, so again by marriage He made one of two.[2]—Thomas Adam

The Puritan ethic of marriage was first to look not for a partner whom you do love passionately at this moment but rather for one whom you can love steadily as your best friend for life, then to proceed with God's help to do just that.[3]—J. I. Packer

When you have a godly husband, a godly wife, children who respect their parents and who are loved by their parents, who provide for those children their physical and spiritual and material needs, lovingly, you have the ideal unit.[4]—Jerry Falwell

Each day of our lives we make deposits in the memory banks of our children.[5]—Chuck Swindoll

The Christian family begins with a personal commitment to God. The starting place for *fixing* the family is fixing the inhabitants who live there. A Christian family begins and ends with each member's personal commitment to God.[6]—Tony Evans

1 Erect an Iron Gate about the Home

The psalmist states, "For he [God] hath strengthened the bars of thy gates; he hath blessed thy children within thee" (Psalm 147:13). Though this text refers historically to the walls and gates Nehemiah constructed, no harm is done to apply it to the home. As the "bars of thy gates" were built around Jerusalem by those under Nehemiah's leadership for their protection, so must both husband and wife under God's direction erect such walls about the home for security. Note that the text states upon completion of the task God "strengthened the bars of thy gate." It was not Nehemiah who strengthened them but God; He only was able to construct them as required.

Build the bars of the gates about the home with the lumber of prayer, the Word of God, worship (private and corporate), submission to God, and abstinence from things that defile and damage (alcohol, drugs, pornography, gambling, etc.), and God will so strengthen them that no enemy will be able to make entry.

Read Together:

He Reads: Psalm 127:1
She Reads: Isaiah 54:11–13

Answer Together:

Psalm 147:13–14 is a conditional promise of divine protection (v. 13a), happiness (v. 13b), peace (v. 14a), and provision (v. 14b). What is the condition you must meet to claim the promise? What practices or things do you need to keep out? Allow in?

Pray Together:

Lord, help us erect the strongest bars possible upon the gates about our home, and then supply Thy strength and power to make them impenetrable.

2
Pray for One Another

Gary Chapman said, "Perhaps if we did more praying for each other, we would have not only greater spiritual intimacy but less unresolved conflict in our marriages."[7]

"Our relationship to God," states David and Claudia Arp, "should foster marital closeness, and nothing brings us closer than praying together. Praying together is the highest tie binding a couple together, and yet it is rare."[8]

How can you get started? The foremost thing is to talk with each other about the possibility of doing it. Discuss objections, fears, concerns, etc., and the benefit to be gained by it. Once it is decided you will pray together, set guidelines such as no preaching to each other in the prayer, a time limit, and when and where it will be done. Third, establish who will be responsible for initiating the prayer time and be the first to pray.

Read Together:
He Reads: Ephesians 1:16–19
She Reads: Psalm 66:17–20

Answer Together:
What specific things might you pray for in behalf of your spouse? Talk about praying together. You might begin with one time a week and gradually do it more often as you both get more comfortable.

Pray Together:
Lord, forgive us for praying for the needs of others while neglecting to do the same for each other and with each other.

3
Time-Starved Marriage

"We'll never find more time," write Les and Leslie Parrot. "But we can 'make' more time. Time is made whenever we decide what matters most."[9]

Neglect of getting enough couple time hinders communication, bonding, increased fortification of the marriage, and the exhibition of love to our spouses that fills their tank with happiness, security and significance.

A great key to a wonderful and happy marriage is simply to make having time with your spouse a top priority (above work, entertainment, sports, television, etc.).

Read Together:
He Reads: Ephesians 5:16–18
She Reads: Ecclesiastes 3:1–8

Answer Together:
Is your spouse starving for more time with you? If unsure, ask. If he or she is, how might your schedule be lightened to afford more time for the one you love more than anything and anyone other than God?

Pray Together:
Forgive us, Lord, for allowing what we deem to be important to rob us from what is all-important—quality time together.

4

Cure for Troubled Marriages

"I challenge those," states Tony Campolo, "who come to me for marriage counseling this way: 'If you do what I tell you to do for an entire month, I can promise you that by the end of the month you will be in love with your mate. Are you willing to give it a try?' When couples accept my challenge, the results are invariably successful.

"My prescription for creating love is simple: do ten things each day that you would do if you really were in love. I know that if people do loving things, it will not be long before they experience the feelings that are often identified as being in love. Love is not those feelings. Love is what one wills to do to make the other person happy and fulfilled. Often we don't realize that what a person does influences what he feels."[10]

"The same Jesus," says Adrian Rogers, "who turned water into wine can transform your home, your life, your family, and your future. He is still in the miracle-working business, and His business is the business of transformation."[11]

Read Together:

He Reads: Ephesians 5:25–33
She Reads: Ephesians 5:22–23

Answer Together:

What are you doing for your mate daily that is a telltale sign of love? If your love for your mate has been smothered with stuff, follow Campolo's counsel—do ten things daily for her/him that you would do if madly in love with her/him.

Pray Together:

Help us, Lord, keep alive the love we have one for another by not taking it for granted but ever cultivating and enriching it through continuous acts of love.

5

Biblical Acceptance of Each Other

"Marriage is a process," writes Stephen Arterburn, "of accepting all that [your partner is and does]. This does not mean you should accept abusive, addictive or other destructive behaviors. Every day is an exercise in acceptance."[12]

Gary Thomas said, "Even if I've never met you, I know one thing that is true about you and your spouse: you're both married to an imperfect mate. I also know another truth about you: the Bible calls you to still respect and appreciate your very imperfect spouse. This is true whether you're a husband (1 Peter 3:7) or a wife (Ephesians 5:33)."[13]

Thomas continues, "Every one of us is married to an imperfect spouse. We confront different trials, different temptations, and different struggles—but each one of us faces the same reality: living as imperfect people, in an imperfect world, with an imperfect spouse. Learning to love, appreciate, and to be thankful for that imperfect spouse is one of the most soul-transforming things you can do."[14]

God accepts us as we are in Christ Jesus. "To the praise of the glory of his grace, wherein he hath made us accepted in the beloved" (Ephesians 1:6). Good News for imperfect husbands and wives!

Read Together:
He Reads: I Peter 3:7
She Reads: I Samuel 16:7

Answer Together:
In marriage, couples vow to accept each other's flaws, scars and all. But this isn't always easy. What "weaknesses," mannerisms or habits (not sinful) have you failed to accept in each other?

Pray Together:
Enable our love for each other to be of such proportion that we accept each other at face value, not what we might wish each other to be.

6

Parenting God's Way

John MacArthur states, "Parenting is hard only to the degree that parents *make* it hard by failing to follow the simple principles God sets forth. To neglect one's duty before God as a parent is to forfeit the blessing inherent in the task—and those who do so take on a burden God never intended parents to bear."[15]

MacArthur continues, "What we desperately need is a return to the biblical principles of parenting. Christian parents don't need new, shrink-wrapped programs; they need to apply and obey consistently the few simple principles that are clearly set forth for parents in God's Word, such as these: Constantly teach your kids the truth of God's Word (Deuteronomy 6:7). Discipline them when they do wrong (Proverbs 23:13–14). And don't provoke them to anger (Colossians 3:21).

"Those few select principles alone, if consistently applied, would have a far greater positive impact for the typical struggling parent than hours of discussion about whether babies should be given pacifiers or what age kids should be before they're permitted to choose their own clothes or dozens of similar issues that consume so much time in the typical parenting program."[16]

What Successful Parents have in common:
1. Encourage their children and bolster their self-esteem
2. Communicate their love to their children
3. Create a positive home environment that includes laughter

4. Nurture spiritual values
5. Show consistent, balanced discipline
6. Make their children proud of them
7. Create community—extended family, neighborhood and church
8. Give children the feeling that they are safe and emotionally secure
9. Model a good marriage
10. Take time to spend time with their children
11. Teach financial values and skills
12. Give children responsibility
13. Are passionate about teaching values and integrity[17]

Read Together:

He Reads: Ephesians 6:4
She Reads: Proverbs 22:6

Answer Together:

Is parenting a blessing or a burden? If a burden, turn it into a blessing by applying the principles of parenting set forth in the Bible.

Pray Together:

Lord, thank you for the blessing and joy in parenting. Help us experience both more fully by following your biblical blueprint for parenting.

7

Spiritual Development of Children

Twelve percent of youth have regular dialog with their mother on faith/life issues, while only five percent have such discussions with their father. Nine percent of youth have experienced regular reading of the Bible and devotions in the home.[18] We are rearing a generation of youth who know little of the Faith and who are clueless as to why they believe what they do.

Dawson McAlister states that ninety percent "of kids active in high school church youth groups do not go to church by the time they are sophomores in college."[19] Rigorous teaching and training in the faith of children as taught in Scripture must be practiced, or the church will lose multitudes more to the god of this age.

Read Together:
He Reads: Proverbs 1:8–9
She Reads: Deuteronomy 6:3–9

Answer Together:
How much time is being spent by you in the spiritual development of your child? What might you initiate in the home to move your child to a greater understanding of God and His Word?

Pray Together:
Heavenly Father, help us rear the child(ren) you have blessed us with not only in the physical and material dimension but also in the spiritual. Grant us grace to make their spiritual growth a priority.

8

Flexibility in Roles in Marriage

"There are necessary roles in marriage," states Frederick Mahan, "[that] vary with the circumstances. Each spouse must be receptive to [change]. Marriages fail because individuals neglect to assume necessary and reasonable roles."[20]

Every culture has its unwritten rules governing marriage roles. Whenever one partner cleaves to the *norm* and the other rebels against it, problems arise. Both partners must realize that marriage roles are not to be dictated by tradition or culture but by the Word of God.

Flexibility (ability to be adaptable) with my spouse means that we are in this thing together, and although there are specific roles unalterably assigned in Scripture to the husband and the wife, the rest are negotiable ("I will do the dishes tonight, you tomorrow night." "I will get up with the baby tonight, you tomorrow night."). Flexibility in roles is especially essential if both work.

Read Together:
He Reads: Colossians 3:19
She Reads: Colossians 3:18

Answer Together:
What role(s) are you expected to play that you count unreasonable? Are you open to roles that may not be comfortable but are

necessary for the betterment of the marriage and family? What might be some of these roles?

Pray Together:

Lord, help us do whatever is necessary for the enrichment of our marriage and family without complaining or nagging.

9

Marital Grace

"Love is a deep unity," states C. S. Lewis in *Mere Christianity,* "reinforced [in Christian marriages] by the grace which both partners ask and receive from God."

Grace [*charis*] is the spiritual favor or blessing of God upon man freely bestowed not only with regard to salvation but also to manifold issues, including marriage. Out of the fullness of Christ Jesus we have and continue to have 'grace upon grace' (John 1:16). No matter how awesome, grand or superlative you think God's grace to be, it yet is that much greater. James underscores my point in saying, "He gives a greater grace" (James 4:6 NASB).

Chuck Swindoll said, "The more the grace of God is awakened in a marriage, the less husbands will attempt to control and restrict, and the less wives will feel the need to 'please no matter what.' It makes marriage easier to manage. Grace releases and affirms. It doesn't smother. Grace values the dignity of individuals. It doesn't destroy. Grace supports and encourages. It isn't jealous or suspicious."[21]

So ask God for added grace not to be jealous, domineering and judgmental (and/or something else) toward your spouse but patient, kind, understanding, and more loving. He is able and willing to give more grace to enable you to be a better spouse.

Read Together:

He Reads: Ephesians 2:3–7
She Reads: 1 John 3:1–3

Answer Together:

What is the grace to which Lewis refers? What is its source? What do you need special grace for with regard to your partner?

Pray Together:

Lord, grant us fresh grace to love and forgive each other in the same manner in which you love and forgive us. Supply grace equal to the need we have with regard to being all we should be to each other.

10

Is Your Child's Desertion from God Your Fault?

Despite what is commonly believed, the Hebrew text (Proverbs 22:6) does not state that God guarantees children reared in a Christian home will remain in the Faith or if they err from it, return back to the Faith when they are older. An obvious reason why God made no such promise is due to man's free will to decide to follow or not follow Him. Outside parental religious training which influences a child's choice are his companions, teachers and worldly appetites (which may allure him away from God). Parents who rear their children in the Faith must not feel guilty if they abandon it. Steering a child spiritually in the way he should go through prayer, worship, biblical instruction, and example certainly raises the likelihood of (but does not guarantee) his continuance in it or return to it should he falter.

Read Together:

He Reads: Proverbs 22:6

She Reads: Proverbs 1:8–16

Answer Together:

Is it an ironclad rule that those reared in a Christian home who desert the Lord will at some point return to Him? What might parents do to insure (as much as possible) their child will not forsake the Lord upon leaving home?

Pray Together:

Father, we long that our family circle in You be unbroken on Earth and in Heaven. Give us wisdom as to all that we may do to insure such is the case. However, should any of our children stumble into sin or unbelief, please draw them back into the fold with Thy cords of mercy and lovingkindness we plead.

11

Witnessing within the Home

"How many others," writes C. H. Spurgeon, "have you brought to Christ? Is it quite certain that you have led any to Jesus? Can you not recollect one? I pity you then! The Lord said to Jeremiah about Coniah, "Write ye this man childless." That was considered to be a fearful curse. Should I write you childless...? Your children are not saved, your wife is not saved, and you are spiritually childless. Can you bear this thought? Do tell them about Christ."[22]

> Will the circle be unbroken
> By and by, by and by?
> Is a better home awaiting
> In the sky, in the sky?
> —Ada R. Habershon

How about it? Will the family circle be incomplete in Heaven? Is your son in? Is your daughter in? If not, don't stop efforts to get them in until they are. Don't allow a pastor or evangelist to rob you of the joy of leading your own children to Jesus Christ.

Read Together:

He Reads: Jeremiah 22:30

She Reads: 2 Kings 4:26

Answer Together:

Are we spiritually childless? What steps have we taken to cultivate the seed of the Gospel in our children in an effort to win them to Christ? What further steps may be taken (family altar, Sunday school, church, etc.)?

Pray Together:

Lord, please use whatever means to draw our child(ren) to saving faith. Help us be diligent in cultivating the seed of the Gospel within their hearts that at the earliest possible age they may be saved. Help us maintain a priority focus on this we pray.

12
God Uses Broken Things

"God uses broken things," states Vance Havner. "It takes broken soil to produce a crop, broken clouds to give rain, broken grain to give bread, broken bread to give strength. It is the broken alabaster box that gives forth the perfume. It is Jacob limping from Jabbok who has power with God and men. It is Peter, weeping bitterly, who returns to greater power than ever."[23] (Hosea 10:12; Matthew 26:7)

You have been hurt sorely, and it's like a blanket that ever envelopes your life with ever changing emotions of anger, bitterness, resentment, and vengeance. God is aware of the hurt and promises healing and blessing if handled in His prescribed way. God promises to work good out of "all things" for the Christian (Romans 8:28).

What a goldmine of comfort is contained in this text if one but has the faith to grasp it. God forthrightly promises to use everything that happens to the believer for his temporal and eternal good. He avows to take even the worst that happens and turn it into a blessing.

"No matter what our situation," comments John MacArthur, "our suffering, our persecution, our sinful failure, our pain, our lack of faith—in those things, as well as in **all** other **things**, our heavenly Father will work to produce our ultimate victory and blessing."[24]

MacArthur continues, "**All things** include circumstances and events that are good and beneficial in themselves as well as those that are in themselves evil and harmful."[25]

Read Together:
He Reads: Hosea 10:12
She Reads: Matthew 26:7–13

Answer Together:
What is the lesson of "broken things?" What broken things have you experienced (broken health, broken finances, broken dreams, broken family, etc.)? How might you apply the teaching of Romans 8:38–39 to that which has been broken in your life or family?

Pray Together:
Father, our hearts are heavy due to the broken thing we have experienced. In our distress we cry unto You for help and comfort. Please never allow this broken thing to injure our fellowship with You

or one another. We do trust the promise that You will use even the worse of broken things for our highest good and Thy glory.

13
Telephone Line to Heaven

Prayer involves "asking" God. "Asking" works because it's the authorized and anointed means given to Christians by God to have needs met personally and for others corporately. (Matthew 7:7-8) Simply, "asking" works because God promises it will. (Jeremiah 33:3) The Christian is to trust the promise of God about prayer and thus while praying exhibit faith in His ability and power to answer in accordance with His divine will and good pleasure.

Read Together:
He Reads: Matthew 7:7-8
She Reads: Jeremiah 33:3

Answer Together:
What strategy may you formulate to assure more prayer time in a day (watch alarm to sound once on the hour to prompt prayer for thirty seconds, etc)?

Pray Together:
Lord, we fail to pray as we ought to and ask forgiveness. Help us be more prayer focused personally and as a couple (family) corporately. How often it is true that 'we have not, because we ask not'? Henceforth, Father, may such be untrue with us.

14
Happiness in the Home

"Every home," states John R. Rice, "should be a refuge from a sin-cursed world all about us and a likeness of our heavenly Home which God has prepared for them that love Him.

"Happiness in the home depends on having God there and having the home honor Christ. Only where Christ is Lord can happiness have full place. If we expect to have a little bit of Heaven in our home, then we must have Christ there, and His will must be done. Sin brings trouble and heartache. Every sickness, every failure, all the trouble and misunderstanding and heartbreak of the world has been brought by sin. So the only way to have a really happy, blessed home is to have a Christian home, a home where the principles to the marriage are saved people who put Christ first."[26]

Read Together:
He Reads: Psalm 127:1–2
She Reads: Proverbs 3:33

Answer Together:
Have you entered into a personal relationship with Jesus Christ by acknowledging Him alone as Lord and Savior? If not, why not do so right now? To know God's utmost blessing in the home, both husband (father) and wife (mother) must choose to allow Him to rule.

Pray Together:
Lord, help our home be truly a Christian home, a home where You are worshipped, loved and obeyed and an environment as free from the contamination of sin as possible.

15
Husbands' God-Given Purpose

H. A. Ironside said, "The Lord never does anything to tear down or put down His chosen bride! Even when He must discipline us, He does it in love that we may share His holiness (Hebrews 12:6, 10). The application for Christian husbands is obvious. Any thoughts, words or deeds that put down your wife, ridicule her, attack her, or tear her down are not in line with your God-given purpose."[27]

The love husbands must display for their wives is manifested in Christ's love for the church (sacrificial love, caring love, relentless love, and unbreakable love). Martyn Lloyd-Jones states, "His argument is clearly this—it is only as we realize the truth about the relationship of Christ to the church that we can really function as Christian husbands ought to function."[28]

Read Together:
He Reads: Ephesians 5:25, 28–29
She Reads: Ephesians 5:33

Answer Together:

As a husband you are to love your wife in the same way that Jesus loves the church (verse 25). What are the ways Christ loves the church (His bride)? Are you exemplifying the same love traits to your wife, or are you guilty of demeaning or abusing her in thought or deed? As a wife, how might you reverence your husband (verse 33)?

Pray Together:

Lord, as a husband I confess my failure to love my wife as You love the church and as I love my own self. Help me henceforth change this mindset and behavior, that I might love her as she deserves and as I desire.

16

God's Divine Order in the Home

"One of the root problems in the home of Ahab and Jezebel was the reversal of God-assigned roles," states W. A. Criswell. "Jezebel's dominant leadership in the home was against the divine order, as was Ahab's refusal to assume leadership."[29]

God's Word declares in I Corinthians 11:3 that "the head of every man is Christ; and the head of the woman is the man; and the head of Christ is God." It says further that "God is not the author of confusion, but of peace, as in all churches of the saints" (14:33). God's order for the home is not confusing (though society may attempt to make it so). Simply, it is the Lordship of Christ over both husband and wife, the husband's leadership and authority over the wife, and the wife's submission to her husband.

Read Together:

He Reads: I Kings 21:1–16, 25
She Reads: Ephesians 5:22–23

Answer Together:

What is the biblically designed role for husband and wife? In what ways were the roles reversed between Ahab and Jezebel? What resulted? Is such evidenced in today's culture; and if so, in what ways. Why do marriages which reverse biblically assigned roles fail?

Pray Together:

Help us exemplify Your divinely designed role in marriage.

17
Hedge of Protection about the Home

God erected a hedge of protection from Satan about Job, his family and all he possessed in every direction (Job 1:10). Herein we find the biblical premise for asking the Lord to erect such a hedge about our marriage, home and children. Today and every day make this your incessant prayer as husband and wife.

Read Together:
He Reads: Job 1:7–12
She Reads: Job 1:13–22

Answer Together:
What were the consequences of the removal of the hedge of protection from Job's home? What lesson does it teach? Do you believe that your family presently is hedged in on every side with God's protection? If so, give God praise and glory for His wondrous work in daily protecting your children, spouse and goods.

Pray Together:
Heavenly Father, please hedge our child(ren) and us and our possessions in on every side that Satan may not steal, kill or destroy. We are vulnerable to the enemy, and unless You envelop us constantly with Thy power, surely we will falter. Preserve our home for Thy glory and honor.

18
Defusing Arguments

Spousal arguments often spring from the most minuscule and unimportant things—things that won't matter an hour or day or week later (being a backseat driver, taking too long to get ready, choice of restaurant, music selection in the car, television selection at home, whose turn it is to change Billy, failure to refuel the car, not cleaning up what you mess up in the kitchen, with whose family to spend Christmas, or the house temperature setting). Now really, aren't such things ridiculous to argue over?

If one or the other spouse would realize this, many arguments would be averted.

In the following interview, an elderly man shares a way to keep an argument from escalating, should it occur.

Reporter: "So you are 100 years old. How did you manage to live so long?"

Old man: "Well, son, I got married when I was 21. The wife and I decided that if we had arguments, the loser would take a long walk to get over being mad. I suppose I have been benefited most by 79 years of fresh air and exercise.[30]

Great advice. Take a long walk to return to being levelheaded. Ask the Lord to forgive you for initiating or fueling the argument, and then ask your spouse's forgiveness.

Read Together:
He Reads: Proverbs 16:32
She Reads: II Timothy 2:23–24

Answer Together:
What might you do to defuse potential arguments?

Pray Together:
Heavenly Father, help our communication with each other be seasoned with respect, gentleness, openness and love even in the times of disagreement.

19
Fighting Fairly in Marriage

The Bible does not condone marital fights (arguments); but when they do erupt, both partners must fight fairly. Consider 10 tips for fighting fair.

1. Don't drag up the past.
2. Don't demean your spouse to others.
3. Give your spouse a chance to speak without interruption.
4. Be honest.
5. Accept responsibility if you are guilty.
6. Act mature; avoid the screaming, and certainly abuse.
7. Don't assume you know what your spouse thinks by

mannerisms. Ask for clarification.
8. Don't say a matter is settled when it isn't.
9. Don't make a mountain out of a molehill.
10. Remember you both are on the same team.

Read Together:
He Reads: Ephesians 4:32
She Reads: Ephesians 4:15

Answer Together:
Identify which of the 10 tips stated requires work on your part. What does the Bible state about marital conflict or fights?

Pray Together:
Lord, help us avoid marital conflict; but when it may surface, enable us to confront each other in love, respect and dignity in an effort to fight fairly.

20
Marriage Changes You

"No one who marries," states Stephen Arterburn, "has the stubborn right to stay the same while expecting the other to change. Both must let go of their marriage fantasy. While you may feel disappointed that your life together isn't what you dreamed of before you said 'I do,' the upside is that marriage doesn't allow you to stagnate as a person. You *will* be changed—both of you."[31]

Having a changed marriage depends on each of you *changing yourselves*. You certainly cannot change each other, so don't chase that rabbit.

Change comes about first by the realization that you are still a bridge under construction, that there is much improvement and growth in being a husband/wife remaining. The construction, in fact, will be ongoing, never ending throughout marriage. The very moment you stop working at changing yourself in order to be a better spouse is the moment the marriage begins to weaken and struggle.

Change occurs when it is realized that your spouse is not responsible for your unhappiness or discontentment; you are. As long as you base self-worth, meaning in life, acceptance and joy upon your husband/wife, change will never happen. A personal and deep relationship with Jesus Christ is the key to a life of happiness and purpose. He and He alone is more than sufficient to meet the hunger and thirst of your soul by bringing about an inner change that will manifest itself outwardly.

The wonder of godly personal change is that it positively affects not only you but also your spouse.

Read Together:

He Reads: I Peter 4:8
She Reads: I Corinthians 15:31b

Answer Together:

Are you 'dying to self' so that the needs of your mate are met, or are you stubbornly resisting? What positive changes by you would make the relationship more harmonious and joyful? Have you entered into a personal relationship with Jesus Christ as your Lord and Savior? If not, will you now? Out of love for your mate and God, take a first step, regardless of how small, to implement godly change.

Prayer Together:

Thank you Lord for creating the love of my heart just for me. Help me ever be grateful for my mate's positive virtues and patient in his/her negative traits. Enhance my memory that You alone are the source of my happiness and joy. Whatever changes I need to make to fulfill his/her need, grant the grace to do so.

21

Successful Parenting

"How do you guarantee," says John MacArthur, "that your little child—as cute and cuddly as he or she might be right now—will end up being a joy to you? What kind of shade-providing tree will you plant to protect that precious life from all that will seek to exploit its weaknesses? Ephesians 6:4 [gives the answer]. That's it, and it isn't complicated. You don't have to be a child psychologist, attend a thousand seminars, or buy every child-rearing book on the market to do it."[32]

"Fathers, do not provoke your children to anger by the way you treat them. Rather, bring them up with the discipline and instruction that comes from the Lord" (Ephesians 6:4 NLT). Paul states (perhaps from childhood experience) that fathers must discipline wayward children but not to such excess (overdone criticism and rebuke or too strict discipline) that it results in a broken spirit.

William Barclay declares, "We cannot forget the duty of encouragement. Luther's father was very strict, strict to the point of cruelty. Luther used to say: 'Spare the rod and spoil the child—that is true; but beside the rod keep an apple to give him when he has done well.'"[33]

J. Vernon McGee's take on the text is similar. He says, "The parent is not to vent a bad disposition on a child or punish him in a fit of rage. It is the parents' duty to teach the child the truths of the Scriptures and then to live them before the child. Don't provoke your children to wrath. As a believer, you are to live at home like a believer. "'Fathers' includes the mothers also. However, the emphasis, I think, is on the father because the disciplining and training of the child is actually his responsibility, but it does include the mother also."[34]

Both the discipline and instruction are to be "of the Lord," that which He orders and approves.

"Instilling sound principles of life; training to good habits; cautioning and protecting against moral dangers; encouraging prayer, Bible-reading, church-going, Sunday observance; taking pains to let them have good associates; and especially dealing with them prayerfully and earnestly in order that they may accept Christ as their Savior and follow him, are among the matters included in this counsel."[35]

Having dug deep into the meaning of this text, it is understandable why MacArthur suggests that it encapsulates all that is needed to be a great parent.

Read Together:
He Reads: Ephesians 6:4
She Reads: Deuteronomy 4:9

Answer Together:
Based upon today's scripture reading, what is the most essential responsibility of parents to their children? What might you do to keep the main thing the main thing in parenting? What are ways parents may provoke their child "unto wrath" and its consequence(s)?

Pray Together:

Help us bring our child(ren) up knowing, loving, serving and obeying You.

22

Your Mate a Second Self

"In marriage," William Penn said, "do thou be wise. Prefer the person before money, virtue before beauty, the mind before the body; then thou hast a wife, a friend, a companion, a second self."[36]

C. S. Lewis in *Mere Christianity* said, "The Christian idea of marriage is based on Christ's words that a man and wife are to be regarded as a single body."

In Mark 10:8 (NLT), Jesus said, 'This explains why a man leaves his father and mother and is joined to his wife, and the two are united into one. Since they are no longer two but one, let no one split apart what God has joined together."

These words are illustrated so beautifully by Leo Tolstoy when he said of someone, "He felt now that he was not simply close to her but that he did not know where he ended and she began."

That is the kind of oneness Jesus was referencing that ought to exist between husband and wife and the type you are to strive after in the relationship with your husband or wife.

Read Together:

He Reads: Proverbs 5:18–19
She Reads: Proverbs 12:4

Answer Together:

What do you think Penn meant when he said our mate should be a second self? How might that be attained? What problems would it resolve? Do you love each other so dearly that it's impossible to tell where your life ends and his/hers begins? What do you believe is meant by "the two shall become one flesh"? In what ways do you both reveal this teaching of Jesus (goals, values, doctrinal beliefs, convictions, etc.)? As one body the husband is to love his wife as he loves himself, and vice versa. Neither may be detached or separated from the other.

Pray Together:

Heavenly Father, as we became one in body in saying "I do" to each other at our wedding, help us grow in understanding of what that fully means. Merge our values, goals, dreams and spiritual beliefs together to the end that we will be each other's "second self."

23

Marital Conflict

"To solve a marriage problem," says R. C. Sproul, "you have to talk with each other about it, choosing wisely the time and place. But when accusations and lengthy speeches of defense fill the dialogue, the partners are not talking to each other but past each other. Take care to listen more than you speak. If you still can't agree on a solution, consider asking a third party, without a vested interest, to mediate."[37]

Jesus told the church at Ephesus their problem was that they had left their first love for Him (Revelation 2:4). It was still there. They just had to decide to return to it. That's the problem with many marriages. The first love for the spouse has fizzled away (covered up over time gradually due to taking the mate for granted, daily routines, work, etc.). It's still there; they must decide to return to it whatever the cost. As Sproul suggests, sometimes in martial conflict it's most advantageous to have a third party to mediate by way of counseling and advisement.

Read Together:

He Reads: I Corinthians 13:4–6

She Reads: Proverbs 10:12

Answer Together:

In the effort for reconciliation, are you guilty of lengthy speeches of accusations and personal defense? If so, how has that worked out? Reconciliation can occur only when you both calmly listen to each other without verbal outbursts of denial and attack and determine to arrive at a doable solution.

Pray Together:

Father, I am sorry for allowing the routines of life (or something else) to smother the flame of my first love for my mate. Whatever the cost, reignite the flames of our first love for each other to blaze as a raging inferno.

24
Marriage, a Total Commitment

"Marriage is a total commitment," says Wayne Mack, "and a total sharing of the total person with another person until death."[38]

Read Together:
He Reads: 1 Corinthians 11:11–12
She Reads: Matthew 19:4–6

Answer Together:
Recite your marital vows together. What in them speaks of a total commitment and a total sharing of the totality of who you are with your mate until death?

I, _____, take thee, _____, to be my husband/wife, and before God and these witnesses I promise to be a faithful and true husband/wife.

"Will you, _____, have _____ to be your husband/wife? Will you love him/her, comfort and keep him/her, and forsaking all others remain true to him/her as long as you both shall live?" ("I will")

(Repeat) "I, _____, take thee, _____, to be my husband/wife, and before God and these witnesses I promise to be a faithful and true husband/wife."

(Rings) "With this ring I thee wed, and with all my worldly goods I thee endow, in sickness and in health, in poverty or in wealth, 'til death do us part."

Pray Together:
Outside of you, Lord, there is none I love more than my life mate. May that love shine through in all I do for him/her. Help me never take for granted that my mate knows how madly in love I am with him/her.

25

Communicate More

Henry Cloud and John Townsend said, "The more you can stop the things that stop your communicating, the more you will be able to find each other's heart, preserving or reestablishing the connection."[39]

A recent survey of one hundred health professionals discovered that the most common cause for divorce was communication problems. The survey revealed that the communication complaints were different between men and women. Seventy percent of the professionals surveyed stated that men cited a woman's nagging and complaining as being the big issue. Eighty-three percent of the experts cited that a woman's top complaint was that her husband failed to validate her opinions or feelings.[40]

Couples often "talk" but seldom really "communicate." Improvement of communication skills would be an asset to most marriages and be a *game changer* as to its success or failure.

Steps to real communication with your spouse:

1. Unilaterally disarm. Give up the right to win. This doesn't mean you simply compromise or be agreeable but that you will genuinely listen to his/her point of view.

2. Bring to the conversation the only thing of which you can be certain—your own thoughts, feelings and perceptions. Instead of attacking or blaming your spouse, focus on YOU. Reveal your hurt and disappointment, things that may be embarrassing or humiliating, and your personal deep-down wants (compliments, acts of appreciation, etc.). Make sure you talk to your spouse with the same respect and decency as you would to anyone else.

3. Listen well to what your partner has to say. Don't enter the conversation thinking you know what is to be said, for you don't. Your opinion or advice is not what is being sought; your undivided attention is. Put yourself aside and focus intently on your spouse, seeking to experience what he/she is feeling. Throughout the conversation let him/her know you are listening and understanding by at times saying so. In identifying with her/him in their burdensome and painful issues you cannot help but become more compassionate for her/him.

4. Finally, you may want to review what was learned from each other and talk about resolution of problems that may have been stated.

The right kind of communication will bring couples closer together, not cause even a greater divide.[41]

Read Together:

He Reads: James 1:19

She Reads: Proverbs 18:3

Answer Together:

Define what is meant by the word *communication*. What is it that blocks communication with your mate (television, computer, entertainment, etc.)? Do you agree that communication is a skill that every couple needs to improve? How might your spouse communicate more freely and effectively with you?

Pray Together:

Help us, Lord, make time to really talk with each other, to open up and share our hearts. May the love of my life know beyond doubt it is never an *interruption* to engage me in conversation.

26

Fights over Money

Larry Burkett, noted financial author, says, "Money is either the best or the worst area of communication in our marriages."[42]

"After years as a financial counselor and working with marriage counselors," states Dave Ramsey, "I know that money and money fights are the #1 cause of divorce, not to mention the thing we fight about the most."[43]

Ramsey continues, "So if you are married and have money fights, you are normal. But if this is a real problem area for you, there is also an opportunity to improve your relationship and maybe even reach agreement with your spouse. I'm not talking about agreement brought on by surrender but rather by each person's getting a vote, understanding the other's view, and finding common ground."[44]

What is it to be equal partners with the purse strings? Harmony and happiness in marriage will only truly occur when both mates partner together with regard to financial decisions.

Gary Chapman states, "There's no room for competition in marriage; you and your mate are equal partners on the same team. Certainly one partner will need to pay the monthly bills and balance the bank statement. But this doesn't mean the bookkeeper controls the money. Together you must develop a plan for processing your finances. The bookkeeper simply follows the plan to which you've both agreed."[45]

Read Together:
He Reads: Matthew 6:21
She Reads: Psalm 37:16–17

Answer Together:
What is the meaning of *money* to you? Do you always feel you both are equal partners on the same team in the area of money? Have you established a financial plan together? Do you feel your spouse is strict on your use of family funds but lenient when it comes to his/her spending? What about household finances do you wish would be handled differently?

Pray Together:
Keep us, Lord, from being selfish financially with each other and help us view each other as equal partners with the management of our money. May the day of "money fights" be forever banished in our home.

27

Marriage's Ultimate Defense

If you had eyes to see, it would be overly evident who is seeking foremost to undermine and destroy marriage—yours, others' and mine. Satan, our arch enemy, dispatches numerous *invisible* demons not only to work havoc in our lives personally but in our families collectively, of which we must ever remain aware and against which we must be vigilant. The apostle Paul states, "For we wrestle not against flesh and blood, but against principalities, against powers, against the rulers of the darkness of this world, against spiritual wickedness in high places" (Ephesians 6:12).

"If the forces which threaten marriages today were just human forces," states Dr. Timothy Faulk, "then conceivably man's wisdom could deal with them. But the human factors are only the visible dimensions of the problem, like that small part of an iceberg which protrudes above the surface. The greatest danger—that which truly threatens—remains concealed from view, and we must ultimately deal with these forces.

"In this field of encounter, human wisdom and human strength count for nothing. Here nothing prevails except the authority of Christ. When He takes charge, those forces which are threatening to swamp Christian marriages will recede and withdraw. But if we sleep on in the back of the boat, we may well be washed overboard (Mark 4:34–41). This is the simple choice which faces marriages today. Will we call out to Jesus and ask Him to take charge of our homes, or will we keep straining at the oars of manmade schemes while the waves around us mount higher and higher?"[46]

Faulk is right in his assessment. The survival of marriage and the family as God designed it is dependent upon His being Lord in and over it, for only He can thwart the demolishing missiles of satanic attack against it (Ephesians 6:13; I John 4:4).

Read Together:

He Reads: I Peter 5:8
She Reads: I John 4:4

Answer Together:

Have you been trying to resolve marital or family issues apart from God? Why is it that Satan targets marriages as strenuously as he does? Are you continuously alert to and thus prepared for Satan's attack upon your home?

Pray Together:

Heavenly Father, be the defender and protector of our home against the fierce attacks of Satan and the demons of Hell.

28
Speaking Aloud Affirmations

Billy Sunday said, "Try praising your wife, even if it does frighten her at first."[47]

Stand face to face with your spouse. Take turns speaking six or so negative words about each other one at a time, and as you do, take a step backward each time. Next, take turns speaking positive words about each other one at a time, and as you do, take a step toward each other. It will be seen that the positive outweigh the negative, bringing you together, whereas the negative talk pushes you apart. Critical, derogatory speech can gradually erode the foundation of a happy marriage.

Read Together:
He Reads: I Thessalonians 5:11
She Reads: Proverbs 18:20–21

Answer Together:
How did the exercise above encourage/affirm you? How might you start consciously affirming one another daily (example: Fill a jar with numerous slips of paper on which are written words of heartfelt affirmations and daily pull one out to share with your mate).

Pray Together:
Heavenly Father, help us to understand that the way we speak to each other is a choice. Grant us the grace to speak words that build up and not tear down.

29
The Five Love Languages

Gary Chapman, the author of *The Five Love Languages*, says there are basically five ways to express love emotionally. Your spouse has a specific love language you need to discover and actualize for him/her to feel loved.

Words of Affirmation. Praise and appreciation for what they do.

Acts of Service. Simple acts of service may shower love down upon your mate like nothing else.

Receiving Gifts. For some, nothing fills their tank more with love than getting a gift on special occasions (birthday, anniversary, Christmas, etc.) and on "nonoccasions."

Quality Time. Your mate's love language may be that of your undivided, undistracted attention (not watching a football game as she tries to communicate). Personally I have learned to pause a television show to listen to my wife. If this is the love language of your wife, you will score big time if you "cease and desist" when she wants to talk and fill her tank up with love.

Physical Touch. This love language includes holding hands, hugging, kissing, sexual intercourse, etc. If this is your mate's love language, nothing will communicate love more than such touches.

Read Together:

He Reads: 1 John 3:18

She Reads: 1 Peter 4:8

Answer Together:

Ask each other, "Honey, how do you feel most loved?" You need to discover how your mate is wired emotionally so the need of love is fully met. As this is learned and applied, the door to a deeper and more intimate relationship will develop.

Pray Together:

Lord, teach us to understand each other emotionally so we can meet each other's need for love, meaning and happiness.

30
Marital Entitlement

Stephen Arterburn states, "Desiring a little freedom is not wrong. But feeling entitled to freedom can easily morph into a pattern of self-centeredness. Why? Because at the heart of entitlement lurks the ugly sin of greed. The more you take, the less you give. And, ironically, you receive less in return—the opposite of what you really want. The answer? Take less, give more, and receive more."[48]

Genuine freedom has restraints. A train is free to travel the tracks, but wreckage occurs when it ventures off them. What restraint does freedom have in marriage? Among others, a tremendous one is to put your spouse and his/her needs and desires ahead of yourself. As with a train, a marriage is headed for shipwreck when either mate gets off this track.

Jesus condemned self-centeredness—the life that centers on *self* to the injury of others.

Read Together:

He Reads: Titus 3:1–2
She Reads: Galatians 5:13

Answer Together:

Why must freedom have restraints in marriage? What restraints have you willing and lovingly accepted for the betterment of the marriage?

Pray Together:

Forgive us, Lord, for venturing off the tracks due to selfishness. Help us put each other ahead of our personal wants and appetites.

31

Handling Anger

John Piper in *Kill Anger Before It Kills You or Your Marriage* states, "In marriage, anger rivals lust as a killer. My guess is that anger is a worse enemy than lust. It also destroys other kinds of camaraderie. Some people have more anger than they think, because it has disguises. When willpower hinders rage, anger smolders beneath the surface, and the teeth of the soul grind with frustration. It can come out in tears that look more like hurt. But the heart has learned that this may be the only way to hurt back. It may come out as silence because we have resolved not to fight. It may show up in picky criticism and relentless correction. It may strike out at persons that have nothing to do with its origin. It will often feel warranted by the wrongness of the cause."[49]

"When you are quick to get angry," states Adrian Rogers, "you can lose so much—your job, friends, children, wife, health, and testimony. There is nothing more debilitating to your Christian testimony than for you to fly off the handle."[50]

Rogers says an essential to controlling anger is not repressing it but confessing it unto the Lord asking for help to keep it in check.[51]

Piper adds additional thoughts on the control of anger: "Think about how you do not want to give place to the Devil, because harbored anger is the one thing the Bible explicitly says opens a door and invites him in. Ponder the folly of your own self-immolation, that is, the numerous detrimental effects of anger to the one who is angry— some spiritual, some mental, some physical, and some relational. Ponder the rights of Christ to be angry, but how he endured the cross, as an example of long-suffering."[52]

Read Together:

He Reads: I Timothy 2:8
She Reads: I Corinthians 13:4–7

Answer Together:

What weapons are available to fight the battle with anger? What are some of the damaging results of uncontrolled anger upon your marriage and family? When your spouse is about to explode in anger, what might be done to extinguish the fuse? Ask your spouse how often you are angry with her/him and/or the children?

Pray Together:

Lord, may our disagreements never evolve into angry fights with each other or with our children. Help us respond to offenses or disagreements with gentleness and kindness, even as You did.

32

Honesty and Openness

"Because marriage," write David and Vera Mace, "is a relationship of shared intimacy, it requires a level of honesty between partners that goes much deeper than social relationships."[53]

Marriage is based upon mutual trust and openness with each partner. Why should you ever be dishonest or deceitful with the one who is flesh of your flesh, the one you love above all others?

To sneak around on your mate is not only a sin against him/her but against God. A foundational pillar of a successful marriage is trust, and when it's absent, the marriage crumbles.

Read Together:

He Reads: Proverbs 6:16–19

She Reads: Ephesians 4:25

Answer Together:

If your spouse asked to review your cell phone contacts, checkbook or appointment book, would there be any objection? The point is that you should be so honest and open with your spouse that he/she so trusts you that playing investigator is entirely unnecessary.

Pray Together:

Heavenly Father, help us be totally honest and open with each other, never lying or being deceitful. May our dependence upon you and our love for each other be so strong that it can always handle the truth, thus eliminating the temptation ever to lie.

33
Characteristics of a Christian Home

"Is Christ," John R. Rice writes, "put first in your home? Do you have thanks at the table? Are little children taught to bow their heads and to be grateful to God for daily bread? Your children can recognize Christ in you when they are accustomed to daily prayer, to gratitude, to reverence in the home. Does your home have Christian mottoes, Scripture verses on the walls? Are the children accustomed to hearing Mother and Father pray? Are they taught to lift their little voices in thanks and in petition? Are they accustomed to the Word of God as the fountain of blessing which Father and Mother have found it to be? I beg you, put Christ in your home if you want happiness there!"[54]

Sadly, "Christian" homes often fail in living up to their name, and our marriages and families are the worse for it.

Read Together:

He Reads: Deuteronomy 5:27–29

She Reads: Deuteronomy 6:6–9

Answer Together:

What evidence would an outsider find that would indicate your home is a Christian home? Is there any difference between your home and that of an unbeliever? If so, in what way? Consider establishing a family altar, a gathering of the family to read from the Bible and pray.

Pray Together:

May you, Lord, be the head of our home and Your Word its constant focus and guide. Help us root our children in Your Word by teaching them all it says, and be their example of a godly person.

34

Nonloving Motives for Sex

John R. Rice well said, "Sex appeal alone is the poorest basis in the world for a happy marriage."[55] But with that said and understood, sex is a gift to married people that bonds them together.

John MacArthur said, "Marriage itself is consummated with the literal bodily union of husband and wife. From that point on, the husband should regard the wife as his own flesh. If she hurts, he ought to feel the pain. If she has needs, he should embrace those needs as his own. He should seek to feel what she feels, desire what she desires, and in effect, give her the same care and consideration he gives his own body."[56]

Solomon declares, "Let your manhood be a blessing; rejoice in the wife of your youth. Let her charms and tender embrace satisfy you. Let her love alone fill you with delight" (Proverbs 5:18–19, TLB).

Marital couples engage in sex for sundry reasons, including love and affection, self-gratification, relief of stress, reconciliation (attempt to appease hurt spouse), marital obligation, payback or payment for a favor—all of which are wrong motives, except the first. Engaging in sex for nonloving motives is paramount to reducing your spouse to a sex object, defying God's design for sex, and making the act an ordeal void of real meaning and significance.

Sexual union with your spouse is to be an act of emotional and physical intimacy enveloped and motivated by love.

Read Together:

He Reads: Song of Solomon 1:7

She Reads: I Corinthians 7:3–4

Answer Together:

Has the motive for sex for either of you been other than love and affection? Do you ever feel used by your mate in having sex? What are some improper motives for withholding sex from your spouse?

Pray Together:

Heavenly Father, help us always engage in the gift of sex out of love and affection for one another.

35

Seven Secrets of Lasting Love

Adrian Rogers states there are seven secrets of lasting love which I summarize with additional comment.

1. *Fortify Faith.* A threefold cord is a man, a woman, and God; and it is not easily broken (Ecclesiastes 4:12). Help each other fully develop in the faith.

2. *Remember Roles.* The head of the home is the husband, as Jesus is the head of the church (Ephesians 5:23–25).

3. *Cultivate Contentment.* The apostle Paul said, "I know how to live on almost nothing or with everything. I have learned the secret of living in every situation, whether it is with a full stomach or empty, with plenty or little" (Philippians 4:12 NLT). With Paul *learn* how to be content without anything except God, each other, and the basic needs of life.

4. *Banish Bitterness.* Attack the problem rather than one another. Resolve not to go to bed angry with one another.

5. *Continue Communication.* [This] is truly what builds intimacy in marriage. Keep talking, not barking at each other.

6. *Refresh Romance.* Don't stop courting after the wedding, but continue flirting without end (Men, keep up the compliments, bringing flowers, opening the door, having dates and sweet talking).

7. *Practice Prayer.* Husband's, humble yourselves and pray with your wife. Wife, encourage joint prayer even if you at the first have to lead in it.[57]

Read Together:

He Reads: I Peter 3:7
She Reads: Ecclesiastes 4:12

Answer Together:

What might you do to keep romance fresh in your marriage? All couples have times of disagreements. Determine never to go to bed angry with each other even if it means several sleepless nights until the matter is resolved. Are money issues causing conflict? Sadly, for many couples their marital vow, though unintended, is not 'til death do they part' but 'til debt do they part.' What steps can you take to insure indebtedness doesn't destroy your marriage?

Pray Together:

Lord Jesus, help us always keep the flame of romance burning in our marriage by fueling it continuously and by extinguishing the flames of that which would kill it.

36

The Model Marriage

Melvin Worthington states, "Marriage is a divine institution. [God established it.] Marriage is a defined institution. God set the parameters for marriage—one man and one woman in a lifetime relationship is the ideal marriage. Marriage is a designed institution. God designed marriage for male and female. Marriage is a directed institution. The directives for a happy, harmonious, and holy home are found in the Bible."[58]

Read Together:

He Reads: Genesis 2:18–25
She Reads: Psalm 127:1

Answer Together:

Discuss your views of each of the four descriptive traits set forth by Worthington. If in agreement, how is your marriage manifesting them?

Pray Together:

Lord, help our marriage be just like the model You designed.

37

Is This Church Right for My Family?

What are the biblical criteria in the selection of a church home?

1. It should embrace the Holy Scripture's inerrancy and infallibility (II Timothy 3:16).

2. It should be doctrinally sound. Where does the church stand on the deity, virgin birth, virtuous life, vicarious death, victorious resurrection, verifiable ascension, and visible return to earth of Jesus Christ at the end of the age for believers? Where does it stand on the depravity of man, salvation by faith through grace alone, Hell, and Heaven?

3. It should be evangelistic, not in belief only, but also in practice (Acts 1:8).

4. It should be mission minded, both for home and foreign missions (Matthew 28:18–20).

5. It should be permeated with love and unity by its members (John 13:35).

6. It should be a people's church, not one governed by a hierarchy where the people never have a voice (Colossians 1:18).

7. It should operate by faith (2 Corinthians 5:7).

Ultimately you must depend upon the Holy Spirit's guidance in the choice of a church home. Ever realize He will not lead you to unite with and support a church that propagates beliefs and teachings contrary to the Holy Scripture.

The selection of a church home for your family will be a game changer. Make sure the best you can that it is the right one for your family.

Read Together:

He Reads: 2 Peter 1:20–21

She Reads: 2 Timothy 4:1–5

Answer Together:

What are we looking for in a church that we are not getting in our present church? Are we happy with what our church embraces morally? How can we become more involved in church? Are we being fed biblically from the classroom and pulpit consistently?

<u>Pray Together:</u>
Holy Spirit, guide our family to unite with the church that will meet our spiritual needs and where we can best serve the Lord.

38

Lust Leads to Adultery and a Broken Marriage

James presents the modus operandi of lust. Satan gives birth to immoral, perverted desires in the heart. If there is a conception, there has to be a father; and in this case it has to be the ruler of darkness. These cravings of sexual desire draw a person from the place of safety with the Lord only to be "baited" to partake of its forbidden pleasure. Ultimately lust results in sin, and the sin in death.

Some want to blame God, blame their spouse, blame friends, blame their genes, or blame circumstances for their sin. The Bible clearly reveals man's personal responsibility for sin; that is, it is his own evil desire that prompts it.

The apostle Paul says not to sow to the flesh (Galatians 6:8). To sow to the flesh is to stroke it mentally or physically instead of renouncing and crucifying it. A person sows to the flesh by the planting of sensual seeds in the mind. Seeds sown that produce lust or acts of physical sexual misconduct include pornography, indecent touches upon the body of another, sensual looks and gazes on another, association with people whose conversation and conduct spark such, and giving place to people or things that continuously fuel it.

The reason so many fall into sexual sin is that they sow to the flesh, positioning themselves for defeat. The key to defeating lust is to sow to the Spirit (Bible study, prayer, submission to the Holy Spirit's prompting, Scripture memory, godly obedience, worship, moral restraint), and in so doing you will reap the fruit of the Spirit (Galatians 6:8b), which is self-control, godliness, kindness, love, patience, gentleness, faith, meekness, and moral goodness (Galatians 5:22–23). In essence, Paul surmises that the secret to victory over the flesh is to give no place to it (Ephesians 4:27), mentally or physically.

Read Together:
He Reads: Ephesians 4:27
She Reads: James 1:14–15

Answer Together:
What is the biblical lesson of sowing and reaping? In what ways is it possible to sow to the flesh? What is the modus operandi of lust according to James? How can lust unchecked lead to adultery and perhaps divorce?

Pray Together:
Heavenly Father, we depend upon Your strength to resist lust and to live in marital harmony.

39

I Promise You Forever

Gary Smalley declares what each spouse should truthfully say to the other in *I Promise You Forever*. (The author formulated the statements under each promise.)

I promise to honor you

"I will value you as a person of immense worth because I choose to do so."

I promise to install an emotional security system for our marriage

"You will always be safe in sharing things with me from the well of your deepest self without fear of being criticized or judged."

I promise to listen and communicate with love

"My ears and heart will be tuned to what you communicate, and you need not ever fear my reaction because of my love for you. With God's help I will strive to openly share with you my needs and consider your feelings and needs in all I say."

I promise to learn what your needs are

"I will from time to time ask what your needs are so I can do a better job in meeting them."

I promise to remember you are God's gift to me

"I will always remember that you are a wonderful treasure God has entrusted to me as my life's mate."

I promise to focus on your value instead of weaknesses

"My love for you supersedes any faults that may ever surface."

I promise to work with you for a win-win solution to our differences

"I realize that I cannot do whatever I like, whenever I like, because you have beliefs, needs and feelings that may differ from mine. I promise never to trample upon them and ever work with you in decision making for a conciliatory solution."[59]

Read Together:
He Reads: Proverbs 31:10–12
She Reads: Proverbs 31:28–31

Answer Together:
With hands united and eyes fastened upon each other, repeat the promises of love cited. Is there any promise you especially need to emphasize to your mate?

Pray Together:
Lord Jesus, today we make these love promises anew and afresh to one another. As we move from this moment, may we always recall this special moment and the commitments made.

40

Give a Hug

A man walking down a city street noticed in a bookstore window a book titled *How to Hug*. Being of a romantic nature, he entered the shop and purchased a copy. When he opened the book, he discovered to his disappointment that it was a volume of an encyclopedia covering subjects from "How" to "Hug." Hopefully neither of you need a book teaching how to hug, but perhaps you may need some encouragement to hug each other more.

When someone touches us, our anterior cingulate cortex—the region of the brain that registers both physical and emotional pain—releases opioids, the body's most potent painkillers, says Naomi I.

Eisenberger (codirector of the Social Cognitive Neuroscience Lab at UCLA).[60] God uses our touches and hugs to one another as healing agents for pain.

It's amazing what a ten-second hug can accomplish before you leave for work in the morning or upon arrival afterwards or when either of you is having a bad day.

Read Together:
He Reads: Acts 20:10
She Reads: Song of Solomon 2:6

Answer Together:
When was the last time without reason you hugged your mate? Take a moment and hug one another now.

Pray Together:
Thank you, Lord, for Thy ever embracing hug about our life which grants security, hope and peace. Help us understand the power of a hug that we may hug each other and our child(ren) more.

41
Love Means You Have to Say You're Sorry

In the movie *Love Story,* one line that was shared twice became very popular: "Love means you never have to say you're sorry." The line first was shared by Jennifer Cavilleri (MacGraw's character) when O'Neal was about to say he was sorry for his anger; the second time it was the last line of the movie, by Oliver, upon his father's saying "I'm sorry" in learning of Jennifer's death. The line was voted #13 in the American Film Institute's list AFI's 100 Years in 2005 of most popular film quotes.[61]

Regardless of its acceptance and quotation, the *line* just isn't true. Love always means you will say you're sorry. Every couple, regardless of Christian stature, has moments they wish never happened in their marriage (a sharp word, inattentiveness, argumentation, rage of temper). Love doesn't mean you never say you're sorry and press ahead as if nothing happened! Absolutely not! Love means the total opposite.

Injurious acts always call for the soothing medicine of confession and request for forgiveness.

Read Together:

He Reads: Luke 7:4

She Reads: Mark 11:35

Answer Together:

Why do you think the quote from *Love Story* is popular? Do you accept it as truth or not? Why or why not? Is it hard to own up to a wrong and tell your mate that you are sorry for it? Is there something you need to confess to her/him, asking forgiveness?

Pray Together:

Lord Jesus, help us always remember that love never takes forgiveness for granted but expresses sorrow for the wrong through confession and repentance.

42

Be an Athanasius

The battle is getting fiercer, and the noose is ever tightening. We must prepare ourselves and our children more and more for the conflict lest shipwreck occurs.

Athanasius, a fourth-century Christian leader who stood stubbornly strong in his beliefs, was confronted by the Roman emperor Theodosius. The emperor said to him, "Athanasius, the whole world is against you." Athanasius replied, "Then Athanasius is against the whole world."

May Athanasius' belief and backbone be instilled into us and our children through the study of God's Word, formation of sound biblical convictions, and cultivation of spiritual walk!

Read Together:

He Reads: Daniel 3:8–29

She Reads: Joshua 24:15

Answer Together:

What steps may be taken to fortify your family against the spiritual darkness that is permeating the world? What lesson may be drawn from the three Hebrew children in Daniel 3? In the midst of moral and spiritual decadence, Joshua made a firm decision for his family, one he would not back down from. Will you do the same?

Pray Together:

Heavenly Father, help us stand for truth and the right even if it means standing alone. Grant us wisdom as to how to rear our child(ren) to do the same.

43

Children as Arrows in Your Hands

The psalmist states children are "as arrows" in the hand of a mighty man (Psalm 127:4).

Children, like arrows, must be developed with the right components (biblical values, convictions, beliefs, discipline) *and shaped correctly* (by discipline, example, and instruction). It is far better for children to be shaped by parents than by the White House, schoolhouse or playhouse.

Children, like arrows (with some exceptions), go where they are aimed. The primary reason why some children turn out bad is because a parent's aim was bad.

Children, like arrows, are purposed for battle. The apostle Paul states that we are in a constant war against Satan and his cohorts. As parents, equip your child to fight the good fight of faith, driving the enemy back in the name of Jesus Christ.

Children, like arrows, are message bearers. Children are to take the message of King Jesus into the entire world, seeking to bring the lost to a saving knowledge of Him. As gospel arrows, they are able to go where you may never go and do so more swiftly (some as missionaries, evangelists, pastors).

Read Together:

He Reads: Psalm 127:4–5
She Reads: Psalm 128:1–6

Answer Together:

As overwhelming as the truth is that your hand is upon the bowstring that delivers the arrow (child) into this sinful world, find hope in knowing that God's hand is upon your hand directing and empowering it as much as it is allowed to. As a parent, have you been trying to rear your child without God's help? How focused have your eyes been on the target (goal) for your arrow(s)? How good a job are you doing in fabricating a good arrow with the right components to insure it will not be warped?

Pray Together:

Lord, help us shape our arrow(s) after Thy master design and aim them steadfastly at the target of Thy perfect will and plan for their life. Place Thy hand of strength and guidance constantly upon ours upon the bowstring.

44

When Empty Arms Become
a Heavy Burden

The Bible is replete with numerous instances where a barren woman in response to prayer by herself or with her husband was blessed with a child.

Hannah was in bitterness of soul because she was childless (I Samuel 1:10). She prayed for a child, and God blessed her with Samuel (I Samuel 1:20).

Sarah was childless. Abraham prayed for her to conceive (Genesis 15:2–3), and God blessed with Isaac (Genesis 21:1–3).

Isaac's wife, *Rebekah,* was barren, yet when he prayed for her to conceive, she did, giving birth to Jacob and Esau (Genesis 25:21–26).

The wife of Manoah was barren, but undoubtedly after his prayer for her to have a child, God blessed with the child Samson (Judges 13:2–3).

In II Kings 4, we learn that the Shunammite woman who was barren bore a child (vv. 17–18) when her desire was told to Elisha.

In the New Testament we read of how Zacharias and Elizabeth prayed for a number of years for a child and God gave them John the Baptist (Luke 1:7, 13). Added to these testimonials are many which might be added from the present time.

Certainly it is biblical for a barren couple to pray for a child. Pray fervently and in faith that God will answer with a child, always ending it with the words of Jesus in the garden as He faced Calvary: "Nevertheless not my will, but thine, be done" (Luke 22:42). When He blesses with a child, rejoice and give Him all the glory. If He doesn't, rejoice and give Him all the glory. As with all aspects of the life of the Christian, the promise of Romans 8:28 applies whether or not we bear children.

Read Together:

He Reads: Jeremiah 33:3

She Reads: James 1:6–7

Answer Together:

How long should you pray for a child before giving up? Pray as long as God places in your heart the burden or until a peace settles upon your soul one way or the other. Did Hannah make a deal with God regarding His opening up her womb? Was that what enabled her pregnancy? Why or why not? Should God think it best for you to remain barren, how will you handle that decision? Infertility in a marriage can be tough. It's most important that such couples trust God implicitly and not blame the other for not being able to have children. Adoption may be a possibility.

Pray Together:

Lord, even as you blessed Hannah, Elizabeth, Sarah, and others with a child, we beseech You to do so for us. At Your word we know this can happen instantly despite the long years in waiting and praying. We long to be blessed with a life of Thy creating and to experience the joy and love that child brings. Grant this our prayer in keeping with what is best for us and Your glory.

45

When the Family Hurts

Recall that when Lazarus died, Mary and Jesus wept, and others wailed (John 11:34–35). Referencing this text, John R. Rice declared:

"Why did Jesus weep? He knows that in a few minutes He will call Lazarus out of the grave....Oh, but He weeps for the tears of Mary and

Martha and others. He weeps with all the broken hearts in the world. He weeps with every mother who loves her [dead] baby, every husband who stands at the casket of his wife. He weeps with every mother or father who weeps in the night over a prodigal boy or wayward girl....But those tears are for me, too, and for you and all who have trouble and sorrow in this world....He is troubled with our troubles....He enters into every sorrow."[62]

When you hurt, Jesus hurts. He is the sympathizing Savior.

The Great Physician now is near,
The sympathizing Jesus;
He speaks the drooping heart to cheer.
Oh, hear the voice of Jesus!

Sweetest note in seraph song;
Sweetest name on mortal tongue;
Sweetest carol ever sung:
   Jesus, blessed Jesus!

Read Together:
He Reads: John 11:34–35
She Reads: John 14:18

Answer Together:
Times of hurt ought to bring us to our knees, for the believer's true source of strength and comfort comes through prayer from the throne of God. Express unto God and each other the anger, pain, sorrow, and doubts you are battling.

Pray Together:
Lord, help us always support each other in the times of hurt and difficulty; help us be friends to lean upon and draw strength from, friends who undergird with prayer. May the cloud of hurt never obscure Your abiding presence to comfort and sustain.

46
Praying with and for One Another

You have seen the bumper stickers and heard the slogan for years: "The family that prays together stays together." I believe that what it advocates is true. There are various approaches a couple may take in praying together.

Scripture prayer. Personalize it for your mate. For example, you might pray Psalm 94:22 in this fashion: "Lord, today be Mary's defense and rock of refuge as she encounters difficulty or hurt."

Silent prayer. You may at first feel most comfortable praying silently or for your mate to voice the prayer.

Conversational prayer. While conversing, stop and pray about a matter under discussion. You can do this silently or verbally.

Spurs to prayer. Expand the prayer shared at the end of each devotional entry in this volume (use the prayer cited as a rocket launcher for your own).

Read Together:
He Reads: Philippians 4:6–7
She Reads: Colossians 4:2

Answer Together:
What are the benefits as a couple in praying together? Are you willing to commit to praying together? If so, what is the best time? Prayer time together doesn't have to be long, especially at the start. Of the various approaches cited, with which are you both the most comfortable?

Pray Together:
O Lord, help us overcome timidity or the busyness of life to stop to pray together daily. Help us understand that praying together and for each other fortifies our marriage and family.

47
Avoiding Financial Disaster

Research shows that the more couples pool their money, the happier they are. Couples who pool eighty percent of their money are much happier than those who pool only seventy percent or less. Marriages where all income is retained by the spouse who earned it are the least happy.[63]

Dave Ramsey states that separation of financial accounts is disaster in a marriage; to have a combined marriage, you need a combined checking account.[64]

Ramsey elucidates, "When we do a budget and handle our money together in one checking account and live our lives unified, we are sharing our dreams. We are sharing our fears. We are becoming more and more unified. It'll add a level of unity to your marriage like nothing else will. Marriage counselors often use the budget and the single checking account as a marriage healing tool....The very nature of a quality marriage is that you are interdependent. You're not a good husband when you want to be independent of your wife. You're not a good wife when you want to be independent of your husband. It's the very nature of marriage."[65]

The attitude in marriage that says "this is mine, and that is yours" goes against biblical teaching. Jesus said that when a man and woman are united in marriage, they become "one flesh [identity]." How can a couple who is *one* stand separate with regard to possessions?

Read Together:
He Reads: Matthew 6:21
She Reads: Proverbs 24:3–4

Answer Together:
Do you agree or disagree with Ramsey's view on the single checking account system in marriage? Cite its pros and cons. Obviously, based upon what Ramsey said, a single checking account is not synonymous with tyrannical rule of finances in the home by either spouse.

Pray Together:
Help us, Lord, lay aside our independence financially. Since we are one entity ("the two shall become as one"), all money belongs to both of us. Help us trust each other with the little or much that we possess and in so doing become more fully the *one entity* You intended.

48
The Christian View of Marriage

John Piper said, "The main meaning of marriage is to display the covenant-keeping love between Christ and His church. In other words, marriage was designed by God most deeply, most importantly, to be a parable or a drama of the way Christ loves His church and the way the church loves and follows Christ. This is the most important thing for all husbands and wives to know about the meaning of their marriage."[66]

Isn't it amazing that God's design for your marriage is that it be a testimonial of His love for the church and her love and submission to Him by the way you as a husband love your wife and the way she responds in submission and love to you?

Read Together:
He Reads: Ephesians 5:23; 25–26
She Reads: Ephesians 5:22; 24

Answer Together:
What is God's design for marriage? As husband and wife, how might you fulfill that design? Contrast how God loves the church with how you are to love each other.

Pray Together:
Lord, may our union and love one for another be a testimonial to that of Yours for the church.

49
A United Front to Your Children

John Piper writes, "Children need one united front coming from Mom and Dad. Work through your differences and then stand united."[67]

Parenting as a Team

Prepare for dealing with behavior problems by discussing the discipline to be exacted. Numerous such problems are predictable.

Set some disciplinary rules by which you will abide. For example:
Never exact punishment that exceeds the nature of the wrong;
Never use your hand to punish;
Never discipline when angry;
Discipline only in private.

Always explain the reason for the punishment prior to its being administered and affirm love for the child afterwards. If in doubt about the measure or means of discipline to be exacted, discuss the matter together. Confront each other in private upon disciplinary disagreement; never go behind each other's back talking negatively of one another to the child regarding the punishment exacted.

Manifest the "I've got your back" attitude with your spouse. Always present a united front when disciplining the child. Choke down the urge to battle each other in front of your child regarding the discipline to be exacted.

It's okay to disagree in a gentle manner with your spouse, but ultimately give unwavering support unless the punishment is abusive or totally inappropriate. Don't allow the child to pivot you against each other; if you do so, he wins. Be open to compromise with your spouse regarding the form of discipline.

Having a game plan regarding discipline and actually following it is difficult for sure, but if followed, it will be most beneficial to all concerned.

Much of what has been said about parents working as a team in the discipline of their child may be adapted to decisions made in response to their child's requests. In an effort to get what they want, children adopt the strategy "divide and conquer" with their parents. Parents who disagree regarding something their child wants to do or get must work through it in private so as to stand as one in the decision made.

Read Together:
He Reads: Colossians 3:21
She Reads: I Corinthians 14:33

Answer Together:
What are the negatives of not being united as parents in discipline/decisions rendered? What rules governing discipline and decision making have you formulated or will you formulate? Who primarily handles the discipline and decision making in the home? Is that working well? Are you giving a united front to your child in discipline and decision making?

Pray Together:
Help us, Lord, be united in the decisions and discipline we exact upon our children.

50
Stressed Out Moms and Dads

As a mom are you stressed out? If so, you are not alone, for a whopping seventy percent say that mothering is "incredibly stressful."[68]

Factors that contribute to this emotional state may include fatigue (trying to balance work outside the home with mothering within it), attempts to have your children "keep up with the Joneses," financial worry (even at a subconscious level), sleep deprivation.

> Unchecked stress can hurt our health and our family's well-being. Chronically stressed moms tend to be more insensitive to kids. Studies also show that a parent's ability to manage stress is a strong predictor of the quality of her relationship with her children and how happy her children are.—Dr. Michelle Borba[69]

How do you know if your stress is harming your children and home? The answer to the following two questions (if answered honestly) will reveal if it is or not. First, the home climate test. Is the home a place where you and the children can relax and enjoy each other—a place of laughs and fun together? Second is the mother memory test.[70] If you asked your children to describe you, would they say you are calm, always approachable, good to listen, and fun to be around? Or would they say you are always distracted from them by the phone, computer, or television and easily irritated and stressed out?

If you (or your husband) parade a wiped out, stressed out, irritable presence in the home, then it's time to take steps to resolve the stress. Remember, the emotional health and happiness of your children depend on an environment of love; calm, pleasant tone of voice in correction, contrasted to screaming; and quality time (which signals they are highly prized, valuable treasures to you).

Read Together:
He Reads: I Corinthians 13
She Reads: Proverbs 31:10–12; 26–28

Answer Together:
Paul, in the love chapter of the Bible (I Corinthians 13), draws a wondrous painting of the traits of true love. The virtues of love he depicts must be manifested between husband and wife and with their children. What are these virtues of love? Which of these virtues need strengthening? What might be done today to relieve the stress you experience (destress things)?

Pray Together:
Lord, help us trust You with the pressures we face with parenting, take a deep spiritual breath in times we feel stress, and regain composure so that our home will always be an environment of calm, relaxation, peace, laughter, and wondrous interaction with our kids.

51
Won by a Mother's Love and Tracts

A young man was rebellious and indifferent to his mother's appeal to be saved. This mother was relentless in her effort to win her son to Christ to the point that she would put gospel tracts in inconspicuous places, such as under his pillow or cereal bowl. Finally, at age 16, the tracts hit home, and he was saved. This young man was Eddie Martin, one of Southern Baptists' greatest evangelists and soul winners who preached in 1,500 crusades/revivals during his ministry.[71]

Read Together:
He Reads: Luke 1:37
She Reads: I Samuel 1:26–28

Answer Together:
In addition to prayer, what else might you both do to bring your child to salvation in Jesus Christ? What tool did Eddie Martin's mother use with great success to bring him to Christ? It is essential that regardless of the numerous times the appeal is rejected you never give up. Imagine what might not have been had Mrs. Martin given up one tract sooner.

<u>Pray Together:</u>

Father, we intercede for our child that the Holy Spirit may open his eyes to spiritual truth and deep conviction regarding his need of forgiveness through Jesus Christ. Lead us in what to do and not to do in our quest for his salvation.

52

Home Dedication

Let us look at God's Word and see what He has to say about the dedication of our home.

<u>Read Together:</u>

He Reads:

Psalm 127:1

Except the LORD build the house, they labour in vain that build it: except the LORD keep the city, the watchman waketh but in vain.

Deut. 20:5

What man is there that hath built a new house, and hath not dedicated it?

Nehemiah 12:27

And at the dedication of the wall of Jerusalem they sought the Levites out of all their places, to bring them to Jerusalem, to keep the dedication with gladness, both with thanksgivings, and with singing, with cymbals, psalteries, and with harps.

She Reads:

Ezra 6:16–17

And the children of Israel, the priests, and the Levites, and the rest of the children of the captivity, kept the dedication of this house of God with joy,

And offered at the dedication of this house of God an hundred bullocks, two hundred rams, four hundred lambs; and for a sin offering for all Israel, twelve he goats, according to the number of the tribes of Israel.

The dedication of a home is a commonplace event in the Bible, and it is with great joy we dedicate yours at this time. Please repeat, "We dedicate this home," after each of the following statements.

To Thee, O God, who has united us together as husband and wife and blessed richly:

Husband and wife: We dedicate this home.

To Christian growth through prayer, the Word, and patient discipline:

Husband and Wife: We dedicate this home.

To a Christian environment in what is said, watched, and read:

Husband and Wife: We dedicate this home.

To private and corporate worship, Bible reading, and prayer:

Husband and Wife: We dedicate this home.

To the rearing of children in the knowledge, fear, and love of the Lord by precept and practice:

Husband and Wife: We dedicate this home.

To faithful service to God within and without its walls:

Husband and Wife: We dedicate this home.

To guard it zealously against untruth, unholy companions, immorality, alcohol, and other deviant devices of Satan:

Husband and Wife: We dedicate this home.

To faithfulness to the local church:

Husband and Wife: We dedicate this home.

To God, our Heavenly Father, to Jesus Christ, our Savior and Lord, to the Holy Spirit, our Companion and Comforter whose divine presence we shall ever welcome, the unseen Guest at every table and the silent Listener to every conversation:

Husband and Wife: We dedicate this home.

Today, O God, we stand at the threshold of this new home and declare openly with Joshua:

Husband and Wife: "And if it seem evil unto you to serve the LORD, choose you this day whom ye will serve; whether the gods which your fathers served that were on the other side of the flood, or the gods of the Amorites, in whose land ye dwell: **but as for me and my house, we will serve the LORD**" (Joshua 24:15).

Pray Together:

Heavenly Father, we dedicate our home unto Your divine purposes, honor and glory. May all who enter its doors so sense your presence that they depart saying, "Surely the Lord was in this place."

53

The Suffering of Saints

The suffering of Job was not the result of his sin. Included in the reasons as to why God allows suffering are: (1) to develop our faith (42:1–6), (2) to lead to increased blessing (42:10–16), and (3) to benefit other sufferers.[72]

Sometimes the reason for one's suffering is unclear at the first but will be manifest in time, if not here then in Heaven. Lazarus' sickness and eventual death puzzled Mary and Martha (John 11:3), but four days later its purpose was revealed (John 11:40, 45). David testified *after* suffering, "It is good for me that I have been afflicted; that I might learn thy statutes" (Psalm 119:71). Paul states the reason for his "thorn in the flesh" was to keep him from becoming conceited (II Corinthians 12:7).

Read Together:

He Reads: Job 1:8; 42:1–6
She Reads: Job 42:10–16

Answer Together:

What are three reasons why God allows suffering? In times of suffering, were these reasons experienced? Understanding the reasons for our suffering is encouraging and certainly makes the ordeal bearable.

Pray Together:

Lord, in times of suffering (sickness or otherwise), grant grace that it may be borne courageously and patiently that Your purposes for it may be fully realized.

54
Leave Father and Mother—Really?

In marriage God states the man/woman is to "*leave* his father and his mother" (Genesis 2:24). What does this mean? Dr. Timothy Faulk states, "Well, it certainly does not mean that you abandon or utterly forsake them. Nor does it mean that you make a great geographical move."[73]

Dr. Ed Wheat relates, "Of course, the bonds of love with parents are lasting ones. But these ties must be changed in character so that the man's full commitment is now to his wife and the wife's commitment is now to her husband. The Lord gave the man this commandment, although the principle applies to both husband and wife, because it is up to the man to establish a new household that he will be responsible for. He can no longer be under authority, for now he assumes headship of his family."[74]

Faulk continues, "To leave your parents means that your relationship to your parents must be radically modified. It means that you establish an adult relationship with them and that you must be more concerned about your mate's ideas, opinions, and practices than those of your parents. It means that you must not be slavishly dependent on your parents for affection, approval, assistance, and counsel. You must also eradicate any inauspicious attitudes toward your parents, or you will be tied emotionally to them regardless of how far you move from them. You must stop trying to modify your mate simply because your parents do not like them. The instruction God is providing us simply means that the husband and wife relationship must be the priority human relationship."[75]

Read Together:
He Reads: Matthew 19:5
She Reads: Mark 10:7

Answer Together:
Failure to obey this directive in marriage greatly hampers it at its start. Share with each other some of its detrimental effects. Have either of you not left mother or father as God commands? Although, as Faulk points out, the Scripture doesn't state a couple is to geo-

graphically *leave* their parents, sometime such is needed for the couple to stand on their own without interference. Why?

Pray Together:

Lord, help us rightly deal with overaggressive parents/in-laws who mean well in proffering advice and help but who are interfering with our happiness and life.

55

Hard of Hearing or Hard of Listening

A wife took her husband to see an audiologist. "I want to see if he is hard of hearing or just hard of listening!"

James underscores the value of listening in saying, "Wherefore, my beloved brethren, let every man be swift to hear, slow to speak" (James 1:19). Knowing the danger that a man might hear but not listen, Jesus said, "He that hath ears to hear, let him hear" (Matthew 11:15). To really listen or not is a conscious decision; the one requires discipline and patience, while the other is effortless.

Dictionary.com defines listen: "to give attention with the ear; attend closely for the purpose of hearing; give ear; to pay attention." Most husbands (including this one) have to admit that at times they are guilty of *hearing but not listening*.

Read Together:

He Reads: Proverbs 18:13
She Reads: Luke 8: 18a

Answer Together:

Husband, have you been guilty of answering your wife while she was still talking? What does Proverbs 18:13 state about such a habit? Wife, do you really listen to what your husband says, not just his words? Luke 8:18a admonishes that we take heed how we hear (listen). What might be done to assure that you both really hear what the other says? Poor listening skills will injure any marriage.

Pray Together:

Lord, help us work hard at really listening to one another. Thank you for always listening to us when we call upon you.

56
The Deadly Problem That Kills Marriages

We all face the problem of being self-focused (looking out for good ol' number one first), and this is the deadly problem that kills good relating, according to Dr. Larry Crabb. "If your marriage is troubled," Crabb states, "look hard at your spouse to identify *his* or *her* hurts and wounds and frustrations, and then do whatever is in your power to help. The obstacles that you need to remove are those that interfere with your progress toward other-centeredness, not with self-expression. Learning to be other-centered then is the foundation for *masculine* and *feminine* relating."[76]

Easier said than done, right? The flesh fights hard to retain its rights to be number one and will not surrender easily. Paul's battle with the flesh led him to confess, "I don't really understand myself, for I want to do what is right, but I don't do it. Instead, I do what I hate (Romans 7:15 NLT)." Later he came to understand that the key to denying self was found in the infilling (control, dominion) of the Holy Spirit (Romans 8:4–5).

To be other-centered and not self-centered in marriage, you will need to make the same discovery.

Read Together:
He Reads: Romans 7:14–25
She Reads: Philippians 2:3

Answer Together:
What obstacles need removing that interfere with your being *other-centered* with your spouse? What hurts, wounds and frustrations is your spouse facing that are within your ability to help? What is it to be Spirit-filled and live the Spirit-filled life? (Ephesians 5:18; Galatians 5:16–18).

Pray Together:
Father, with Paul we pray that daily we may die to self that personal ego will not jeopardize our fellowship with either You or one another. Holy Spirit, take full control of our heart, empowering it to thwart tendencies to elevate self over the other.

57
The Christian Home Is Different from That of the Unbeliever

What makes the Christian home different from that of the unbeliever? Is it that the Christian's home is free from arguments, disagreements, difficulties, and sin that exist in the non-Christian home?

Jay Adams, Christian counselor and professor, states that the primary difference between the Christian and non-Christian home is that the former is a place where sinful people face the problems of a sinful world with God's supernatural power and resources (Colossians 2:3).[77]

Therefore, the huge difference between the two is *Who* is Lord of their home and to *Whom* they turn in facing the trials and troubles of marriage and family life. Outwardly, both homes may look the same by casual observance, but upon closer examination their distinct and defining difference is clearly seen.

In the Christian home when fault occurs, its acknowledgement (to self and/or spouse and/or child) is followed by confession (repentance) to the Lord which results in forgiveness (I John 1:7; 10). The Christian family in times of sorrow, distress, conflict, and failure ever relies upon the promises of God as revealed in Scripture and rests in Him for help and deliverance, unlike that of unbelievers.

Read Together:
He Reads: Colossians 2:3
She Reads: 2 Corinthians 10:4

Answer Together:
Imperfect people make up homes of the believer and nonbeliever, so the occurrence of failure and wrong exist in both. What then is the *game changer* for the Christian family; what makes it vastly different from that of the ungodly?

Pray Together:
Father, thank you for our Christian home. Continue to grow us in grace that it may continuously evolve into the home of Your design.

58
When Is a Child Old Enough to Be Saved?

Scholars were asked the question, "When should children come to Christ?"

One scholar answered, "At thirteen"; another said, "At ten"; another replied, "At six." A little girl then gave her striking answer: "Whenever they understand who God is." She was more correct (though not fully) than the scholars.

C. H. Spurgeon surmises the best when a child may be saved. "As soon as a child is capable of being lost, it is capable of being saved. As soon as a child can sin, that child can, if God's grace assist it, believe and receive the Word of God....Believe that children can be saved just as much as yourselves. I do most firmly believe in the salvation of children. When you see the young heart brought to the Savior, do not stand by and speak harshly, mistrusting everything."[78]

Jonathan Edwards was saved at age 7, Isaac Watts was saved at age 9, and Fanny Crosby was saved at age 11. The vast majority of people are saved under the age 21.

Read Together:
He Reads: Matthew 19:14
She Reads: Luke 18:17

Answer Together:
Prior to today's devotion, what did you deem the "age of accountability" to be saved? Understanding of the basic tenets of the faith, not one's age, is the determining factor for salvation. What are these foundational truths a child must understand to be saved? What is meant by Jesus' words in Matthew 18:3?

Pray Together:
Lord, help us instill in our child foundational truths of the Gospel so that at the earliest possible time he may experience conviction of sin and trust your Son, Jesus, as His Lord and Savior. Enable us to be keenly sensitive when that time arrives.

59
Unrealistic Expectations for Your Marriage

During World War II, the 23rd Headquarters Special Troops stationed in France had a phantom military regiment. Skillfully, these soldiers staged the illusion of real troops, artillery, trucks, and other equipment (primarily by the use of inflated lookalikes) that from the air appeared real, fooling the Germans.

Hollywood has done a great job in creating the illusion that marriage is one never ending stroll down primrose lanes, uninterrupted happiness and joy, fulfillment of one's grandiose dreams and desires; and as the song says, "love is all they need" to succeed. But it is all a phantom, an apparition that exists only in Hollywood or your mind.

James Dobson says, "There is no way a marriage between two imperfect human beings can deliver on that expectation. The late counselor Jean Lush believed, and I agree, that this romantic illusion is particularly characteristic of American women, who expect more from their husbands than they are capable of providing. The consequent disappointment is an emotional minefield."[79]

Many brides, as the Germans, are fooled by an illusion, the resemblance of something real, and must awaken to reality lest expectations are shattered (and they will be) and divorce result.

Walgreens aired commercials about a "perfect place" in which it depicted things that could happen only within its city limits. Hollywood expectations of your marriage exist in only such a place.

You must reject whatever unrealistic, unbiblical, and unattainable expectations you have conjured up about your husband or wife, whether they stem from parents, friends, or Hollywood. Identify them for what they really are, merely a phantom of your imagination.

Read Together:
He Reads: John 8:44
She Reads: 2 Corinthians 11:14

Answer Together:
Do either of you have a phantom about marriage? What expectation did you have about your spouse that you now realize was a phantom, an unattainable one? About yourself?

Pray Together:
Heavenly Father, the enemy has done a remarkable job in creating an illusion of what marriage and our expectations for one another are to be like. Help us see it for the illusion that it is and base our expectations upon Your Word and that which is real.

60
Benefits of Disciplining Your Child

W. A. Criswell states: "The rod of discipline is one means of introducing YAHWEH God to children. As children experience love and learn obedience from parents, they can better recognize God's love and respond to His discipline (Matthew 7:7–11). It is the means of cleansing (Proverbs 20:30); it is a tool for driving out foolishness (22:15); it is a vehicle for breaking the rebellious heart and thereby delivering the child from eternal punishment (23:13–14); it is an effective teaching device (10:13; 29:15); it is prerequisite to a parent's rest and satisfaction (29:17)."[80]

Never discipline when your temper is raging (cool off first), or uncompassionately (heartlessly), or without explanation (purpose of the discipline).

Read Together:
He Reads: Proverbs 13:24; 20:30; 22:15; 23:13–14
She Reads: Proverbs 10:13; 29:15; 29:17

Answer Together:
How is the rod of discipline a means of introducing your child to God, the means of cleansing, a tool for driving out foolishness, a vehicle for breaking the rebellious heart, an effective teaching device, a means to save your child from Hell, and a means to your tranquility and satisfaction? It's important that you both be on the same page with regard to the use of discipline, so talk about it.

Pray Together:
Father, we have learned from experience that your discipline upon us is always done in love, for our best good, and for Your glory. Help us discipline our child in the same manner and for the same purpose.

61

The Neglected Vineyard

The person speaking in the Song of Solomon 1:6 had the responsibility for the upkeep (the pruning, plowing, planting) of vineyards that belonged unto others. It is clear from the text that she was not negligent in this assignment but diligent and determined to keep them so that each would fulfill its purpose to the owner's pleasure. Such faithfulness to her lord (the owner) and sacrificial work is commendable!

However, the passion that led her to serve so zealously in the vineyards of others caused her to neglect her own vineyard, and for that she should be reprimanded. This servant testifies, "They made me the keeper of the vineyards; but mine own vineyard have I not kept." She enabled the vineyards of others to stay pruned and thus bear much fruit, while her own was overtaken with weeds and thorns yielding little or no fruit.

> The wife of a great evangelist said that her husband won the world but let his own son die and go to Hell.

Work in the vineyards of others but not to the neglect of that of your own (heart and home). Embrace the great work of pruning, plowing, and planting in the vineyard of your heart and home through personal and corporate Bible study, prayer, regular pruning of that which is wrong, church attendance, witnessing, and biblical instruction.

Failure to keep the vineyard of the home or heart leads to spiritual famine and devastation.

Read Together:

He Reads: Song of Solomon 1:6
She Reads: Philippians 2:12; II Timothy 3:14, 17

Has hurriedness of life or laziness hindered work in the vineyard of your heart or home? What work in each vineyard needs undertaking?

Family vineyard. Talk together about how to schedule family spiritual times, the removal of things that are injurious spiritually or morally, and faithful attendance at church.

Personal vineyard. Decide to roll up the sleeves and work diligently in your vineyard at becoming the godliest person possible.

Lord, we confess that sometimes we do a great job in working in another's vineyard (counseling, mentoring, supplying needs, etc.) while doing a poor job in our own. Help us keep our own vineyard (heart and home) well as we endeavor to keep the vineyards of others.

62
Ten Nonnegotiables for a Happy Marriage

God is in absolute control. He is the ruler over every detail of marriage and family life.

Friends will not interfere or hinder the marriage. Night out with the *old gang* is history if they are proving to be a detriment to the marriage. In fact, old friends may need to become former friends to make way for beneficial friends for both spouses and the marriage. Oswald Chambers says in *My Utmost for His Highest*, "Friendship is rare on earth. It means identity in thought and heart and spirit."[81]

The husband is God's ordained leader in the home; the wife, the helper.

Worship with fellow believers is prioritized and prized.

Acceptance for each other is embraced totally despite *warts, blemishes and wrinkles.*

In times of storms that shake and rattle the boat of marriage, both partners trust the unseen hand of God to sustain (Romans 8:28).

The husband will love his wife as Christ loved the church (passionately, sacrificially, patiently, selflessly, endlessly). John MacArthur said, "What higher motive could there be for the husband to love his wife? By loving her as Christ loved the church, he honors Christ in the most direct and graphic way. He becomes the embodiment of Christ's love to his own wife, a living example to the rest of his family, a channel of blessing to his entire household, and a powerful testimony to a watching world."[82]

Communication channels are always open.

An attitude of trust between both partners exists (if eroded, it must be rebuilt).

Both embrace marriage as a permanent "till death do us part" commitment.

Read Together:
He Reads: Psalm 127:1
She Reads: Philippians 2:10

Answer Together:
Which of the ten nonnegotiables stated does Satan attack the most often and most fiercely in your family? Why? What might be done to strengthen that area? There are many other nonnegotiables of a happy marriage. Share several. What is it for God *to build the house?*

Pray Together:
Lord, we want you to build our house into the home of Your heavenly design. We commit, with firm resolution, to our assigned roles to hold fast to the nonnegotiables cited in today's thought.

63
Never Think Divorce

Marriage is a divine institution established by God between a man and woman designed for a lifetime. Jesus forthrightly stated that a husband and wife were "one flesh" and pictures His unending and abiding love for His bride, the church (Ephesians 5:24–31). Jesus is the "Bridegroom" of the church (the bride, the redeemed family of God), and this union will never be divorced. In marriage it is essential that the home be built upon biblical principles, worship and prayer; that the husband love the wife as Christ loves the church (Ephesians 5:25); and that the subject of divorce never be broached.

Adrian Rogers states, "Now some couples leave divorce as an option if problems arise. But couples that get divorced and those that don't have basically the same kinds of problems. The difference is not in the problems but in their commitment.

"Others rationalize, 'I owe it to myself to be happy.' There's a Greek word for that: bologna! When you were at the marriage altar, you made a vow. You owe it to God, your spouse, your children, and yourself to keep that vow."[83]

Read Together:
He Reads: Matthew 19:4–6
She Reads: Genesis 2:24

Answer Together:
In the marriage vow you said "for better or worse" regarding remaining with each other. If things have become worse, what might be done for the marriage to be better? It's imperative that divorce is not considered an option. Avail yourselves of counseling by your pastor or certified Christian therapist if the situation warrants. You owe it to each other, your children and God to work hard at turning that which is *worse* into that which is far *better*.

Pray Together:
Heavenly Father, mend the brokenness of our relationship to one another. Help us acknowledge personal fault for what has happened and immediately take the necessary steps to correct it. Turn our marriage back into that which is wonderful and happy.

64
Seven Common Mistakes of Parenting

Parents make mistakes in parenting; some are recognized and changed immediately, while others sadly go unchecked, affecting a child's physical, spiritual and/or mental health.

Included in the mistakes parents make in parenting are:

1. Giving them too many choices. Fewer are better than more with regard to choices afforded to children lest they become overwhelmed and frustrated.

2. Praising children for all they do in time turns them into praise junkies. If there is no praise or payoff, they refuse to do what is asked or expected.

3. Trying to make them happy by bowing to their every wish or demand. Children need to rely upon God, not others or stuff, for satisfaction, joy and meaning in life.

4. The use of shame or threats to gain their obedience always backfires. You should never give the impression you will stop loving them or send them to stay with others if they fail to comply.

5. Neglect of bedtime conversation ("How was your day?" "Anything happen you want to share?" "What do you plan to do tomorrow?") and Bible devotion.

6. Taking the pacifier from them before they are ready. It is their security. When they feel secure without it they will stop on their own.[84]

7. Disciplining by anger. Dr. James Dobson states: "The best way to get children to do what you want is to spend time with them before disciplinary problems occur—having fun together and enjoying mutual laughter and joy. When those moments of love and closeness happen, kids are not as tempted to challenge and test the limits. Many confrontations can be avoided by building friendships with kids and thereby making them want to cooperate at home. It sure beats anger as a motivator of little ones!"[85]

Read Together:
He Reads: Colossians 3:21
She Reads: Proverbs 29:15

Answer Together:
Did any of the stated mistakes surprise you; if so, which ones? How might you avoid these mistakes? What other parenting mistakes might you add to this list that must be avoided?

Pray Together:
Lord, we need Your wisdom and guidance to parent so as to rear healthy children mentally, physically and spiritually. Point out the mistakes we presently are making that they may be avoided in the future.

65
Have Couple Time

Having fun times by doing activities together that each enjoy strengthens the marriage by deepening the relationship. It's important that couples have periodical *couple's time* (without the children) to bond more deeply and affectionately.

A friend shared that for the first time since their children arrived they were to have several days alone at a ski resort. I responded, "Hooray. So happy for you both."

Couples should schedule getaway times, occasions to do what the other enjoys, and weekly date nights.

Read Together:
He Reads: Proverbs 5:18–19
She Reads: Proverbs 12:4

Answer Together:
What activity does your mate enjoy in which you may participate? Ask each other, "What is it that you would like us to do together?" What have you done lately together (without the children) that you felt enriched your relationship? What couple time can you schedule for this week?

Pray Together:
Heavenly Father, bind us together more and more through what we do together. Help us not become so preoccupied with earning a living, keeping the house, and rearing children that we neglect each other, causing our relationship to dissipate.

66
Helping Your Children Honor Your Spouse

As a father, it is your task to *teach* your children by example and word to honor their mother. Treat her as the princess on the throne in the home, and your children will have a worthy example to follow.

Wife, you are equally to raise the bar of the opinion of your children about their father. Praise him; speak of your admiration and appreciation of him in their presence.

Never should parents undermine the honor each duly deserves from their children, but ever bolster it.

Read Together:
He Reads: Proverbs 31:28
She Reads: Romans 12:10

Answer Together:
What are you doing to cause your child to honor their mother or father more? Have you been guilty of belittling each other before them? If so, how might that hurt the children's view of their mother or father? Arguments between parents ought to be reserved for the private bedroom, not the public showroom.

Pray Together:
Lord, help us consistently treat each other with such respect, love and honor that our children will grow up honoring and respecting us.

67
The Ministry of Laughter

Dr. Marvin E. Herring of New Jersey's School of Osteopathic Medicine said, "The diaphragm, thorax, abdomen, heart, lungs, and even the liver are given a massage during a hearty laugh."[86] Laughter is medicine prescribed by the Great Physician for a broken, crushed spirit. Solomon says, "A cheerful heart is good medicine, but a broken spirit saps a person's strength" (Proverbs 17:22 NLT).

The grief is so horrendous and the loss so devastating, it's really difficult to even want to laugh. Laughter is like the prescribed medicine the doctor orders for a physical ailment; it may not be desired, but it certainly will speed up the healing.

Research indicates that laughter produces endorphins in the body that produce the sense of well-being. Other physical benefits of laughing noted by health care professionals include:

Decrease in stress hormone levels
Strengthening of the immune system

Muscle relaxation
Pain reduction
Lowering of blood pressure
Cardiovascular conditioning
Natural antidepressant[87]

Dr. William Fry from Stanford University said that one minute of laughter is equivalent to 10 minutes on the rowing machine.[88]

So laugh. It's a gift from God. "Then was our mouth filled with laughter, and our tongue with singing" (Psalm 126:2). Neuroscientist Jodi Deluca, Ph.D., of Embry-Riddle Aeronautical University said, "It doesn't matter why you laugh. Even in small doses, it improves your overall quality of life."[89] Personally, I turn to the Andy Griffith show for laughter therapy. It's impossible to watch Andy and Barney without laughing.

Laughter is contagious and infectious. Your laughter will prompt your spouse to laugh. Laughter eases tension and defuses conflict while lengthening life. Follow the DOCTOR'S advice and daily take your laughter medication.

Read Together:
He Reads: Proverbs 17:22
She Reads: Psalm 126:2

Answer Together:
Recall and share a time that you both laughed together. Sometimes laugher is spontaneous; other times it is spurred by a humorous joke or video or show. Determine to be intentional on sharing things that bring laughter to your spouse.

Pray Together:
Lord, thank you for creating the medicine of laughter that not only aids in healing the grief-stricken, ministers to the sick, prevents some sicknesses, and lifts the troubled, but also strengthens marriages and families. Fill our mouths often with laughter, we pray.

68

Weathering Life's Storms

Corrie ten Boom said everyone has just been through a storm, is going through a storm, or is about to face a storm. Often storms develop quickly and unexpectedly. Gospel singer/songwriter Tommy Dorsey faced such an unexpected, devastating storm.

In 1932, when Dorsey was age 32, he and his wife, Nettie, lived in a small Chicago apartment. One hot August afternoon, he was the featured soloist at a revival meeting, an engagement he did not want to do. Nettie was pregnant with their first child, and the time was drawing near when she would deliver. He kissed her good-bye and set out in his Model A to the revival. Soon he discovered he had left his music case and turned around to get it. He found Nettie sleeping. As he paused, something strongly told him to stay, something he later wished he had obeyed.

He arrived in St. Louis and sang again and again in the revival. Upon sitting down, he received a message that read: YOUR WIFE JUST DIED. He immediately phoned home, and all he could hear were the words "Nettie is dead. Nettie is dead."

Upon arriving home, he learned Nettie had given birth to a boy. Sadly, the boy died that night. He buried them both in the same casket. The grief overcame him to the point he felt God had done him an injustice, and desire to ever serve God or write gospel songs vanished.

On one of those dark days of grief, he determined it was God who told him to stay with Nettie and not travel to St. Louis. Had he listened, he would have been with her when she died. He said, "From that moment on I vowed to listen more closely to Him."

Professor Frye, who seemed to know what he needed, took him to Madam Malone's Poro College, a neighborhood music school. In the quietude of that place before a piano, Dorsey said, "Something happened to me then. I felt at peace. I felt as though I could reach out and touch God. I found myself playing a melody, one I'd never heard or played before; and the words in my head—they just seemed to fall into place:

Precious Lord, take my hand.
Lead me on; let me stand!

I am tired; I am weak; I am worn.
Through the storm, through the night,
Lead me on to the light.
Take my hand, precious Lord; lead me home.

"The Lord gave me these words and melody; He also healed my spirit. I learned that when we are in our deepest grief, when we feel farthest from God, this is when He is closest and when we are most open to His restoring power. And so I go on living for God willingly and joyfully, until that day comes when He will take me and gently lead me home."[90]

Read Together:

He Reads: Isaiah 4:6
She Reads: Psalm 55:8

Answer Together:

What storms have you experienced personally? As a couple? How did you cope? How can you help others weather similar storms? How would you adapt or apply today's Scripture reading to weathering life's storms?

Pray Together:

Almighty God, thank You for sustaining us through the fierce storms already encountered that certainly would have shipwrecked our lives and possibly marriage. Thank You for being our strong tower and refuge of protection in which we may always flee when the storm of sorrow, adversity, failure, rejection, or conflict arises.

69

Healing through Helping

Dr. James Dobson said, "This is one of the powerful paradoxes of the Christian life: When we share someone else's pain, we often shed some of our own. When we help others, we end up helping ourselves. When we lift another's burdens, ours lighten."[91]

In Isaiah 58:7-9 (TLB) we read, "No, the kind of fast I want is that you stop oppressing those who work for you and treat them fairly and give them what they earn. I want you to share your food with the hungry and bring right into your own homes those who are helpless, poor, and destitute. Clothe those who are cold, and don't hide from relatives who need your help. If you do these things, God will shed his own glorious light upon you. He will heal you; your godliness will lead you forward, goodness will be a shield before you, and the glory of the Lord will protect you from behind."

The text clearly states that destructive habits, attitudes, and thoughts are conquered through repentance and fasting (v. 6). However, a second less recognized truth it states is that helping the poor and needy provides personal emotional healing. Give, and it shall be given unto you. Give love, encouragement and goods (clothes, shelter, food) to the hurting, and not only will they be helped, but "God will shed his own glorious light upon you. He will heal you." In helping heal the wounds of others, your own wounds will be healed.

Read Together:

He Reads: Galatians 6:2
She Reads: Philippians 2:4

Answer Together:

What insights about bearing the burden of others did you glean from today's Scripture reading? What do you do, to whom do you turn when you are feeling down, discouraged or depressed? Have you found the statement by Dobson and the text by Isaiah to be true when dealing with pain or trouble?

Pray Together:

Lord Jesus, help us suffer as good soldiers without complaint or rebellion, bearing a good witness to all men. Help us use our pain for gain by investing it in the work of helping others who are troubled and downcast.

70
When Death Invades the Home

Probably the best things that can be shared to strengthen and comfort you in sorrow are said without words. You need friends to love on you, simply listen to you, talk and cry (not dialogue), journey with you on the roller coaster of emotional sorrow that has its highs when God is felt near and dear and its possible lows of wondering if God has abandoned you. You need friends who will be your Safe Place where you can be yourself, cry, talk, question, or doubt—without putting in their two-cents' worth unrequested.

Queen Victoria illustrates my point. Once she heard that the wife of a common laborer had lost her baby. Compassionately she called on the woman and spent some time with her. Neighbors afterward made inquiry as to what the queen had said. "Nothing," replied the grieving mother. "She simply put her hands on mine, and we silently wept together."[92]

You need friends who will primarily reach out to you with a gentle, loving touch or a hug, who will allow their spirit and yours to communicate without the use of words. Charlie Walton in his book *When There Are No Words* explains the power of a hug in the hour of grief.

"Pain doesn't come in pounds or ounces or gallons. You just feel like you are standing before a mountain that you are going to have to move one spoonful at a time. It is a task you can never hope to complete...a mountain that you can never hope to finish moving. But...as you stand surveying that mountain of grief...a loved one steps forward with a hug that communicates clearly. You can almost picture that person stepping up to your mountain of grief with a shovel and saying, 'I cannot move the mountain for you...but I will take this one shovelful of your grief and deal with it myself."[93] Walton continues, "Every hug helps to dilute the pain...to move the mountain. Don't be selfish with your mountain. Don't be a martyr about your grief. There is plenty of mountain to keep you busy the rest of your life...and...if your friends hadn't been willing to help...they wouldn't have showed up with those spoons, shovels and hugs."[94]

In the wilderness, a man became lost. He was approached by a man who met him, and the following conversation ensued. "Sir, I am lost. Can you show me the way out of this wilderness?"

"No," said the stranger, "I cannot show you the way out of the wilderness; but maybe if I walk with you, we can find it together."[95] Though unable to tell us the way out of our sorrow, compassionate friends will walk with us until we find it.

Read Together:
He Reads: Psalm 91:4
She Reads: Psalm 147:3

Answer Together:

Don't fence people out in times of sorrow but allow them to bring their spoons, shovels and hugs to remove a little bit of that fierce and painful mountain from your life. What have you discovered to be really helpful from others in your journey through sorrow? What was hurtful? What might others have said or done to comfort you better? How can you use your pain for gain personally and in helping others?

Pray Together:

God of all comfort, our hearts are broken, and it is unto you alone we look for strength, comfort and healing. Sustain us in this sorrow with thy Holy word and the eternal Hope it promises in seeing our saved loved one again in Heaven. Thank you for friends who have arrived in Your name with shovels, spoons and hugs to bear some of the horrendous pain and grief.

71

The Power of the Tongue

Tongues are more terrible instruments than can be made with hammers and anvils, and the evil which they inflict cuts deeper and spreads wider.[96]—C. H. Spurgeon

In the classic movie *A Christmas Story*, during recess on a cold winter day two boys surrounded by classmates argue whether a person's tongue will stick to the school's flagpole. One of the boys "triple-dog dares" the other to stick his tongue to the pole. He does, and it gets stuck. As his classmates returned to class, there he remained with his tongue frozen to the flagpole in great pain. Of all the right uses of the tongue, this certainly was not one of them!

This humorous scene points out how the tongue brings trouble and pain when it is misused. Solomon said, "Whoso keepeth his mouth and his tongue keepeth his soul from troubles" (Proverbs 21:23). Or, as The Message translation puts it, "Watch your words and hold your tongue; you'll save yourself a lot of grief."

Of all places, the tongue must be controlled within the home.

Avoid a *Harsh Tongue*. Harsh words are but an invisible sharp razor that cuts and pains deeply the person on the receiving end (Psalm 52:2)

Avoid a *Belittling Tongue*. "Do not use harmful words, but only helpful words, the kind that build up and provide what is needed, so that what you say will do good to those who hear you" (Ephesians 4:29 GNT). Never speak to your spouse or children in a way that makes them think they are nobodies. Words ought to lift others up, not pull them down.

Avoid a *Hasty Tongue*. "Seest thou a man that is hasty in his words? there is more hope of a fool than of him" (Proverbs 29:20). "He that refraineth his lips is wise" (Proverbs 10:19). Be slow to speak, and learn when to be silent. This will prevent many arguments and fights.

Billy Graham said, "More friction and tensions are caused in a family by tone of voice than for any other one reason."[97] As husbands and wives, we must make sure the tone of our voice is gentle, soft and kind even in times of disagreement or conflict.

Read Together:
He Reads: Proverbs 21:23
She Reads: Proverbs 29:20

Answer Together:
In your own words describe what it means to have a harsh, belittling and hasty tongue. Which of these would your spouse say you were guilty at times of using? How many arguments or fights among you both have been ignited by the use of one of these hurtful tongues? In tomorrow's devotion we will consider how the tongue may be controlled.

Pray Together:
Heavenly Father, help us use our tongue to splash out love and laughter in the home instead of pain, hurt and divisiveness.

72
Muzzling the Tongue

So how can you "muzzle the tongue"? David states, "I will guard my ways that I may not sin with my tongue. I will guard my mouth with a muzzle" (Psalm 39:1). How can you muzzle the mouth to say only things pleasing to God?

1. Be determined to abstain from the sins of the tongue.

2. Fill your mind with biblical, wholesome truth. What's in the well of the heart is what comes out its faucet (the tongue).

3. Lay the tongue on the altar of sacrifice. James tells us, "No man can tame the tongue." And he is right. But Jesus can. So rely upon His super-duper-natural strength to speak rightly (Philippians 4:13).

4. "Don't give place to the devil." That is, don't condone bad talk at any time about any person. Say a loud NO always to unhealthy talk.

5. Apply Greg Laurie's acronym T.H.I.N.K. as a guide to healthy speech.[98]

T   Is it true? If not, don't speak it (Proverbs 12:17).

H   Is it helpful or hurtful? (Proverbs 12:18).

I   Is it inspiring, uplifting, encouraging? (Proverbs 17:22).

N   Is it really necessary to say? Much of what is said to others about others is best left unsaid (Proverbs 13:3).

K   Is it kind or demeaning? (Ephesians 4:32).

Is it true, helpful, inspirational, necessary, and kind? If not, don't say it.

We all need to muzzle, bridle, control our tongue and use it more to tell others about Jesus and His awesome love. A good prayer for you to pray is Psalm 141:3: "Set a watch, O LORD, before my mouth; keep the door of my lips."

Read Together:

He Reads: Proverbs 12:18

She Reads: Ephesians 4:31–32

Answer Together:

What might you do for your speech to be seasoned with kindness, gentleness and loving warmth to your husband/wife/child? As life mates, if not careful we may say a word in rage or haste to one another that cuts so deeply it will take weeks if not years to heal. For love's sake, think before you speak.

Pray Together:

Lord, help us more fully understand the power of words to build up or tear down, bring laughter or tears, unite or divide. With the psalmist we cry, "Set a watch, O LORD, before my mouth; keep the door of my lips."

73

Two Good Forgivers

"We are to forgive," writes Charles Stanley, "so that we may enjoy God's goodness without feeling the weight of anger burning deep within our hearts. Forgiveness does not mean we recant the fact that what happened to us was wrong. Instead, we roll our burdens onto the Lord and allow Him to carry them for us."[99]

C. S. Lewis said, "To be a Christian means to forgive the inexcusable, because God has forgiven the inexcusable in you."[100]

In pondering the great cost of forgiveness, you must agree with William Barclay: "Where there is forgiveness, someone must be crucified (that is, self)." And that someone is you. Recall the words of Paul, "And they that are Christ's have crucified the flesh with the affections and lusts" (Galatians 5:24) and "I die daily" (I Corinthians 15:31).

Death must occur to the "Big I," as Bertha Smith called it, if forgiveness is to be manifested. The idea of death to the flesh encompasses a willingness to sacrifice your rights, desires and rewards so that the guilty (he who hurt you) may be fully forgiven and placed in right standing with you. Though costly, forgiving our spouse pays us back in the weight of gold.

Billy Graham's wife, Ruth, often said, "A good marriage consists of two good forgivers."[101] And she was right.

Read Together:

He Reads: Matthew 18:21
She Reads: Colossians 3:13

Answer Together:

What does it really mean to forgive others (spouse included) as Jesus has forgiven you? Forgiveness is not rendered based on whether he/she deserves it but upon the example and precept of Christ. If there is a lack of forgiveness with regard to anything toward your spouse, it is time to bring it to the cross and let it go.

Pray Together:

God, help us in our marriage be two good forgivers. In those times when our flesh says or does something that hurts the other, help the offended to forgive despite the hurt and pain.

74

Your Aging Parents

As you grow older, never forget that your parents are getting older and the command to honor them remains in effect to their death.

Dennis Rainey states, "Honoring your father and mother is the forgotten commandment today, even among pastors and counselors, but it may be a key step to restoring relationships with our parents and growing toward maturity."[102]

Honor them by treating them with the dignity they deserve despite their old age and frailties. Honor them by discovering their needs either by observation or inquiry and then supplying those needs. Honor them by frequent contact (visits, phone calls, emails, etc.). Never forget you are still their world though they may not be yours. Honor them by including them on special occasions (Christmas, Easter, birthdays, Thanksgiving). Honor them through various expressions of love such as a bouquet of flowers or gift card or by being their handyman for the day. Honor them, if still in the home, by compliance to their wishes. Honor them by doing those little things that can brighten an otherwise *dark* day.

It is so easy for married children to allow their parents' world to be totally eclipsed by their own.

Stay sensitive to that which they daily encounter in their world and help bear the burden.

Don't tell me how good a Christian you are (because it isn't true) if you are failing to care for your father and mother.

"If God," states Billy Graham, "gives you responsibility for aging parents, seek what is best for them, not what is most convenient for you. And keep in contact with them."[103] Graham added, "If ever we needed to put the Golden Rule into action, it's with our aging parents."

He Reads: Exodus 20:12

She Reads: Matthew 7:12

If your parents suddenly died, would you have any regrets regarding your treatment of and care for them? As a spouse, are you hindering your wife/husband from honoring her/his parents in the highest possible manner in violation of God's command? How can you be more intentional in honoring your parents? How does the Golden Rule apply to your treatment of your parents?

Heavenly Father, thank You for our aging parents who cared for us with great sacrifice and cost as children and beyond. Help us count no cost too great to repay them in some measure for all they did for us by doing for them what they no longer can do for themselves.

75

Raising Godly Children in a Godless Age

Billy Graham offers godly advice to Christian parents.[104]

"*First*, take time with your children. Your children not only require a great deal of your time, but they long and hunger for it. Perhaps they do not express it, but the hunger and longing are there just the same. Love them; spend hours with them. Cut out some of your so-called 'important social engagements' and make your home the center of your social life. God will honor you, and your children will grow up to call you blessed (Proverbs 31:28).

Second, give your children ideals for living. Teach them moral and spiritual principles of life. Show them that only the morally and spiritually right attain genuine satisfaction in life.

Third, set your children a good example.

Fourth, plan activities for your children. Plan things together as a family.

Fifth, discipline your children. The Devil's philosophy is: "Do as you please." Children are going to be in society what they are in the home. The Bible, from Genesis to Revelation, teaches that parents ought to lovingly discipline their children.

Sixth, teach your children to know God, and bring them up in the church. Very seldom do parents have trouble with children when the Bible is read regularly in the home, grace is said at the table, and family prayers take place daily.

Read Together:

He Reads: Isaiah 28:13
She Reads: Proverbs 31:28

Answer Together:

How much *quality* time do you spend with your children daily (not time in which you have a phone to your ear or iPad in your lap)? Are you introducing your children to God and His Word a little bit here, a little bit there, "word upon word and precept upon precept"? Do you habitually read the Bible or a Bible story and have prayer with your children?

Pray Together:

Lord, thank You for the wonderful gift of children. As with Hannah, we believe you have lent our children to us for their godly upbringing. Help us teach them about You and Thy wondrous Word that they will become Christians at an early age and live for You all their life.

76

Does Jesus Live at Your House?

"Does Jesus live at your house?"
I heard a child once ask.
Her little brow was furrowed
As she struggled with a task.
I saw her eyes were shadowed;
Her face marked with a tear;
The voice, a wee bit wistful
For the answer she might hear.
"He used to live at our house
With Mamma—Daddy, too.
But now He's gone away somewhere.

I don't know what to do;
For Daddy's not the same today,
And Mamma laughs no more.
They never bother much with me;
They say I'm just a bore.
"It didn't used to be this way
With Jesus in our home,
For every night my daddy came,
When all my curls were combed,
To help me say my bedtime prayer
(And Mamma helped me, too);
And they'd smile and tuck me in,
But now—they never do.
"Could you tell me where Jesus is,
For everything seems black?
We want Him in our house again;
We want Him to come back.
And when He comes we'll keep Him,
For we truly need Him so—
If Jesus lives at your house,
Oh, don't ever let Him go!"
The child then turned and left me
While I pursued my way
And thought of many home fires
That could be bright today.
Does Jesus live at your house?
How much these words portend!
Yea! On this question's answer
Our hopes—our all—depend.[105]

Sadly, the poem is true of far too many Christian homes. Neglect of family prayer, devotions, and church attendance coupled with obsession to make money or excel in job performance and the pursuit of the pleasures of this world slowly but surely extinguish the home's fire for God.

If the allegiance your family has for God is dissipating, now is the time to reestablish it. Return to family prayer, devotions, and church faithfulness, and rearrange your priorities both within and without the home.

Read Together:
He Reads: Genesis 18:19
She Reads: Joshua 24:14–15

Answer Together:
What can you do to instill Christian truths in the members of the household? Could your little girl/boy say of your home what the little girl in the poem stated about hers? Satan would love to destroy your Christian home. What defenses can be set in motion against him?

Pray Together:
Almighty God, we choose for our home to be ever under Your authority. Help our home honor You in its decisions, conversations, entertainment, and conduct.

77
Make Things Right with Your Parents

Suddenly your parents may die; and with their death, opportunities for reconciliation, expression of gratitude and love, obedience, and the blessings of their presence will forever be gone. Harriet Beecher Stowe (1811–1896), author of *Uncle Tom's Cabin,* said, "The bitterest tears shed over graves are for words left unsaid and deeds left undone."[106] Today say what needs to be said and do what needs to be done to make things right with your mom and/or dad. Tomorrow sadly may be too late.

Read Together:
He Reads: Proverbs 3:27
She Reads: Galatians 6:10

Answer Together:
If your parents died today, would you bear the bitterest tears for words left unsaid and deeds left undone with regards to them? Will you go to them today saying what needs to be said and doing for them what should be done? If on the outs with your parents, take the high road and initiate reconciliation.

Pray Together:
Lord Jesus, help us not procrastinate in telling our parents of our deepest love, gratitude and appreciation and in doing for them what needs to be done.

78
Parents Who Are at Odds with Their Child

A recent study comparing the U.S. with Israel, Spain, Germany, and the U.K. revealed that the relationships between adult children and their aging parents were the most "disharmonious" in the U.S.[107] The pivotal reason for this, according to psychologist Joshua Coleman, is that "the primary determinant for whether family members remain close in the U.S. is based on how the relationship makes the individuals within those relationships feel."[108] And the greatest longing for parent and child is to feel loved, accepted and respected, no matter the circumstance.

In disagreements that divide, it's essential as the parent that you take the initiative in reconciliation. "But it was their doing. They spoke the harsh words and violated the rules of the household. Why should I be the first to step up to the plate to seek resolution?"

Because as an adult your maturity level to resolve conflicts is far greater than the emotional roller-coaster maturity of adolescence. To stubbornly say, "Until he comes to me to apologize, I will have nothing to do with him" not only likely delays reconciliation and intensifies the problem but also wounds the spirit of both the child and yourself further.

What's wrong with the parent's saying to the rebellious child, "I am ready to listen to your side of the story calmly and lovingly," or, "I am sorry for my outburst of anger over what you did; I'm ready now to talk about it calmly," or, "I really want to hear you out; I possibly misunderstood what happened," or, "I now realize my wrong that led to our estrangement and am deeply sorry for what I did or said." And most certainly say, "I want you to know that I love you beyond comprehension and will regardless whatever you do."

The wayward son of Luke 15 recalled the care, provision, and love of his father for him, as well as the sin he committed against his father. He resolved to confess it to him, and this prompted his return. The boy's father, in catching a glimpse of the returning son, ran to meet him and greeted him with loving forgiveness, making full restoration possible. It is when such happens that the wounded spirits of parent and child are healed.

Read Together:

He Reads: Luke 15:11–24
She Reads: I Corinthians 13:4–6

Answer Together:

At what cost are you willing to be reconciled with an erring son or daughter? Will you take the initiative in being reconciled with him/her? What does the father of the prodigal son teach in the matter of reconciliation with one's children?

Pray Together:

Heavenly Father, we bring our prodigal son/daughter to You, begging their receptiveness to our effort in reconciliation. Help us approach him/her in heartfelt love and affection and a meek and gentle spirit. Do whatever is necessary to awaken our son/daughter in the far country and bring him/her home to You and us.

79

Battlements for the Home

The rooftops of the homes in Moses' day were flat. This posed a great danger, for they were used for worship, recreation and solitude. It is because of this that the Lord said, "When you build a house with a flat roof without erecting a battlement (safety wall 3½ feet tall) around it and someone falls off and dies, you will be held responsible."

God is clearly saying to fathers and husbands, "Men, you must build your home for the safety of your family. You must build your home so that your family will be protected. If your wife, child or grandchildren get morally or spiritually injured due to your not erecting strong battlements about the home, I will hold you accountable."

The need of spiritual safety walls about the home is dire. Families are being destroyed. The divorce mill is grinding our homes into ruin. Children are being lost more and more to the world, the Devil and humanism. The home that God ordained in the Garden of Eden is becoming extinct.

Erect at least four battlements of protection about your home.

The Battlement of Defiance.

Upon Surgical Operating Room doors, a sign reads, "Keep Out." Safety of the patient depends upon an environment free from any possible contamination from the outside. For the safety of all within your home, you must place such a sign upon every entrance to your home: "Keep Out" to all that would possibly corrupt and defile.

The Battlement of Discipline.

How we need fathers who will teach their children that they mean what say they and create within them a spirit of willing obedience both to God and them. Solomon states that if we really love our children we will discipline them so they will obey. He says, "A youngster's heart is filled with foolishness, but physical discipline will drive it far away" (Proverbs 22:15 NLT). Again he says, "Punishment that hurts chases evil from the heart" (Proverbs 20:30 TLB).

The Battlement of Doctrine.

Doctrine is simply "a set of guidelines" to govern the home. And there is none better for the sanctity and preservation of the home than the Bible. God promises not only to protect the home which is built upon the Word of God, but also to prosper it (Deuteronomy 6:1–9).

The Battlement of Devotion.

A fourth wall of protection to be erected about the home is that of devotion to Jesus Christ. You must become madly in love with Jesus to the extent that you practice what you believe in the church, the workplace, and the home. May your child never say, "My daddy hardly believes what he says in church, or else he would never treat my mother the way he does," or, "He does not believe what he says in church, or else he wouldn't talk or act the way he does."

Fathers are intended to be an image of God the Father, the high priest, the king, the judge, the counselor, the provider, and the avenger of wrong to his family! Paul declares "For a man indeed ought not to cover his head, forasmuch as he is the image and glory of God" (I Corinthians 11:7). He represents God in a particular sense in which woman and children do not.

Erect these four battlements—Defiance, Discipline, Doctrine and Devotion—about your home, and it will be protected from the enemy. Some of your children may climb over the battlements, being drawn away by the beckoning call of sin. But if you wall them up well now, they will have a ladder ever attached to their back to use one day to climb back into the arms of God.

Read Together:
He Reads: Deuteronomy 22:8
She Reads: Ephesians 6:4

Answer Together:
What kind of image of God are you (father, husband) manifesting to your wife and child? What battlements do you need to erect in the home? Which battlements do you need to refortify?

Pray Together:
Lord Jesus, help me as the head of my household be diligent in erecting these four walls of protection and ever keep them in good repair.

80
Lessons from Mothers of the Bible

Mothers of the Bible reveal traits of successful motherhood.

Eve, the first mother, is best remembered for being deceived by Satan in the Garden of Eden (Genesis 3:1–6). She teaches mothers to be aware of and alert to Satan's schemes to destroy their family. Mothers should pray constantly a hedge of protection about their husband and children.

Eve also teaches mothers that when they face times of greatest vulnerability (grave trials, trouble, crisis), Satan will say, "Did God really say…?" in an effort to get them to doubt God's care, love and provision. Unlike Eve, as a mother, rebuke him in the name of Jesus. Never doubt from God in the night what you believed in the light!

The Widow of Zarephath (I Kings 17:7–16) knew the sorrow of burying her husband, of being a single parent, of being impoverished, and of facing life alone. In her need, she yet gives what food remains to Elijah, trusting God to care for the needs of her son and herself. God honored her faith and made provision daily for them. Widow mother, God will do the same for you if you but rest upon Him as she did for provision. God is well acquainted with your hardship and struggle.

Hannah (1 Samuel 1:27–28) prayed for a child, and God answered with her birth of Samuel.

Hannah said, "The Lord hath lent him to me." Understand as Hannah did that your child or children first belong unto God and then to you. He has lent them to you for their spiritual upbringing and physical care. As Hannah did, allow and encourage your child to fulfill God's plan for their life even if it includes vocational Christian service, as was the case with Samuel.

Bathsheba's (II Samuel 12: 22-24) child by David died in infancy. The greatest grief and pain belong to mothers whose child dies, and it is for these mothers that my heart pains. With David and Bathsheba, find comfort in knowing you have not lost your child to death. A person is not lost if you know where he is. They knew their son was with Jesus in Heaven, and thus David declared, "I cannot bring my son back, but I can go to be with him." Grieve, yes indeed, but amidst grieving trust God for the eternal hope of one day seeing your child again.

Eunice (II Timothy 1:5; 3:15) taught Timothy the Scripture in his childhood, and he turned out to be one of Paul's greatest associates and Christianity's greatest saints. My mother, as Eunice, first taught me of Jesus, and thus I could sing: "Jesus loves me this I know, for my mother tells me so." I remember my mom above all as a mother who raised her children to fear God and live for Him. Mother, don't be remembered for being a great cook, having a great garden, or for social success, but as a godly mother who reared her children in the whole counsel of God.

Read Together:

He Reads: I Samuel 1:27–28
She Reads: II Timothy 1:5; 3:15

Answer Together:

How will you be remembered, mother? As a mother with a cigarette in one hand and a beer can in the other? As a mother who sent her children to church but who didn't go herself? As a mother who usurped the authority of her husband in the home? Or as a Proverbs

31 mother, a mother of faith—a mother who instilled the Word of God in her children as Eunice did?

Pray Together:

Almighty Father, anew I commit myself to being a godly mother, to the rearing of my children in your Word and Way. For success in this great task, I plead for Your strength and wisdom to constantly be showered upon me.

81
Ten Words That Will Safeguard Marriage

Obviously it was a wise and experienced man who told Dr. Timothy Faulk that there were ten words that would both safeguard and strengthen any marriage. The ten words are: "I was wrong. I'm sorry. Forgive me. I love you." Make these ten words a foundational block in your marriage, and it will soar into a lasting and loving relationship.[109]

The words are short and simple but at times most difficult to actually speak due to fleshly pride and just pure stubbornness. But said they must be with sincerity in times of wrong toward your mate. And when this is done, your mate is to forgive. The apostle Paul admonishes, "Be kind to one another, tenderhearted, forgiving each other, just as God in Christ also has forgiven you" (Ephesians 4:32).

Read Together:

He Reads: Matthew 5:23
She Reads: Colossians 3:13

Answer Together:

Practice saying to each other the ten words that will safeguard your marriage (perhaps in sincerity they need to be said now). The last three words explain why as a husband/wife you ought to say the other seven to your mate upon hurting them.

Pray Together:

Lord, help us ever be tenderhearted and dead to destructive pride toward one another. Help us be quick to confess wrong committed to each other and to forgive when sincerely asked.

82

Parental Favoritism

In a study conducted by psychologist Karl Pillemer at Cornell University and his colleagues, seventy percent of mothers stated they showed favoritism for one of their children. The children perceived the favoritism; only fifteen percent said they received equal treatment.[110]

"It doesn't matter if you are favored or not," according to Pillemer, "the perception of unequal treatment has damaging effects for all children. The less favored kids may have ill will toward their mother or preferred sibling, and being the favored child brings resentment from siblings and the added weight of greater parental expectations."[111]

Parental favoritism is the elevation of one child in the family above another. It surfaces first in Scripture in the family of Abraham and Sarah (Genesis 21:9–15). Sarah wanted Ishmael removed from the family, while Abraham did not. In Genesis 25:28, the favoritism of Isaac and Rebekah is recorded: "Isaac loved Esau, because he did eat of his venison: but Rebekah loved Jacob." Further the Scripture reveals that Jacob loved the sons of Rachel more than he loved the sons of Leah.

Parental favoritism is a sin (James 2:9) that all parents want to avoid in their heart for obvious reasons. It sends the wrong message to the slighted children that they do not match up with their brother/sister and are thus inferior. It leads to problems between spouses due to one's partiality toward a child, the crushed and broken spirit (low self-esteem) of the child "loved" less, and family disunity; and it fosters such sibling rivalry that sibling relationships may be damaged for a lifetime.

As a parent, avoid comparing one child to another or favoring the sickly child over the healthy, the weaker above the stronger, the smarter above the slow learner, or the achiever above the under-achiever. Certainly some children by their rebellious, noncompliant lifestyle would make it easy for their parent to favor their submissive and obedient sibling. Nonetheless, shower love, acceptance and affirmation equally.

"The best way to prevent favoritism, I have found," states Dr. Judith Kleinfelds, "is to communicate clearly you are treating your children equally with regard to presents, privileges and expensive outlays like paying for college. And then do it."[112]

Parental favoritism is a temptation that lurks in nearly every household of two or more children. Stay on guard against it.

Read Together:

He Reads: James 2:9
She Reads: Genesis 25:28

Answer Together:

Why does James call favoritism a sin (James 2:9)? As a child, was a brother/sister favored by your parents above you? In what ways was a sibling favored above you, or were you favored above your siblings? If your children were asked if one of their siblings was favored above the others by you, what might they say? What is the harm of parental favoritism?

Pray Together:

Lord Jesus, help us value and love our children equally as You do those in Your family. Prevent us from falling gradually into the trap of preferring one above the other.

83

Dedication of Your Child

The New Testament never speaks of infant baptism; rather, it states that only those who express faith in Jesus Christ are to be baptized. Based upon this truth, Baptists do not include baptism in the dedication service of an infant.

The baby dedication ceremony was initiated by Hannah several thousand years ago when, in answer to prayer, God blessed her with the child Samuel (I Samuel 1:27–28). She immediately dedicated Samuel's *whole life* to God for His divine purpose.

Mary and Joseph took the Baby Jesus to Jerusalem to present Him unto the Lord (Luke 2:22). At that time Simeon and Anna held him and pronounced God's blessing upon him (2:27–28; 38). The final verse in the narrative of Jesus' dedication states, "And the child grew, and waxed strong in spirit, filled with wisdom: and the grace of God was upon him" (2:40).

The essence of a child dedication service is more about the parents' dedication than anything else. It is they who commit themselves to rear the child in the admonition of the Lord by instructional teaching, godly guidance, and holy example. It is the parents who dedicate the child to the Lord (infants obviously are clueless as to what is occurring) for His designed plan to be fulfilled with the child, as did Hannah with Samuel. The minister, upon the occasion, solicits the prayers of saints in the baby's behalf and exhorts the parents to rear the child in a Christian home, ever instilling in him the Word of God. He offers a prayer of thanksgiving, protection and dedication for the child (a scriptural promise such as Jeremiah 29:11 is claimed for the child).

Read Together:
He Reads: I Samuel 1:27–28
She Reads: Luke 2:22–34

Answer Together:
Were you dedicated to the Lord as an infant? Have you dedicated your children to the Lord in a public church ceremony? Do you believe there is biblical precedent for you to do so?

Pray Together:
Heavenly Father, our hearts overflow with joy because You have favored us with a child. It is our utmost desire to bring him/her up at the foot of the Cross, ever pointing him/her to You. Help us rear our children in such a manner that they will be saved at an early age and live for you all the days of their life.

84

Growing Old Together

With the season of "old age" comes deterioration of many members of the body that hamper life as it once was. I read a story about three elderly people who were sitting in rocking chairs on the front porch of their rest home. One said to the others, "You know, I don't hear so well anymore, and I thought it would bother me more than it does. But there isn't much that I want to hear anyway."

The second woman said, "Yes, I've found the same with my eyes. Everything looks blurred and cloudy now, but I don't care. I saw just about everything that I wanted to see when I was younger.

The third lady thought for a moment and then said, "Well, I don't know about that. I sort of miss my mind."

When a grandson asked his grandfather how old he was, he teasingly replied, "I'm not sure."

"Look in your underwear, Grandpa," he advised. "Mine says I'm 4 to 6."

As a Christian, I am not afraid to die, for I know on the other side of old age is Heaven. It's just that I don't like losing all these parts along the way!

Dr. James Dobson encapsulates better than anyone else what both husband and wife need from one another as they move into the latter decades of their lives together.

"In conclusion, let's return to the relationship between men and women as it pertains to the process of aging. What does a woman most want from her husband in the fifth, sixth, and seventh decades of her life? She wants and needs the same assurance of love and respect that she desired when she was younger. This is the beauty of committed love—that which is avowed to be a lifelong devotion. A man and woman can face the good and bad times together as friends and allies. By contrast, the youthful advocate of 'sexual freedom' and noninvolvement will enter the latter years of life with nothing to remember but a series of exploitations and broken relationships. That short-range philosophy which gets so much publicity today has a predictable dead end down the road. Committed love is expensive, I admit; but it yields the highest returns on the investment at maturity."[113]

A popular Christian song, "I Will Be Here" by Steven Curtis Chapman, contains a promise every husband ought to make to his wife. In part Chapman says,

I will be here,
And you can cry on my shoulder
When the mirror tells us we're older.

I will hold you, to watch you grow in beauty,
And tell you all the things you are to me.
We'll be together, and I will be here.
I will be true to the promises I've made
To you and to the One who gave you to me.
I will be here.

Read Together:

He Reads: Psalm 92:12–14
She Reads: Proverbs 16:31

Answer Together:

As a wife, what is the greatest fear you have in growing older? As her husband, what might you do to alleviate that fear? If a young couple, what might you do to begin preparing financially and spiritually for the fifth, sixth, and seventh decades of marriage?

Pray Together:

Heavenly Father, continuously merge our hearts and lives together. Help us enjoy and embrace each other, regardless of the season of life.

85

Marital Ruts

A man sought advice about his marriage. He loved his wife, and she loved him, but something was wrong. He said, "We're stuck. I just feel like we're stuck in a rut, and I have no idea what to do about it!" Do you ever feel your marriage has become stuck in a rut? If so, you're not alone. Many couples would acknowledge having experienced the snare of the rut and a joyous, liberating escape from it.

Here are some ways to get your marriage out of a rut.

Remember the better times. Remember! Remember! Don't ever forget. Keep remembering over and over and over again the sweet days you enjoyed together. Remember the first time you saw each other and how the bells and whistles went off in your head. Remember the first date. Remember the courtship. Remember the proposal. Remember the marriage ceremony and then the honeymoon. Remember when she said, "I'm pregnant" and watching her give birth to your child(ren). Remember the first home (it may have been a trailer, but it seemed as a castle). Remember trusting God for enough money to pay the rent or get food for the baby. Remember the battle of the Christmas tree (getting the thing to stay up) and putting together the toys for the children for Christmas day.

Remembering is good medicine for what is ailing any marriage. God knows the value of remembering; that is why He instructs His children time and again in holy Scripture to remember His person, provision, protection, deliverance, and Lordship!

Break the routine. Dare to change. Schedule weekly date nights. Plan several getaways for several days over the next six months in special places free from *work* or other interruptions.

Engage in an activity. Explore what both of you can do and enjoy together and do it (tennis, walking, running, hunting/fishing, outlet or mall shopping, camping, etc.).

Worship and serve God together.

Affirm one another. I heard of a couple that had been married fifty years. On their fiftieth anniversary, the wife asked, "Why in all these fifty years haven't you told me you love me?"

The old timer replied, "I told you that when we got married and would have told you had I changed my mind."

Wives like to be told of a husband's love over and over again. Wives like to know she still would be your choice if you married all over again. Wives need the husband's genuine words and acts of appreciation and affirmation. Zig Ziglar said, "If you treat your wife like a thoroughbred, you'll never end up with a nag."[114]

Touching and hugging. Touching, snuggling, hugging with your mate communicates more than words can say and further bonds you together. If this is new to the marriage, such may feel somewhat awkward or artificial; but the more engaged you are, the greater the ease and delight.

Pray together. Regularly pray with each other. Ask God to lift your marriage out of its ruts and renew its first love and joy.

Read Together:

He Reads: James 3:17–18

She Reads: Psalm 139:23–24

Answer Together:

Is your marriage in somewhat of a rut? What activity can you both begin doing together? What is the funniest thing you remember in your courtship? What destination would you like to visit again or for the first time? Will you put it on the calendar today?

Pray Together:

Heavenly Father, grant deliverance from the rut to which our marriage is presently captive (or keep our marriage from getting into a rut).

86
Being a Christ-Centered Spouse

There are three kinds of men (I Corinthians 2:14–3:1). The natural man is he who is dead in trespasses and sin and blind to either the reality or need of Christ. The carnal man, though saved, lives a life centered on the appetites of the flesh to the neglect of that which is spiritual. Disobedient, thus dwarfed, this believer fails to grow, mature, or develop spiritually. He is a defeated Christian, not knowing the victory that walking under the control of the Holy Spirit enables, and is dependent upon another to do for him what he cannot or will not do spiritually—like a baby is dependent upon its parent.

The spiritual man is the believer who lives under the control and dominion of the Holy Spirit. This believer continuously crucifies the lust of the flesh, the lust of the eyes, and the pride of life, denying self to the pleasure of the Lord.

Marriage is greatly benefited and advanced when both spouses identify with the spiritual man.

Read Together:

He Reads: I Corinthians 2:14–16
She Reads: I Corinthians 3:1–3

Answer Together:

Which of the three kinds of man pictures you? If it is the natural man, why not here and now invite Jesus Christ into your life as Lord and Savior? If it is the carnal man, step down off the throne of your life, allowing Christ to reign unchallenged. Why not together submit and surrender to Jesus' Lordship over each of you personally and over your marriage corporately?

Pray Together:

Forgive us, Lord, for usurping Your authoritative rule in our life and marriage. Please forgive us of our sin and retake the throne of absolute control in our lives and marriage.

87

Baby Brings Problems

Nearly two-thirds of couples see their relationship decline within the first three years of their child's birth (Relationship Research Institute).

Couples spend more time on decorating the nursery and shopping for the right baby outfits than on personally preparing for the birth. This failure means they will be suddenly facing numerous unexpected landmines that are problematic to the marriage once the child arrives.

A couple's failure prior to the child's birth to iron out a harmonious plan with regard to whose responsibility it will be to cook the meals, get up several times throughout the night to feed or change the baby, do the household chores like washing clothes and dishes, and paying bills causes grave issues of conflict. The conflict only increases when the couple plays the "who did what for the baby" game ("I am getting up more at night with the baby than you!"). Lack of sleep for both parents can cause a short fuse in temper that may easily be ignited.

Adding to the marriage conflict is the absence of real dialog, sex, and attention being paid to one another.

The arrival of the bundle of joy can bring a distancing between mother and father unless they work hard at communication skills (soft and gentle tones and kindly asking instead of telling what they desire of each other) and understanding and fulfilling their responsibilities.

Read Together:

He Reads: I Peter 3:7
She Reads: Proverbs 31:11

Answer Together:

[For older couples] What counsel in the way of preparing themselves would you give a young couple who are expecting their first child? Do you know such a couple you could talk to in this regard?

[For young couples] What do you need to do to prepare yourselves for the arrival of the child?

Pray Together:

Heavenly Father, as we prepare for the arrival of our baby, help us personally prepare so that the child will not divide us but bring us more and more together.

88

The Curse of the iPhone

You cannot communicate with your child while checking your iPhone or texting. Although cell phones are a blessing, they also easily become a curse when they are stealing away undivided attention from your child. It goes without saying that this is equally true with regard to communication between spouses.

This form of communication says to your child that what you are doing is far more important than he/she is doing. I am sure this is not what is intended; nonetheless, that is what is loudly communicated.

So the next time that beautiful child wants to talk to you about what he/she did at school or church or at home while you were at work, turn the iPhone off, lay it aside, put it on vibrate, and stoop down to eye-to-eye level with him/her and really listen and communicate.

Unless you do, there may come a day when he/she no longer tries to talk with you, believing mother or father is too busy to be interrupted.

An essential to rearing children successfully is cultivating their openness, willingness and freedom to bring to you the good and bad that happens while they are toddlers, children and teens. The open door into the heart (its secrets, fears, dreams, desires) of your children begins at their birth but opens continuously throughout childhood and adolescence.

Read Together:
He Reads: James 1:19
She Reads: Mark 4:24a

Answer Together:
Think back over this day checking to see if there were times when your child tried to talk with you but was put "on hold" due to iPhone matters. What steps will you take to ensure that such does not occur again? Is this also a problem with regard to communicating with your spouse?

Pray Together:
Lord Jesus, thank You that when we want to talk with You we are never slighted, ignored or put on hold due to an iPhone, television program or sports event. Help us model Your 24/7 availability to us before our child.

89
Tone Down the Tongue with Your Mate

Adrian Rogers shares the Seven Deadly Games of the Tongue marriage couples play all too frequently.[115]

The Judge

Judges blame and condemn their partners. We should never condemn our mates.

The Professor

Professors like to talk down to their spouses (putdowns and belittling).

The Psychologist

[Psychologists] constantly analyze their mate's motives. The problem with this game is that nobody knows all the motives of other people (1 Corinthians 4:3–4).

The Historian

Historians correct all the details of their partners' speech.

The Dictator

Dictators use force in their marriages—verbal or physical.

The Critic

Critics condemn and criticize their partners. But perhaps even worse, they compare....And especially never criticize factors over which your spouse has no control—like his or her parents or physical traits.

The Preacher

They assume that they are their spouses' conscience. They use the Bible as a club, beating on their spouses' conscience with the Word of God.

Read Together:

He Reads: James 3:8

She Reads: I Corinthians 4:3–4

Answer Together:

Which of the tongue games would your spouse state you at times play with him/her? What is the downside of playing such games of the tongue with your spouse? How does God desire you to use the tongue with your spouse? (Ephesians 4:29)

Pray Together:

Heavenly Father, please help us use our tongue to build one another up, not tear down. Help us ever be mindful of what we say and the tone in which it is said.

90

When We Have to Say Good-bye
(Death of a Child)

"Thou shalt come to thy grave in a full age" (Job 5:26). C. H. Spurgeon states of this text, "'Ah!' says one, 'that is not true. Good people do not live longer than others. The most pious man may die in the prime of his youth.' But look at my text. It does not say thou shalt come to thy grave in old age—but in a 'full age.' Well, who knows what a 'full age' is? A 'full age' is whenever God likes to take His children home....There are two mercies to a Christian. The first is that he will never die too soon; and the second, that he will never die too late."[116]

David's baby was seriously ill, so he fasted and prayed unto God for the child's healing. The child died. Upon hearing the news, David took a bath, put on fresh garments, went into the house of God, and worshiped. Upon returning home, he broke his fast and enjoyed a good meal (II Samuel 12:20–21).

David, by God's grace, accepted the death of his child, though he didn't understand it. It is doubtful that you presently or ever will understand the death of yours, but by God's grace, faith must be extended to trust Him by submitting to it as His divine will.

"When parents experience the death of a child [like David did]," remarks John MacArthur "one of the first questions they are likely to ask is, 'Why did my child have to die?' Generally, the emphasis in asking the question is 'Why did *my* child have to die?'

"...There is no easy answer to that question. The answer begins with the fact that life is marked by difficulty and sorrow. We live in a fallen world. We live in a world flawed by disease and sin. Trouble comes to us as part of our human condition.

"...God is omnipotent. He is also omniscient. As a result, some of His purposes and plans we cannot know this side of eternity. God may have allowed a child to die for reasons that will never be understood—reasons that may involve the lives of the parents, the lives of siblings, the life of the child himself, the lives of others unknown by the parents or child.

"There is a question even more potent than the question 'Why did my child have to die?' That question is 'What does God desire for me to do in the midst of this tragedy?' The question of 'Why?' has no satisfactory answer. The question of 'What now?' can turn a person from grief to action, from loss to healing, from sorrow to joy, and from feelings of utter devastation to feelings of purpose."[117]

David knew the Scripture well enough that he could say with confidence that though he couldn't bring his child back, he could one day be with his child in Heaven. The Holy Scripture is the believer's indispensable source of comfort in the hour of sorrow. Many are the passages within the Bible that speak comfort to the sorrowing heart (Psalm 23; John 14; Romans 8:37–39; 1 Corinthians 15:51–58; 1

Thessalonians 4:13–18; Revelation 7:9–17; Revelation 21:1–4; and Psalm 90).

Scripture will be medicine to your broken heart like none other, granting healing. Take one step at a time at your own pace, but do what David did, and the peace and comfort of God will rule your heart.

Read Together:
He Reads: II Samuel 12:20–21
She Reads: Psalm 90

Answer Together:
What was David's hope with regard to his deceased child? Share some of God's promises that speak of reunion with our saved loved ones in Heaven. Express to your spouse what you need most from him/her in this grievous hour. If you have other children, how will you help and comfort them? How can you turn your pain into gain through helping other parents who experience the death of a child?

Pray Together:
God of all comfort, we look to You for strength, peace and hope to walk this path of sorrow. Grant us grace to accept what we don't understand so we can rest the "why" in Your eternal loving arms, knowing we can trust You explicitly always to do what is right.

91
Helping Your Child Cope with Death

I have gleaned and summarized from a blog by Dr. James Dobson some helpful guidelines in helping your child deal with grief.[118] Included in what his blog cited are a few of my own.

~ Children should not only be permitted to cry but encouraged to cry as long as there is need. "Don't cry" should not be uttered by parents to their children. Crying may last a few days to several months, recurring at intervals, and that is okay.

~ Children must never be told they are acting 'babyish' for crying.

~ Children must never feel ashamed for crying.

~ Children should be allowed their private time to grieve if needed; if not, physical contact with others will be healing medicine.

~ Children should be told the truth about death. Simply to say, "Daddy has gone on a vacation" or "Mommy has taken a trip" or "Brother has moved away" only confuses the child more and delays the inevitable explanation of what has really happened. The use of such language to a young child speaks of a soon return of their loved one which will never happen.

"We can say," states Dr. James Dobson, "'Your mother is gone for now, but thank God we'll be together again on the other side!' How comforting for a grieving child to know that a family reunion will someday occur from which there will never be another separation! I recommend that Christian parents begin acquainting their children with the gift of eternal life long before they have need of this under-standing."[119]

~ Children should be encouraged but not forced to view the body of daddy or mommy, etc. Such will help in understanding the finality of physical life.

~ Children are prone to feel guilty for a parent's or sibling's death if they were angry or disobedient prior to it—they tend to believe it was their anger or disobedience that caused mommy or sister to leave (die). Assure them such is not the case.

~ Children should be allowed to ask questions, some which you may not be able to answer. Remember that young children take what you say literally.

~ Very young children's mentality is not mature enough to understand that everyone and everything will die, that death is certain and final. It is beyond their limited comprehension to under-stand that though daddy died, he will not be home from work tomorrow as usual.

Read Together:
He Reads: II Corinthians 1:3–4
She Reads: Isaiah 43:2

Answer Together:
Why should your child understand it's okay to cry? Did you experience a death as a child? How were you told to handle it? Do you wish there had been more guidance? How might you help your son/daughter cope with death? Don't be hesitant to ask for help from a trained licensed Christian therapist or counselor.

Pray Together:

Dear Lord, as You comfort us in our grief, help us likewise comfort our child. Help him/her understand what death and life hereafter in Heaven means.

92

Space Invaders

James Dobson states a factor that leads to divorce is the breaching of your spouses needed space. He says, "Space invaders: By space invaders, I am not referring to aliens from Mars. Rather, my concern is for those who violate the 'breathing room' needed by their partners, quickly suffocating them and destroying the attraction between them."[120]

Space is imperative for you separately and also jointly. Understand and guard the "breathing room" your husband/wife needs in order to personally renew and be refreshed in soul, mind and body. Jealousy for your mate cages him/her and causes relationship suffocation. To allow your spouse the freedom to have "space" requires loving trust. If our Lord and Savior Jesus Christ saw the need of "breathing room," certainly you should (Mark 6:31).

As a couple you need space jointly (away from the children, friends and work)—something which may often be a challenge. Make an appointment with each other in a datebook at least twice a month to have "breathing room" together (a weekend getaway, date night or a day at the outlet).

Likewise, as a family jointly you need space free from the television, work, cell phone, or computer to really breathe and bond together. Protect the family "breathing room" at the mealtime table, at family devotions, and at vacation times (it's healthy and fun to have others tag along on vacations, but sometimes it needs to be "us four and no more.")

Read Together:

He Reads: Mark 6:31
She Reads: Mark 6:45–46

Answer Together:

Why do you think Jesus often withdrew from the hustle and bustle of the day to be alone? What benefits are there to having personal, couple and family "space"? What are the enemies of making such possible, and how might they be thwarted?

Pray Together:

Lord Jesus, teach us the great benefits of allowing each other to have personal "space." Help us protect the needed "space" for ourselves individually and jointly as a couple or family. Enable us to say no consistently to people, pleasure and work that would interfere.

93

Trusting Your Partner

Successful and happy marriages are built on trust. How is it developed and maintained?

The meaning of trust

Webster defines *trust* as "belief that someone or something is reliable, good, honest, effective, etc."

Google defines it as "firm belief in the reliability, truth, ability, or strength of someone or something ('relations have to be built on trust')."

The KJV Bible Dictionary states trust is "Confidence; a reliance or resting of the mind on the integrity, veracity, justice, friendship or other sound principle of another person."

One Old Testament definition of "trust" *(batach)* means "to be careless." What a beautiful picture of trust! *Batach* means trusting your spouse so absolutely you are free to be yourself without fear of criticism or reprimand in their presence. As the expression goes, "you can let your hair hang down" and be yourself.

Based on these definitions, trust may be surmised to mean in the context of marriage that firm belief or confidence in one's spouse that he/she is truthful, honest, reliable, dependable, trustworthy and "carefree."

The development of trust

Whereas love is freely given, trust is a virtue that must be earned. It is neither unconditional nor irrevocable. It is wrong for a spouse to demand to be trusted when clearly he/she has been deceitful, untruthful, unreliable, and/or unfaithful. On the other hand, a spouse ought to be trusted if he/she has a proven track record that envelopes all it means.

A key essential in building trust is to tell the truth, the whole truth, and nothing but the truth to each other (where you've been, what you did, with whom you were, etc.). Sharing anything but the truth not only is a sin against God but is also a killer of trust in your marriage.

Extend forgiveness when trust is violated

"Forgiveness reflects," John MacArthur states, "the character of God. Unforgivingness is therefore ungodly. That means unforgiving-ness is no less an offense to God than fornication or drunkenness, even though it is sometimes deemed more acceptable."[121]

The deserving of forgiveness is not the issue

It is doubtful that your spouse who inflicted great pain to you deserves forgiveness. That is most likely not the case. Kent Crockett states, "We base our forgiveness on what God has done for us, not on what another person has done to us."[122]

Forgiveness ought to be granted, not because someone deserves it, but because God out of His infinite love forgave you and tells you to do the same with those who sin against you. "And be ye kind one to another, tenderhearted, forgiving one another, even as God for Christ's sake hath forgiven you" (Ephesians 4: 32).

To trust again or not

Certainly one's heart is ripped open and deeply hurt upon an unfaithful or deceitful act by a spouse. At the very moment this hap-pens, trust is completely lost, and the natural knee-jerk reaction is to decide never to trust him/her again. But don't give up on your spouse or marriage. Grant forgiveness. It certainly is worth giving change a chance to rebuild the relationship. Apologies must be followed by a change in behavior by your spouse and strict accountability to you.

The nature of what fractured the trust will determine the period of time it will take for it to be regained.

Read Together:

He Reads: Proverbs 31:11
She Reads: II Corinthians 7:16

Answer Together:

How can we safeguard the firm trust we have in each other? Occasionally it may be good to ask your spouse, "Have I in anyway lessened my trustworthiness with you?"

Pray Together:

Heavenly Father, may our trustworthiness to each other never be questioned but continuously affirmed by the life we live. Help us daily fuel the flame of trust so it will be always escalating and unshakeable.

94
Corrie ten Boom and Forgiveness

In 1947, Corrie ten Boom was in Germany to share a message upon God's forgiveness. Just as the talk was finished, she saw approaching her a guard from the Ravensbrück prison camp where her sister, Betsie, and she had been bitterly treated for concealing Jews in their home. He thrust forth his hand saying, "A fine message, Fräulein! How good it is to know that, as you say, all our sins are at the bottom of the sea!"

Corrie recounts that moment: "And I, who had spoken so glibly of forgiveness, fumbled in my pocketbook rather than take that hand. He would not remember me, of course—how could he remember one prisoner among those thousands of women? But I remembered him and the leather crop swinging from his belt. It was the first time since my release that I had been face to face with one of my captors, and my blood seemed to freeze."

The man said, "You mentioned Ravensbrück in your talk. I was a guard in there. But since that time I have become a Christian. I know that God has forgiven me for the cruel things I did there, but I would like to hear it from your lips as well. Fräulein,"—again the hand came out—"will you forgive me?"

Corrie said, "And I stood there. Betsie had died in that place—could he erase her slow, terrible death simply for the asking? It could not have been many seconds that he stood there, hand held out; but to me it seemed hours as I wrestled with the most difficult thing I had ever had to do. For I had to do it—I knew that. Forgiveness is an act of the will, and the will can function regardless of the temperature of the heart. *Jesus, help me!* I prayed silently. *I can lift my hand. I can do that much. You supply the feeling.*"

Corrie mechanically thrust her hand into his outstretched hand, saying, "I forgive you, brother! With all my heart!"[123]

What is the severity of your wound caused by another in contrast to the atrocities Corrie ten Boom experienced? Probably mild at best. It's past time the mean or cruel words or act another dished out upon you be released unto the Lord and placed at the foot of the cross beneath His precious blood. Only in so doing will the heart pain and animosity be healed, the inner peace abide due to being obedient to the Lord, and the possibility of reconciliation occur.

It has been said of Abraham Lincoln that "his heart was as great as the world, but there was no room in it for the memory of wrong." If victimized by betrayal, spurned love and trust, abandonment, or slander, forgive the person(s) responsible. As with Lincoln, allow no room in your heart for the memory of wrong.

Read Together:
He Reads: Matthew 18:21–22
She Reads: Romans 12:19

Answer Together:
Is a hurt a family member or friend caused interfering with his/her relationship with you? Will you take the first step in reconciliation by forgiving? Share in your own words what today's Scripture states about forgiveness. Will you apply their teaching?

Pray Together:
Lord Jesus, as You are gracious and merciful to forgive me when I sin, help me forgive others when they sin against me.

95
Powerful Impact of a Father's Example

General Robert E. Lee, while his children were yet young, left home early for a morning walk in the snow. As he walked, faintly he could hear the sound of little footsteps behind him. Looking back, he discovered his little son Curtis, who was imitating his every move and walking in the same tracks he had made in the fresh fallen snow. The little boy was struggling to make sure each of his steps fell in the exact footprint left by his dad.

"When I saw this," Lee told one of his friends long afterward, "I said to myself, *It behooves me to walk very straight when this fellow is already following in my tracks.*"

What a lesson for dads! Should your child step in the exact footprints you leave, what kind of person will he become? Will your footprints lead him to engage in intoxicating beverages, gambling, drugs, pornography, unfaithfulness to his wife when he marries, and/or other dishonorable acts?

Or better, will your footprints lead him to honor and fear God, show faithfulness to his wife when he marries, be involved in church, abstain from dishonorable and defiling acts, engage in Christian service, and lead a life of honor and integrity?

Far too many fathers are like safety pins—they point one way, only to walk another. Be unto your child a godly example both in what you say and in what you do. May your child never say, "My daddy hardly believes what he says in church, or else he would never treat my mother the way he does" or "He does not believe what he says in church, or else he wouldn't talk or act the way he does."

Read Together:
He Reads: Deuteronomy 6:6–9
She Reads: Proverbs 23:24

Answer Together:
Honestly, father, what kind of influence upon your child are you exerting? How will you be remembered by your child upon your death? From what activities ought you to desist for the child's sake and for the glory of God? While people or other things cannot convince

you to stop an evil indulgence, will you stop for the love and best interest of your child?

Pray Together:

O Lord, help me cut from my life that which is sinful before You and harmful to my child. May I ever influence my child in the upward, heavenly direction by precept and example.

96
Love Bank Deposits and Withdrawals

Husbands and wives have a love bank. Its balance is dependent upon the frequency and size of love deposits received and withdrawals made by each other. Prior to marriage, many men made huge deposits of love into their future wife's bank but fail to do so now that they are married, leaving her bankrupt in love.

In the romantic book Song of Solomon, Solomon pictures a lover making huge deposits of love into the lady he is courting by saying she is beautiful (1:15 NLT), is a lily among thorns (2:2), and has a voice that is pleasant and a face that is lovely (2:14 NLT). He says, "You are beautiful, my darling, beautiful beyond words (4:1 NLT); you are altogether beautiful, my darling, beautiful in every way (4:7 NLT); you have captured my heart (4:9 NLT); your love delights me (4:10 NLT); and your smile is flawless (6:6 NLT)."

It is so obvious that this man's love deposits won the day in the woman's heart. She said, "I am my lover's, and he claims me as his own" (7:10 NLT). She continues, "Place me like a seal over your heart, for love is as strong as death. Many waters cannot quench love, nor can rivers drown it" (8:6-7 NLT).

When a husband makes huge deposits of love into his wife's love bank, as this man did, the response from her will be the same as with this lady. Borrow some of his words and sincerely address them to your wife regularly, along with loving deeds, and she will forever say, "I am my lover's, and he claims me as his own."

Wives also need to make love deposits into their husband's bank. The woman of the text says to her lover, "Kiss me and kiss me again, for your love is sweeter than wine. How fragrant your cologne; your name is like its spreading fragrance (1:2-3 NLT); you are so handsome, my love, pleasing beyond words! (1:16 NLT)." The remainder of the book shows her shoveling bunches of love into his bank by her words and deeds.

You may claim not to be a romantic, but putting some romance back into your marriage by the use of words and acts of affirmation and appreciation certainly will make it stronger and happier.

Read Together:
He Reads: Song of Solomon 1–4
She Reads: Song of Solomon 5–8

Answer Together:
When was the last time you made a huge bank deposit in your spouse's bank? What was it? What big love deposit can you made in your spouse's bank this week? Have you made a withdrawal from your spouse's love bank via of argument, bitter disagreement, neglecting, etc.? Determine to make more love deposits and fewer withdrawals and your marriage will be bliss.

Pray Together:
Heavenly Father, help us make more frequent and greater love deposits into each other's bank and fewer withdrawals.

97
Get Personal Documents Together

In the event of your death, family members should not have to look in every crook and crevice in search of personal documents.

Gather up important documents, including funeral plans, life insurance policies, birth certificate, checking/savings accounts, last will and testament, personal loans to others, and user name/passwords to Internet accounts.

Examine the documents and passwords, discarding what no longer is valid.

Store the documents in a central place (bank deposit box, home safe, file cabinet, shoe box, etc.).

Make the location of these documents known to your loved ones, and make this location easily accessible to them.

Review the documents annually, making it a habit to update them upon your birthday each year, if necessary.

<u>**Read Together:**</u>

He Reads: Psalm 39:4

She Reads: Psalm 90:12

<u>**Answer Together:**</u>

In event of the death of both of you simultaneously, are plans clearly established for the custody of your child? Do you have a will, and if so, is it up to date? Does an attorney, relative or child (if old enough) know exactly where your needful documents are stored? In the event your husband dies, do you have knowledge of bills payable, safe deposit boxes and insurance papers, and do you have access to checking/saving accounts? Spend some time now talking through these important matters.

<u>**Pray Together:**</u>

Lord Jesus, knowing the days of our life are numbered, teach us to be prepared for the step of death personally by always walking harmoniously with You and one another and by having prepared legal documents specifically stating our desire for our child and estate.

98
Coping with Your Spouse's Death

The wife of author and theologian C. S. Lewis died of cancer three years after they were married. In *A Grief Observed*, Lewis shares the process of grieving he experienced, from which the excerpt below is taken.

"No one ever told me that grief felt so like fear. I am not afraid, but the sensation is like being afraid: the same fluttering in the stomach, the same restlessness, the yawning. I keep on swallowing. At other times it feels like being mildly drunk or concussed. There is a sort of invisible blanket between the world and me. I find it hard to take in what anyone says—or perhaps hard to want to take it in. It is so uninteresting. Yet I want the others to be about me. I dread the moments when the house is empty. If only they would talk to one another and not to me."[124]

C. S. Lewis continues:

"Getting over it so soon? But the words are ambiguous. To say the patient is getting over it after an operation for appendicitis is one thing; after he's had his leg off is quite another. After that operation, either the wounded stump heals, or the man dies. If it heals, the fierce, continuous pain will stop. Presently he'll get back his strength and be able to stump about on his wooden leg. He has 'got over it.' But he will probably have recurrent pains in the stump all his life and perhaps pretty bad ones, and he will always be a one-legged man.

"There will be hardly any moment when he forgets it. Bathing, dressing, sitting down and getting up again, even lying in bed will all be different. His whole way of life will be changed. All sorts of pleasures and activities that he once took for granted will have to be simply written off—duties too.

> The death of a loved one is like an amputation of an arm or a leg which you will live without for the rest of your life.

"At present I am learning to get about on crutches. Perhaps I shall presently be given a wooden leg. But I shall never be a biped [two-footed] again."[125]

Though I have not experienced the horrendous sorrow of Lewis, my observation of those who have indicate he is right. For those from whom their life partner is taken, their life will never be "two-footed" again.

"Oh, I bear testimony for Him this day," states C. H. Spurgeon, "that you cannot go to God and pour out your heart before Him without finding a wonderful comfort. When your friend cannot wipe away your tears, when you yourself with your best reasoning powers and your most courageous efforts cannot overcome your grief, when your heart beats fast and seems as if it would burst with grief, then as God's child, you will pour out your heart before Him.

"God is a refuge for us. He is our fortress, our refuge and defense. We only have to go to Him, and we will find that even here on earth God will wipe away every tear from our eyes."[126]

Read Together:

He Reads: Matthew 5:4
She Reads: Isaiah 43:2

Answer Together:

To whom are you looking for help in this hour of grief? Are you leaning more upon the shoulders of man than those of God?

Pray:

Heavenly Father, I rely upon you for the strength, comfort and grace to get through this horrendous hour of grief.

99
Mentoring the Young Wife and Mother

A friend of E. F. Brown on furlough in England was asked: "What is it you most want in India?"

And his surprising answer was: "Grandmothers."

E. F. Brown said, "Old women play a very important part in society—how large a part one does not realize till one witnesses a social life from which they are almost absent. Kindly grandmothers and sweet charitable old maids are the natural advisers of the young of both sexes."[127]

Such is exactly what the apostle Paul believed and taught. In Titus he states that older women are to coach young women with regard to the responsibilities and privileges of Christian womanhood (Titus 2:3-5). Aged men are likewise to coach younger men similarly in regard to Christian manhood.

Specifically note that older saintly women are to instruct young married women "to love their husbands, to love their children, To be discreet, chaste, keepers at home, good, obedient to their own husbands" (Titus 2:4-5). Older godly women from teaching, training and experience have discovered the secrets to being wonderful Christian wives and mothers and ladies. It is this knowledge they are to pass on to the young wives and mothers.

To learn from the experience of successful older saintly women about marriage and family life is worth more than hundreds of books on the keys to a successful marriage or parenting. Seneca said, "The road to learning by precept is long; but by example, short and effective."

The young wife and mother ought to seek out a saintly older woman for instruction, guidance and encouragement.

Read Together:

He Reads: Titus 2:1–2; 8–10
She Reads: Titus 2:3–5

Answer Together:

As an older woman, whom may you invite to sit under your instruction and guidance? As a young wife and mother, whom will you ask to be your spiritual mentor?

Pray Together:

Lord Jesus, all that I have learned from experience and from Your Word about being a godly woman, wife and mother, I want to share with the younger wives and mothers. Grant me the courage and ability to do so effectively.

100

Mentoring the Young Husband and Father

Older saintly men are to mentor young men with regard to the responsibilities and privileges of Christian manhood (role of husband, father, Christian leader, etc.).

The Bible is replete with spiritual men who mentored other men for growth in godliness and ministry.

Jethro taught his son-in-law, Moses, how to delegate (Ex. 18).
Moses taught Joshua how to lead effectively (Deut. 31:8; 34:9).
Moses groomed Caleb to lead (Num. 13; 14:6–9).
Samuel anointed David as king and protected him (I Sam. 16:13).
Jonathan and David mentored each other (1 Sam. 18:1–9; 19:1–7; 20:1–42).
Barnabas taught Paul (Acts 4:36–37; 9:26–30; 11:22–30).
Barnabas restored John Mark (Acts 15:36–39; II Tim. 4:11).
Paul poured his life into Timothy (Acts 16:1–3; Phil. 2:19–23; I and II Tim.).
Paul instructed Titus (II Cor. 7:6, 13–15; 8:17; Titus).

"I cannot overestimate," states Chuck Swindoll, "the impact that a mentor can have in another life, and I am reminded of that anytime I look at my own. I am a living legacy to a handful of men who took an interest in me, saw potential where I did not, and encouraged me to become something more."

John MacArthur, in *The Footsteps of Faith*, comments on the power of example. "Thomas Brooks said, 'Example is the most powerful rhetoric.' He was right. The single greatest tool of spiritual leadership is the power of an exemplary life. Along with the principles for living that the Bible gives us, we need models to follow because we tend to be creatures led more by pattern than precept. We are better at following a pattern or a model than we are at fleshing out a precept or principle. What makes examples so powerful? Why is it 'the most powerful rhetoric'? An example shows us what principles can't."[128]

As an older saintly man, the need is tremendous and desperate that you take under your wings a younger man instilling in him the essentials to godliness, being a Christian husband and father, and modeling before him what a godly man (husband, father) looks like.

As a young husband and father, you can learn volumes that will enhance the happiness and success of your marriage from older godly men.

Read Together:
He Reads: Titus 2:6–10
She Reads: Acts 9:27

Answer Together:
As an aged man, whom will you endeavor to mentor? As a young husband and father, whom will you ask to be a spiritual coach?

Pray Together:
Father, help me invest what you have taught me and I have learned about being a godly husband and father with younger men. Conquer any fear and fill me with courage for the task.

101
Couples Mentoring Couples

Eighty-two percent of couples report they would like a mentor couple to walk with them. Research further reveals that couples who have marriage mentors are happier and healthier.[129]

"But mentoring," states Les and Leslie Parrott, "is in short supply these days. In our modern age, the learning process has shifted. It now relies primarily on computers, classrooms, books, and videos. In most cases today the relational connection between the knowledgeable and experienced giver and the receiver of that wisdom has weakened or is nonexistent—especially in the early years of marriage."[130]

Newlyweds Tom and Wendy sought out help from Les and Leslie Parrott who suggested they be aligned with a mentoring couple. Following the mentoring, they wrote, "Our mentoring relationship with Nate and Sharon ended up being the most important thing we have ever done to build up our marriage. It was nice to have another couple know what we were going through and remain objective at the same time."[131]

As a godly couple, you certainly can be a "Nate and Sharon" to many "Tom and Wendy's," strengthening their relationship and marriage. Focus on the Family provides a course by Les and Leslie Parrott on marriage mentoring (http://www.marriagementoring.com/focus) that will equip you for the task.

Marriage couple mentoring doesn't require much time (perhaps once a quarter for a year), perfection in one's own marriage, degree in counseling, or always being available to those being mentored. Yet, it is a *game changer* for many marriages. Consider taking a young couple under your knowledgeable and experienced wings, and see that couple's relationship and happiness soar.

As a young married couple, pray about what godly couple should be asked to be your mentoring couple and invite them to do so.

Read Together:
He Reads: II Timothy 2:2
She Reads: Proverbs 27:17

As an older couple, discuss the possibility of being a mentor to young couples. As a young couple, invite an older saintly couple to be your mentor.

Pray Together:
Lord Jesus, help us perform a ministry of encouragement, guidance and help to young couples.

102
Pressed beyond Measure

"Come, my brethren and sisters," declares C. H. Spurgeon, "are any of you down; are you almost beneath the enemy's foot?...Think what Jesus has given you: your sins are pardoned for His name's sake, your Heaven is made secure to you, and all that is wanted to bring you there; you have grace in your hearts, and glory awaits you; you have already grace within you, and greater grace shall be granted you; you are renewed by the Spirit of Christ in your inner man—the good work is begun, and God will never leave it till He has finished it; your names are in His book, nay, graven on the palms of His hands; His love never changes, His power never diminishes, His grace never fails, His truth is firm as the hills, and His faithfulness is like the great mountains. Lean on the love of His heart, on the might of His arm, on the merit of His blood, on the power of His plea, and the indwelling of His Spirit."[132]

Pressed beyond measure, yes, pressed to great length;
Pressed so intensely, beyond my own strength;
Pressed in my body and pressed in my soul;
Pressed in my mind till the dark surges roll.
Pressure from foes and pressure from dear friends;
Pressure on pressure, till life nearly ends.

Pressed into knowing no helper but God;
Pressed into loving His staff and His rod;
Pressed into liberty where nothing clings;
Pressed into faith for impossible things;

Pressed into living my life for the Lord;

Pressed into living a Christ-life outpoured.

—Annie Johnson Flint (1866–1932)

Read Together:

He Reads: Psalm 34:17

She Reads: Psalm 146:5–6

Answer Together:

Are there times that you identify with Annie Johnson Flint? What pressure is weighing upon you now? In such times how might the words of C. H. Spurgeon help? How might your spouse help bear the pressure you experience?

Pray Together:

Heavenly Father, thank You for the pressures I experience, for they drive me to depend upon and trust You more. Help me soar above the pressures instead of being pressed down by them.

103 Helping Your Child Deal with Schoolplace Bullying

Annually, in excess of 3.2 million students are victims of bullying.[133] It is approximated that 160,000 teens skip school *every day* because of bullying.[134] While physical bullying reaches its peak in middle school and declines in high school, verbal abuse remains unchanged.[135] Bullying wounds the heart. It's not a harmless passage into adulthood or a means to make a person stronger. "And children who were bullied as kids," states Paul Coughlin, "suffer more depression and low self-esteem than kids who were not bullied. For many, the problem doesn't go away."[136]

Bill Mayer states, "The emotional scars that result from bullying can last a lifetime. Children who have been bullied may sink into patterns of antisocial behavior such as vandalism or even look to drugs and alcohol as sources of relief. Constant bullying in school can interfere with a child's education and mental and physical health."[137]

Victims of bullying may turn outward (bodily harm to others), as evidenced at Columbine. Statistics indicate that revenge is the number one factor for bullying. Seventy-five percent of school-shooting incidents are linked to harassment and bullying.

But it most often turns inward (bodily harm to self). The Yale School of Medicine has completed a study that included thirteen countries which found an apparent connection between bullying or being bullied and suicide. Suicides related to bullying sadly include Nicolas, age 13; Brodie, age 19; Daani, age 16; Simone, age 15; Kameron, age 14; Alex, age 14; Harry, age 10; Mitchell, age 11; Asher, age 13. And the list goes on and on. In seeing their faces and ages during research my heart was totally crushed knowing that their precious lives were snuffed out too early all due to bullying. Eighty percent of youth who commit suicide do so due to peer victimization and bullying, according to a study by JAMA Pediatrics Network in 2013.

Bill Mayer states, "Because of the aggressive nature of bullying—stronger children dominating weaker children—the problem requires the intervention of parents, educators, and authority figures on behalf of the child being bullied."[138]

1. Discuss bullying with your child early on; it may prompt him to talk to you if it arises.

2. Watch for the warning signs that may signal your child is being bullied (drop in grades, loss of friends, discontinuation in activities once enjoyed, bruises, need for additional money, etc.).

3. If he is bullied, tactfully address the matter with him personally. Being bullied is never a deserved act, regardless what your child may have done. When told by your child he is being bullied, be cautious never to ask, "What did you do to cause it?" Rather, ask, "What can we do to stop it?"

4. Speak to his teacher about the bullying and the bully. If the teacher fails to intercede, approach the principal. Teachers are able to deal with the bullying without the bully knowing you told of his action. In watching out for your child, they can catch the person red-handed and put a stop to it once and for all.

5. Keep a record. Write down in a journal or on your PC tablet a record detailing the bullying encounters. Include the bully's name, type of bullying (verbal, cyber, or physical), and date. Such information may prove to be of immense value to authorities should the bullying escalate.

6. Tell your child to tag along with a friend to avoid being alone with the bully in the restroom, locker room, or bus stop.

7. Prevent it from happening. The saying that an ounce of prevention is worth a pound of cure is certainly true with regard to bullying. For example, though unintentional, your child may set himself up to be bullied by his dress and grooming.

8. Constantly affirm to your child his invaluable worth and that his value has suffered no loss despite the negatives hurled upon him by the bully. Remind him that his value to God is not based upon what others say or do to him but upon the fact God made him in His own image, and that he will never depreciate in value to God. Drive home the fact that God's love is not dependent upon performance or how others respond to him or popularity or great intellect, that it is an unconditional love. No yardstick can measure it. This awesome love cannot be fully described or defined, just accepted and experienced (Ephesians 3:18–19).

9. Encourage your child not to retaliate. It's understandable that he may want to fight back when bullied, but urge him to resist.

10. Pray for the bully.

Read Together:
He Reads: Romans 12:19–20
She Reads: Psalm 18:3

Answer Together:
Did you experience bullying as a child? What impact did it have upon your life? What might you do to prepare your child for the possibility of being bullied? If your child is the bully, then he must be confronted and corrected.

Pray Together:
Heavenly Father, help us rear our child to the end that he will have self-confidence, a healthy self-esteem, and knowledge of Your eternal love and care for him. As his protectors, lead us in how to handle and squash any bullying he encounters.

104

Help Your Child Memorize Scripture

Plant the good seed of Scripture in your child's heart. It will be an investment that will have eternal dividends. David, the psalmist, said "I have hid thy word in my heart that I might not sin against God" (Psalm 119:11).

Chuck Swindoll wrote, "I know of no other single practice in the Christian life more rewarding, practically speaking, than memorizing Scripture....No other single exercise pays greater spiritual dividends! Your prayer life will be strengthened. Your witnessing will be sharper and much more effective. Your attitudes and outlook will begin to change. Your mind will become alert and observant. Your confidence and assurance will be enhanced. Your faith will be solidified."[139]

N. A. Woychuk offers several suggestions for assisting children in memorizing Scripture.[140]

1. Read the verse(s) to be memorized aloud with expression and enthusiasm, explaining the meaning simply.

2. Memorize the verse along with the child.

3. Do not insist on repetition of the verse by the child every time.

4. Make a song out of the verse which you sing with the child over and over again.

5. Read the verse to the child at breakfast, at family devotions, and at bedtime.

6. Discuss the meaning of the verse with family members so the child may contribute to the family circle.

7. Dramatize the verse(s) that lend themselves for such a purpose (like Psalm 1, you can "walk," "stand," and "sit").

8. Schedule a set time for Scripture memory.

9. Communicate praise for the child's effort to learn verses.

10. Select verses that reveal something about Jesus Christ and your child's relation to Him.

Read Together:

He Reads: Deuteronomy 6:6–7
She Reads: Joshua 1:8

Answer Together:

Share with each other verses of Scripture you memorized as a child and tell how they impacted your life. Based upon the husband's reading for today, how can you instill Holy Scripture into your child and not sin against God's commandment? What is the value of Scripture memory?

Pray Together:

Help us, O Lord, hide the Word of God in our hearts and in the hearts of our children, that we may not sin against Thee, and live a life most pleasing to You.

105 Separation Doesn't Equal Divorce

In the event of separation rather than divorce, the advice of Gary Chapman is timely. He states, "I don't think separation equals divorce. Separation can lead to an absolutely wonderful marriage if we are willing to deal with the problems that led to the separation."[141] Chapman suggests treating the trauma of separation with a 9-1-1 approach. "If it were a physical problem, we would put you in intensive care and look after you day and night until you either died or got better. Separation says this marriage is in serious trouble; it needs intensive care."[142]

Seven helps to saving your marriage

Thoroughly get yourself right with God. "It often happens," states Wayne Mack, "that when couples get their relationship to God straightened out, their relationships with each other begin to straighten out as well."[143]

Issues that are killing the relationship should be shared with your spouse, the sooner the better.

Inquire of your spouse the reasons he/she wants a divorce. Listen closely, tight-tongued and respectfully to the offenses he/she cites against you.

Humbly acknowledge the wrong, asking forgiveness and pledging to change the behavior and work hard at resolving the problems with the marriage.

Avoid bargaining. Instead of bargaining, make efforts at genuine reconciliation.

Seek out a godly licensed Christian therapist or pastor for individual and joint counseling.

Earnestly pray, asking the Lord to soften your spouse's heart to be open to reconciliation.

First and foremost, work hard at saving the marriage. Remember, many marriages that have experienced separation have become great successes following counseling and joint effort. However, when it reaches a point where it is irreconcilable and divorce occurs, personal healing is available from the hands of our gracious Lord Jesus Christ.

Read Together:
He Reads: Ephesians 4:32
She Reads: Proverbs 3:5–6

Answer Together:
Are you walking in agreement with the Lord? To what lengths are you willing to go to save your marriage? Will you agree to marital counseling in an effort to reconcile and strengthen the relationship? Ultimately, are you willing to work hard at resolving the problems that have breached your relationship?

Pray Together:
Heavenly Father, please rekindle the love we once had for each other so our marriage may survive this storm. Guide us in the steps of reconciliation. Hinder Satan from destroying our family, relationship and home, we beg.

106
Marriage Killers

James Dobson states there are numerous "dragons" that can rip a relationship into shreds if given the opportunity. Among them he cites the following:

Overcommitment and physical exhaustion (too tired to spend quality time together)

Excessive credit and conflict over how money will be spent

Selfishness

Unhealthy relationships with in-laws (in-laws smothering your relationship)

Unrealistic expectations (Marriage is not unmitigated joy or never being in want. There is no way a marriage between two imperfect human beings can deliver on that expectation.)

Space invaders (failure to give each other "breathing room")
Sexual frustration and its partner, the greener grass of infidelity
Business success or collapse (agitation over business loss vented toward spouse, or its success creating problems in marriage)
Getting married too young
Alcohol and substance abuse
Pornography, gambling, and other addictions [144]

It may take only one "dragon" or a combination of "dragons" to kill your marriage. Don't discount any "dragon's" ability to devour your relationship gradually or suddenly. Erect a hedge of protection about your home against these fierce foes of a holy and happy marriage, and the likelihood of your marriage being successful is increased a thousandfold.

It only takes a little crack in a sidewalk for weeds to spring up, ultimately doing serious damage. The same is true with regard to your marriage. Don't ignore them; these marriage killers will wreck your marriage and life if left unattended.

Read Together:
He Reads: Proverbs 30:8
She Reads: Song of Solomon 2:15

Answer Together:
Do you know of a marriage that was slain by any of the stated "dragons"; if so, identify the "dragon(s)"? Which "dragon" would be the most likely to attack your marriage? What steps may you take to assure its defeat? Is there any additional "dragon" you might add to our list?

Pray Together:
O Father, hedge our home about with a protective barrier so that no "dragon" may penetrate. When we see a "dragon" invade another's home, help us take tactful and prompt steps for its defeat.

107
What It Means to Fall in Love
Adrian Rogers well said, "You know, the great miracle is not love at first sight. It is love after a long, long look."[145]

Infatuation and Love

Infatuation is based on fleeting feeling; love, on emotion and the will. Infatuation is for a moment in time; love is forever. Infatuation is self-serving, seeking personal pleasure; love is selfless. Infatuation fades with separation; love grows. Infatuation is something one falls into; with love one grows into it.

"Within this Christian vision of marriage," states Timothy Keller, "here's what it means to fall in love. It is to look at another person and get a glimpse of what God is creating and say, "I see who God is making you, and it excites me! I want to be part of that. I want to partner with you and God in the journey you are taking to His throne. And when we get there, I will look at your magnificence and say, 'I always knew you could be like this. I got glimpses of it on Earth, but now look at you!"[146]

It is my conviction that God through His sovereignty orchestrates for the Christian whom he/she is to wed. In meeting such a person, the divine connection will be manifest as love for him/her develops and grows.

Read Together:
He Reads: Colossians 3:12–14
She Reads: Proverbs 19:14

Answer Together:
What role does God play in the Christian's selection of a life-mate? Is it possible to push ahead of God and marry outside His will? What is the Christian's view of love? How does it differ from that of the world?

Pray Together:
Father, thank You for uniting us as husband and wife. May our love ever grow into full blossom for each other.

108 Differences between Men and Women

In his book *More Communication Keys for Your Marriage*,[147] Dr. H. Norman Wright list sixteen differences between men and women.

1. Men and women are very different by nature in the way they think, act, respond, etc. These differences can be complementary but very often lead to conflict in marriage.

2. A woman is an emotional feeler; a man is a logical thinker.

3. For a woman, language spoken is an expression of what she feels; for a man, language spoken is an expression of what he's thinking.

4. Language that is heard by a woman is an emotional experience; language that is heard by a man is the receiving of information.

5. Women tend to take everything personally; men tend to take everything impersonally.

6. Women are interested in the details, the nitty-gritty; men are interested in the principle, the abstract, the philosophy.

7. In material things, women tend to look at goals only; men want to know the details of how to get there.

8. In spiritual or intangible things, the opposite is true. Men look at the goals; women want to know how to get there.

9. Men are like filing cabinets. They take problems, put them in the file, and close the drawer. Women are like computers; their minds keep going and going and going until the problem is solved.

10. A woman's home is an extension of her personality; a man's job is the extension of his personality.

11. Women have a great need for security and roots; men can be nomadic.

12. Women tend to be guilt-prone; men tend to be resentful.

13. Men are stable and level off; women are always changing.

14. Women tend to become involved more easily and more quickly; men tend to stand back and evaluate.

15. Men have to be told again and again; women never forget.

16. Men tend to remember the gist; women tend to remember details and distort the gist.

"Given these interesting facts," states Dr. Timothy Faulk, "we should look at the physical differences and how the total being is involved not only in the relationship but how mind, body and spirit are involved in the communication process."[148] Understanding that men are from *Mars* and women are from *Venus* and why they are deemed such can only enhance marital relationship.

Read Together:
He Reads: Psalm 139:13–14
She Reads: Jeremiah 1:5

Answer Together:
How does understanding the mental, physical and spiritual make-up of each other enhance marriage? In Dr. Wright's list, which facts surprise you most? Which can be the most helpful to your relationship? What is it you wish that your spouse understood about you more?

Pray Together:
Lord Jesus, though we are co-equals, we are in numerous ways different according to divine design. Help us better understand and embrace these differences in each other.

109
The Date Night Opportunity

Many marriages consist of two working professionals whose relationship is like two ships passing in the night. Demands of the office and stress of finances hinder couples from the personal time they need to connect and converse, the lack of which will ultimately lead to marital conflict if not divorce.

One solution to the problem is having a Date Night weekly.

A recent report entitled "The Date Night Opportunity" (The National Marriage Project at the University of Virginia) found that couples who deliberately set aside time to connect and have fun at least once a week were three and a half times more likely to report being "very happy" in their marriages.

Despite the positive benefit of having a weekly "Date Night," couples age 25–50 with two or more children have one

Once a week: 4 percent
Once a month: 21 percent
Once every two to three months: 21 percent
Once every four to six months: 18 percent
Once every seven months or less often: 36 percent[149]

Enhance your relationship with each other; better the marriage by blocking off one night a week to spend together *alone*.

Read Together:
He Reads: I Corinthians 13:5
She Reads: Romans 12:9–10

Answer Together:
How often is your relationship like two ships that pass in the night? Will you, husband, invite your wife out on a date this week? Are you aware of a couple whose marriage is starved for more time together? Will you share the value of a weekly date night with the couple?

Pray Together:
Lord Jesus, let not our work obligation cause our love relationship to suffer. Help us put in place a weekly date night together that will provide personal time to connect, converse and have fun.

110 Divorce Myths

R. C. Sproul shares six myths about divorce.

1. When love has gone out of a marriage, it is better to get divorced.
2. It is better for the children for the unhappy couple to divorce than for them to rear their children in the atmosphere of an unhappy marriage.
3. Divorce is the lesser of two evils.
4. You owe it to yourself.
5. Everyone's entitled to one mistake.
6. God led me to this divorce.

Marriage is established and regulated by a God of truth. The problems of marriage cannot be resolved by myths."[150]

Marriage is a divine institution established by God between a man and woman designed for a lifetime (Matthew 19:4–6). Jesus forthrightly stated that a husband and wife were "one flesh" and picture His unending and abiding love for His bride, the church (Ephesians 5:24–31). Jesus is the "Bridegroom" of the church (the bride, the redeemed family of God), and this union will never be divorced. Likewise, the husband and wife are one flesh, united by God's ordaining authority, and must not be severed. "What God has joined together, let no man put asunder" (Matthew 19:6). God said, "I hate divorce" (Malachi 2:16). The apostle Paul frankly said, "A wife must not separate from her husband" (I Corinthians 7:10), and, "Let not the husband put away his wife" (verse 11). It is noteworthy that Paul used the word *divorce* and *separate* interchangeably.

The bottom line regarding marriage is that it is to last a lifetime with a single mate, not multiple partners, or until one's partner dies, at which time the person is free to marry "in the Lord" again. Refuse to allow divorce myths to trump God's Word.

<u>**Read Together:**</u>

He Reads: Matthew 19:9

She Reads: Matthew 19:6

<u>**Answer Together:**</u>

What was God's design for marriage from the beginning? Has God changed His mind? If this is God's attitude, then why do you suppose there are so many divorces among Christians? What are some preventive measures against divorce that may be taken while you are married? What is a myth? How does it apply to some reasons for divorce, according to Sproul?

<u>**Pray Together:**</u>

Heavenly Father, protect our marriage from all that sows the seed of divorce.

111

Winning Your Spouse to Christ

A wife's mission with her husband is the same as it is with all who are lost. She is to endeavor to bring him to faith in Jesus Christ. Peter states, "Likewise, wives, be subject to your own husbands, so that even if some do not obey the word, they may be won without a word by the conduct of their wives" (I Peter 3:1, ESV).

The text offers great help to wives in winning their unsaved husbands as much by what it doesn't say as by what it does. It doesn't say wives are to divorce their unbelieving husbands (I Corinthians 7:13–14). It doesn't say wives are to continuously preach or argue the need of salvation to their lost husbands. It doesn't say wives are exempt from being in submission to their lost husbands.

Peter says in one word what the Christian wife's role is in winning her unsaved husband. She is to win him by her *conduct*, by living an exemplary Christian life (including submission) before him. That's it. The wife is to so live a devoted and faithful life before her unsaved husband that he may be won to Christ "without a word."

Bible scholar William Barclay puts it this way: "It is by the silent preaching of the loveliness of her life that she must break down the barriers of prejudice and hostility and win her husband for her new Master."[151]

Lee Strobel states, "It was my agnostic wife's conversion to Christianity and the ensuing positive changes in her character that prompted me to use my legal training and journalism experience to systematically search for the real Jesus. After nearly two years of studying ancient history and archaeology, I found the evidence leading me to the unexpected verdict that Jesus is the unique Son of God who authenticated His divinity by returning from the dead."[152]

In verse 7, Peter turns the table, giving instruction to the believing husband about how to win an unsaved wife. The husband is to submit to the unsaved spouse, not in authority or headship which God has established for him, but rather unto her needs. He likewise is to live an exemplary Christian life so she may be won to the faith.

Read Together:
He Reads: I Peter 1:1–7
She Reads: I Corinthians 7:13–14

Answer Together:
Though you were sincere, in what efforts have you engaged to win your spouse that are unscriptural? What strategy does Peter offer in winning your spouse that differs from your own? How often do you pray for your husband's/wife's salvation?

Pray Together:
Lord Jesus, as a wife (husband), help me so live a life of virtue consistently that my husband (wife) may come to faith in You, I beg.

112
Bonding with your Mate

Bonded, as defined by dictionary.com, means "Textiles made of two layers of the same fabric or of a fabric and a lining material attached to each other by a chemical process or adhesive." Google defines it as "(of a thing) joined securely to another thing." In a marital relationship it therefore simply means two people that are securely attached to each other by the adhesive of love and affection for each other and God. The bonding (adhesive attachment) with the couple can and should grow.

Are you deeply, securely bonded to your mate? Drs. Donald Joy and Desmond Morris suggest twelve gradual steps for bonding with your mate in courtship and marriage.

1. Eye to body (spark of interest in someone)
2. Eye to eye (eyes fastening momentarily on each other, indicating interest)
3. Voice to voice (exchange names, data, and agree to date)
4. Hand to hand (think of the first time your husband held your hand)
5. Hand to shoulder (how did it make you feel, wives, when your husband, in courting, put his arm around your shoulder on a date?)
6. Hand to waist (walking around with arms around each other's waist at school spoke of your commitment to one another)
7. Face to face (Wow! Remember that first good-night kiss?)
8. Hand to head (stroking her hair or wiping the mustard off his face)
9. Hand to body (steps 9–12 occur in marriage)
10. Mouth to body
11. Touching below the waist
12. Intercourse

Regardless of age or years married, you both need to continuously, slowly, but affectionately engage in these twelve steps to intimacy and bonding. It may just make you feel like high school or college sweethearts again, restoring luster, excitement and intimacy to your marriage.

Read Together:
He Reads: Song of Solomon 3:3–4
She Reads: Song of Solomon 1:2

Answer Together:
Walk through the first seven steps together, recalling how you met and the bonding that occurred. Wife, if you would like your husband to do what he did then, tell him. Are you as a couple experiencing *bonding* growth, and if so, by what means?

Pray Together:
Father, help us keep the romantic love and bonding experienced in courtship ever alive in our marriage. You, O Lord, are the supreme

adhesive in our marital bonding. Glue us more and more into one, we pray.

113   The Model "In-law"

Moses worked forty years in Midian for Jethro and married Zipporah, Jethro's daughter (Exodus 2:21). At the time the Lord called Moses to go to Egypt to deliver the Israelites from captivity, vicious contention between Zipporah and him developed over the circumcision (4:25–26) of their two sons, which resulted in their separation. Zipporah took the two sons back to Midian to live with her father, Jethro. Moses went to Egypt alone to deliver the Israelites (18:2).

As the Israelites were in the Wilderness of Sin, Moses' father-in-law, Jethro, brought Zipporah and the two sons back to Moses. Jethro initiated the reconciliation (vv. 2–3) and was responsible for saving the marriage. By the way, we never read in Scripture that Jethro ever criticized or demeaned Moses. Certainly Moses was extremely thankful for an in-law like Jethro who sought to bring him and his wife together, not further divide them.

W. A. Criswell stated, "Isn't that a model? Instead of the in-law adding to the divisiveness and destruction of the home and the family, the in-law, Jethro, is the instrument by which the family is put together again. That's a model for all of our in-laws. Help the children. Bless them. Minister to them. Make it possible for them to have a beautiful home life together."[153]

Moses shares with Jethro all that God did in the Exodus deliverance of the Israelites from Pharaoh's hands (v. 8), and Jethro, a pagan, is converted to belief in Jehovah God (vv. 11–12).

What a beautiful story! First Moses' father-in-law, Jethro, convinces his daughter to give their marriage another chance; then Jethro's son-in-law, Moses, leads him to faith in Jehovah God. Oh, that all marriages would have in-laws like unto these!

Note finally that when it came time for Jethro to return home, he departed alone (v. 27), something which indicates his effort worked in reuniting the couple.

Read Together:

He Reads: Exodus 18:2-7
She Reads: Exodus 18:8-12; 27

Answer Together:

Are your in-laws' dispositions like that of Jethro? Do you feel that they really support your marriage and would battle to save it like Jethro did? What might you do to have better relations with them? Are your in-laws unsaved? If so, endeavor to bring them to faith in Jesus Christ, as Moses did.

Pray Together:

Heavenly Father, help us be the kind of *in-law* to our spouse's parents that Moses was to his wife's. Help us take steps to diffuse any misunderstanding or disagreement that may exist with them.

114 Grandparenting Conflicts

I recall hearing grandparents tell me over the years, "Just wait until you have grandchildren. There's nothing like it." Now that we have three, I can frankly say those grandparents were not wrong. Grandparenting is joy indescribable and an experience unutterable. In fact, if I had known how wonderful it was to have grandchildren, I would have had them before I had my children!

However, it is laden with potential conflicts with the grandparent's daughter/son or daughter-in-law/son-in-law in at least twelve regards (what is stated in the parentheses is the grandparent's possible objection).

1. Over what they eat (not enough veggies; too many burgers)
2. About correction (they get by without punishment too much)
3. About the gifts you give (when stored in a closet or exchanged at the store)
4. Over the baby's name (grandparents politic for the name; when rejected, bitter feelings may arise and linger)
5. Regarding at whose home they will spend the holidays (can be contentious)
6. Concerning equal time (same time the other set of grandparents get, or else)

7. About whom they are allowed to date (you only want the best, certainly not who they are seeing at present, and say so)
8. What activities are allowed (protest their doing things your parents never would have allowed)
9. Their dress code (they shouldn't be seen in public wearing such attire)
10. About viewing habits (too much computer or television)
11. About going to church (they need to be in an evangelical church every Sunday)
12. When the grandchildren are not treated equally (it's unfair to give more attention to one child than the other)

Yes, as grandparents we have our own preferences about all these things (and of course we are always right!) because of our desire to see our grandchildren happy, safe and healthy and to have them learn about God at an early age. BUT we always must remember that they are not ours to rear. Therefore, walk softly and choose carefully what to say and not say, refusing to interfere with their parents' supervision and philosophy of child rearing (unless physical or emotional abuse occurs) unless asked.

Read Together:
He Reads: Proverbs 17:6
She Reads: II Timothy 1:5

Answer Together:
What do you count as the greatest responsibility you have with your grandchildren? What conflicts have you encountered in being a grandparent? What lessons have you learned in grandparenting?

Pray Together:
Lord Jesus, help us invest Your truth into the lives of our grandchildren so they will grow up being Thy choice servants. Keep us mindful of the limitations stated and permission granted by their parents, that we never jeopardize our time with them.

115 The Role of Grandparents

Jay Kesler said, "Grandparents have always played an important role in providing stability and support for families."[154] Kesler further states that the family in ancient times had the involvement of the extended family, especially grandparents, for such was crucial to the survival of the children.[155] The same is no less true today.

A woman came to her pastor and said, "When should I start the religious training of my child? When will he be old enough? Is it too early to start at six years of age?"

The pastor said, "No, that's too late."

She said, "Well how about six months?"

He said, "That's too late."

She said, "Then when should I start?"

He said, "With his grandparents."

I agree. The spiritual training and teaching of our grandchildren begin long before they arrive, while his mother/father are still under our roof. Let's do a good job (if it's not too late) in their spiritual training and education so that they will be great, successful parents.

The biblical role of grandparents

1. God wants you to be a Blessing Giver

"The memory of the righteous will be a blessing" (Prov. 10:7). You are to so order your life spiritually and morally before the grandchilddren that you are a blessing unto them now and after your death. Presently, can you say their memory of you will be a blessing? Will they remember you as a saintly person, praying person, loving person, and caring person?

2. God wants you to be a Pattern Setter

"The righteous man leads a blameless life; blessed are his children after him" (Proverbs 20:7).

God wants you to be a track setter for your grandchildren in living a life of devotion to Him, by a life of integrity, by faithfulness to the church, by an unwavering stance on biblical teaching, by spiritual disciplines, and in your love for each other.

3. God wants you to be a Message Bearer

"Even when I am old and gray, do not forsake me, O God, till I declare your power to the next generation, your might to all who are to come" (Psalm 71:18). Grandparents are to undergird the parents' task in the religious training of their grandchildren, ever sowing the seed of the Gospel so that at the earliest possible age they will receive God's gracious gift of salvation through faith in the Lord Jesus Christ.

A 2003 Barna research poll revealed that children ages five through thirteen have a thirty-two percent chance of being saved, and that the percentage drops drastically to four percent for kids ages fourteen to eighteen. God is counting on us to bear His glorious message of salvation to our grandchildren while their hearts are receptive. Additionally, bear the message of biblical morality to them when they are old enough to hear and understand.

4. God wants you to be a Pray Intercessor

"I exhort therefore, that, first of all, supplications, prayers, intercessions, [and] giving of thanks, be made for all men" (I Timothy 2:1). Martyn Lloyd Jones stated, "Always respond to every impulse to pray. The impulse to pray may come when you are reading or when you are battling with a text. I would make an absolute law of this—always obey such an impulse."[156] You can often stand in the gap for your grandchildren regarding their schooling, home life, sibling relationships, health, and outside influences—and you should. God hears the prayers of the righteous and will speedily answer. Every day I pray a hedge of protection about our three grandchildren (Madison Clark, Jude, and Hudson) that Satan in no wise will be able to "steal, kill, or destroy."

Little may we realize how often the intercessory prayers of grandparents like you were the very thing that protected grandchilddren from harm until Heaven is reached.

Read Together:
He Reads: Isaiah 46:4
She Reads: Psalm 92:14

Answer Together:
Which of the four biblical roles of the grandparent do you find the most challenging? Why? Can you recall an occasion when you strangely were impressed to pray for a grandchild only later to learn he was in need of help at that time? Have you begun sowing the seed of the Gospel in the heart of your grandchildren based upon their age of understanding? How do you want your grandchildren to remember you after your death? What are you doing so that will be the case? Why not take time together to pray for your grandchildren now?

Pray Together:

Heavenly Father, help us fulfill the four biblical roles of grandparenting without staggering. Help us leave a legacy of love and devotion to You so that they, in remembering, will be blessed and challenged.

116

How to Mess Up the Minds of Your Children

The famous Methodist evangelist George R. Stuart, speaking on the home, said "From the proper or improper settlement of the home question comes more of joy or sorrow, more of weal or woe, than from all other questions combined. Build your palaces, amass your great fortunes, pile up your luxuries all about you, provide for the satisfaction of every desire; but as you sit amid these luxuries and wait for the staggering steps of a drunken son or contemplate the downward steps of a wayward daughter, happiness flies out of your heart and your home. There is nothing that can render happy the parents of godless, wayward children. Every drunkard, every gambler, every debauchee, every lost character once sat in Mother's lap [and I add Father's too]. The downfall of every character can be traced to some defect in the home life."[157]

"Do you want to mess up the minds of your children?" asks Chuck Swindoll. "Here's how—guaranteed! Rear them in a legalistic, tight context of external religion where performance is more important than reality. Fake your faith. Sneak around and pretend your spirituality. Train your children to do the same. Embrace a long list of *dos* and *don'ts* publicly, but hypocritically practice them privately... yet never own up to the fact that it's hypocrisy. Act one way but live another. And you can count on it—emotional and spiritual damage will occur."[158]

The adage is true: "Apples don't fall far from the tree." Your children observe even at an early age your conduct, activities, vices, and bad habits, and such will have lasting impact upon their life for evil. Sadly, many children once they leave home abandon the church and Christ; take up dad's/mom's vices of gambling, drinking, profanity, and/or drug usage; and/or treat their spouse wrongly when married all because of the poor example of parents who claimed to be Christians.

Walk a Little Slower, Daddy

"Walk a little slower, Daddy!" said a little child so small.
"I'm following in your footsteps, and I don't want to fall.

"Sometimes your steps are very fast; sometimes they're hard to see.
"So walk a little slower, Daddy, for you are leading me.

"Someday when I'm all grown up, you're what I want to be.
"Then I will have a little child who'll want to follow me,

"And I would want to lead just right and know that I was true;
"So, walk a little slower, Daddy, for I must follow you!"
—Author Unknown

Daddy, in what direction is your child following you?

Read Together:

He Reads: Geneses 18:19
She Reads: Titus 2:7; Ephesians 5:1

Answer Together:

Honestly, do you present yourself one way at church but another at home? What might your spouse and children point to in your life that is hypocritical? Do you agree with Swindoll's statement?

Pray Together:

Lord Jesus, be merciful to us for being hypocritical with our children and others. Help us take off the mask and be a consistent Christian wherever we go, especially at home with our children.

117 Dress Daily for Battle

Ephesians 6:11–18 cites the armor the believer is to put on daily. Ever be ready for Satanic attack upon your marriage, spouse, children, grandchildren, and self by being clothed with this armor.

The Belt of Truth refers to the believer's need to know what truth is as revealed in Holy Scripture and to walk in it.

The Breastplate of Righteousness refers to the believer's commitment to a life of righteousness (holy attitude/actions) and avoidance of all unrighteousness.

The Gospel Shoes picture the believer's assurance of salvation and his or her willingness to share the Good News everywhere with those who are lost.

The Shield of Faith speaks of the believer's need to continuously believe [faith] God when assailed with the lies of the Devil.

The Helmet of Salvation refers to the Holy Spirit's presence in the believer to protect him from domination by carnal and sensual thoughts and the fiery darts of temptation.

The Sword of the Spirit represents the power of Holy Scripture that thwarts Satanic efforts to overthrow God's rule, will and work in the believer's life.

The Knees of Prayer pinpoint the believer's source of power, protection and provision.

Put on All the Armor

Martyn Lloyd-Jones well said, "If you are to be a soldier in this army, if you are to fight victoriously in this crusade, you have to put on the entire equipment given to you. That is a rule in any army....And that is infinitely more true in this spiritual realm and warfare with which we are concerned...because your understanding is inadequate. It is God alone who knows your enemy, and He knows exactly the provision that is essential to you if you are to continue standing. Every single part and portion of this armor is absolutely essential, and the first thing you have to learn is that you are not in a position to pick and choose."[159]

Read Together:
He Reads: Ephesians 6:10–12
She Reads: Ephesians 6:13–18

Answer Together:
What piece of the armor is neglected most by you? What is the only offensive weapon of the armor? Why is it important to daily put on *all* the armor (not simply pick and choose)? Who is it that although unseen is a fierce enemy seeking the destruction of your marriage and home?

Heavenly Father, although our adversary the Devil seeks our destruction and unhappiness, You have given us the equipment and power for his defeat. Help us utilize it.

118   The Prayer of Jabez

"And Jabez called on the God of Israel, saying, Oh that thou wouldest bless me indeed, and enlarge my coast, and that thine hand might be with me, and that thou wouldest keep me from evil, that it may not grieve me! And God granted him that which he requested."—I Chronicles 4:10.

The prayer of Jabez reveals four specific things for which to pray. We should pray for *GRACE*. "Oh that thou wouldest bless me." Jabez prayed for divine enabling. The apostle Paul said, "But by the grace of God I am what I am: and his grace which was bestowed upon me was not in vain; but I laboured more abundantly than they all: yet not I, but the grace of God which was with me" (I Corinthians 15:10). It is God's grace that enables us and equips us for effective service, not education, abilities, or charisma.

We should pray for *GROWTH.* Jabez prays, "Enlarge my coast," or my border, my territory of influence and service. Pray for God to enlarge and expand the coast of your influence and ministry opportunity. Pray for growth spiritually. Additionally, pray that the ministry of the church and its pastoral staff, missionaries and evangelists will be enlarged.

We should pray for *GUIDANCE*. Jabez prayed, "That thine hand might be with me." The 'hand of God' is an expression that denotes the power of God in action. Pray for God's constant guidance regarding decisions to be made and directions to go (Psalm 139:5).

We should pray for *GODLINESS.* Jabez prayed, "That thou wouldest keep me from evil," that it may not pain me or that it might not spoil my life. Pray that God would keep you from sin and its painful consequences (Matthew 6:13). Pray to be holy and wholesome, free from the stain or stench of sin. Pray that your marriage would always be godly from its very core outward. Make your prayer that of Robert

Murray McCheyne: "O God, make me as holy as a pardoned sinner can be."

The kind of praying that Jabez exhibited so impacted his life that he was called an honorable man by God (I Chronicles 4:9).

Read Together:
He Reads: I Chronicles 4:10
She Reads: I Chronicles 4:9

Answer Together:
In what ways is the prayer of Jabez a model prayer? Specifically, in whose behalf might you pray the prayer?

Pray Together:
Personalize and pray Jabez's prayer together.

119
Facing the Dark Night of the Soul

Life is difficult. It always will be difficult. Part and parcel of life are certain heartaches, sorrows, failures, disappointments, and frustrations from which none are exempt. While I was a college student, a chapel speaker said something I have never forgotten, something I hope you will etch upon the walls of your mind. He simply said, "There's a tolerable solution for every intolerable problem you face." I have proved that statement to be true time and again.

Life is hard, but God is good. He promises to walk through every storm, sorrow, bitter disappointment, lonely moment, and failure with you. He can do anything but fail you. Therefore, fear not that which happens to or around you, relying upon Him who will not "fail thee nor forsake thee." Days of emotional and physical upheaval will come, but they will PASS.

The darkness eventually must give way to the light. God promises to still the boisterous winds and waves beating upon the vessel of your life, saying, "Peace be still." Don't panic. Wait on Him. Trust in Him. Soon the raging sea will become as a sheet of glass, and tranquility will reign again. "In his favor is life: weeping may endure for a night, but joy cometh in the morning" (Psalm 30:5).

Read Together:
He Reads: Deuteronomy 31:6

She Reads: Psalm 55:22

Answer Together:
How do you handle the wrenching pain of a broken relationship, a busted dream, disappointment in a friend, and the consequence of a sin committed? How might you comfort, sustain and strengthen your spouse when he/she is experiencing the dark night of the soul?

Pray Together:
Lord Jesus, thank You for granting the courage and strength for me to face the dark night of the soul. Without You, I couldn't have survived.

120
Spiritual Gifts

"A spiritual gift, quite simply, is a God-given ability for service."[160] Spiritual gifts are "special gifts bestowed by the Holy Spirit upon Christians for the purpose of building up the church."[161] *(Nelson's Illustrated Bible Dictionary)*

Every believer possesses at least one spiritual gift to utilize in service to the Lord. A spiritual gift is not to be confused with natural talent. Talent is derived from birth from parents, whereas a spiritual gift is received supernaturally from God at conversion. Talents are possessed by non-Christians and Christians; only Christians have spiritual gifts. Talents often are used to benefit oneself; spiritual gifts are to benefit others (I Corinthians 12:7).

"Spiritual gifts," states Adrian Rogers, "are not toys but tools, not for your enjoyment but for your employment."[162] Gifts are given that believers may glorify God and edify (build up, mature) the body of Christ (the church).

Talents and gifts must be recognized and developed for maximum potential. Both ought to be used to further God's work, but spiritual gifts specifically are given to this purpose. A person talented to speak, sing, administrate, or lead may excel in using these talents outside the Kingdom realm, but not as effectively as *within* it. In other words, a school teacher will not be as effective teaching Sunday

school; a good lecturer will not be as effective preaching; a bank mana-
ger will not be as effective as a church administrator. It is the supernaturally gifted who are able to perform spiritual assignments the most
effectively. At conversion, God may or may not give a gift or gifts that
parallel talents possessed.

John Piper surmises the purpose for spiritual gifts. "The aim of all
spiritual gifts is 'that in everything God might be glorified through
Jesus Christ' (I Peter 4:11). This means that God's aim in giving us gifts,
and in giving us the faith to exercise them, is that His glory might be
displayed. He wants us and the world to marvel at Him and think He
is fantastic. The stupendous reality of God is all encompassing. 'For
from Him and through Him and to Him are all things' (Romans 11:36).
And there is nothing more thrilling, more joyful, more meaningful,
more satisfying than to find our niche in the eternal unfolding of God's
glory. Our gift may look small, but as a part of the revelation of God's
infinite glory, it takes on stupendous proportions."[163]

Gifts vary in nature and responsibility, but all are vitally important to the operation of the Kingdom. Paul writes, "There are diversities of gifts, but the same Spirit. And there are differences of admini-
strations, but the same Lord. And there are diversities of operations,
but it is the same God which worketh all in all" (I Corinthians 12:4–6).

Read Together:
He Reads: I Corinthians 12:7
She Reads: I Corinthians 12:4–5

Answer Together:
Ask your spouse what his/her spiritual gift(s) are and affirm
them. Why is it important to identify your spiritual gift(s)? Are you
both utilizing them in fullest fashion?

Pray Together:
Heavenly Father, help us recognize the spiritual gift(s) You have
blessed us with and put them to good use in our home, church and
neighborhood.

121
Quiet Time with the Lord

To be a developed (mature), not distorted (malformed), believer requires time spent regularly in the presence of God. Your joint quiet time as a couple does not negate the imperative of your own. Five essential things need be observed to have a meaningful, beneficial quiet time.

The Right Spot

Select a place free from interruption where heart focus can be upon Holy God. Distraction is fatal.

The Ready Soul

Exercise discipline to enter this time alertly, not when you are tired or fatigued. Enter it rightly, with sin confessed and heart clean. Enter it receptively, with mind open to hear and receive from the Lord.

The Regular Span

How much time ought you to spend in the quiet time on a regular basis? It should be time enough to include adoration and exaltation of God, mediation upon and digestion of Scripture, and supplication and intercession at God's throne in a beneficial manner. The secret to an effective devotional time is not the quantity of time but the quality of time.

The Required Stuff

In addition to a study Bible, a journal and a pen are needed to record truths learned, directives issued, and impressions gained.

The Routine Sequence

Start the quiet time with a brief prayer of praise and petition for illumination of His Word. Next, having predetermined the targeted Bible passage and with journal and pen in hand, initiate the study. Adrian Rogers stated, "It is more important for you to hear from God than even for God to hear from you."[164]

Read Together:

He Reads: Psalm 5:3
She Reads: Psalm 63:1

Answer Together:

How important is it for the believer to practice a daily quiet time on a regular basis? What ought to be given priority in the quiet time and why? Demands upon a husband and wife can work havoc on a consistent quiet time unless it is scheduled and formatted well. When is the best part of the day for you to have yours?

Pray Together:

Lord Jesus, enable me to have a consistent and beneficial quiet time daily with You. Help me push aside all the pressing demands of motherhood/fatherhood to drink of Your fountain of living waters and feed upon Your table of heavenly manna.

122 The Fellowship of the Unashamed

As a couple, never be ashamed of Jesus in the daytime or night-time, private or public, the bliss of life or the throes of death. Be an example unto all, especially your children, of courage and boldness in living an exemplary life for Jesus Christ in an ungodly age.

Found among the papers of a young African pastor in Zimbabwe after he was martyred was discovered this brazen statement.

"I'm a part of the fellowship of the unashamed. The die has been cast. I have stepped over the line. The decision has been made. I'm a disciple of His, and I won't look back, let up, slow down, back away, or be still.

"My past is redeemed. My present makes sense. My future is secure. I'm finished with low living, sight walking, small planning, smooth knees, colorless dreams, tamed visions, mundane talking, cheap living, and dwarfed goals.

"I no longer need preeminence, prosperity, position, promotions, plaudits, or popularity. I don't have to be right or first or tops or recognized or praised or rewarded. I live by faith, lean on His presence, walk by patience, lift by prayer, and labor by the Holy Spirit's power.

"My face is set. My gait is fast. My goal is Heaven. My road may be narrow, my way rough, my companions few; but my guide is reliable, and my mission is clear.

"I will not be bought, compromised, detoured, lured away, turned back, deluded, or delayed.

"I will not flinch in the face of sacrifice or hesitate in the presence of the adversary. I will not negotiate at the table of the enemy, ponder at the pool of popularity, or meander in the maze of mediocrity.

"I won't give up, shut up, or let up, until I have stayed up, stored up, prayed up, paid up, and preached up for the cause of Christ.

"I am a disciple of Jesus. I must give until I drop, preach until all know, and work until He comes. And when He does come for His own, He'll have no problems recognizing me. My colors will be clear!"[165]

Will you join the young African pastor and me in saying to the Devil and the world, "I will NOT sell out" regardless of cost or consequence?

Read Together:
He Reads: Romans 1:16
She Reads: Matthew 16:26

Answer Together:
Using the Internet, Google Michael Combs' song *Not for Sale* on youtube.com and meditate over the lyrics as it is sung. What does it mean for you as a couple not to be for sale? In what ways do you believe families have sold out Christ? With your job or social events, how has Satan sought to buy you out?

Pray Together:
Heavenly Father, we commit ourselves and family to be a part of the *Fellowship of the Unashamed*.

123   The Agonizing Doubt of Salvation

The assurance of salvation is "the birthright and privilege of every true believer in Christ."[166] This assurance is not only possible, but it is part and parcel of the normal Christian life. Of a certainty, God desires all His children to be confident of their place in His family. The apostle John echoes this emphatic fact. "These things have I written unto you that believe on the name of the Son of God; that ye may know that ye have eternal life" (I John 5:13). The moment one repents and in faith receives Jesus Christ as Lord and Savior, his or her name is written in permanent ink in the Lamb's Book of Life in Heaven. Clearly, one's salvation is not to be a hope-so, think-so, gambling-so, or perhaps-so knowledge but an unequivocal know-so reality. John Stott well stated, "Clearly one cannot enjoy a gift unless one knows that one possesses it. Therefore, if God means us to receive and enjoy eternal life, He must mean us to know we possess it."[167] No one desires more than I do that doubting Christians become shouting Christians.

Doubt that arises from distrust that God saves all who call upon Him in faith and repentance, doubt that salvation is permanent, or an expectation of a "rush" at the time of salvation or afterward reveals ignorance of biblical teaching.

"Is Jesus Christ," asks Adrian Rogers, "the Lord of your life? Jesus said, 'Why call ye me, Lord, Lord, and do not the things which I say?' (Luke 6:46). Here's a riddle I want to solve for you. On the one hand, the Bible says that we know that we're saved because we keep His commandments (I John 2:3). On the other hand, the Bible teaches us that it is possible to sin (I John 1:8–9). The key word is 'keep.' It is the same word used years ago by sailors who navigated by the stars at night. A sailor's goal was to keep the stars. As a child of God, His commandments are the stars by which you navigate your life. Is keeping His commandments the burning desire of your heart? It is, if you've met the Christ of Calvary."[168]

It's time for the doubter to have inner peace, not stress; joy, not despair; and freedom, not bondage. It's time the battle of the mind and soul caused by doubt ended. It's time for Satan once and for all to be driven back. It's time that haunting and agonizing doubt cease to plague forever. To gain this deliverance, the doubter must do one of two things.

First, trust God that He in fact did what was promised when the conditions of salvation were met (new birth). "Whenever our conscience condemns us, we will be reassured that God is greater than our conscience and knows everything" (1 John 3:20, GWT). Believe God over the accusing doubt Satan has sown in the mind.

Second, admit the conditions of salvation were not understood and/or sincerity of heart was not exhibited (counterfeit salvation) and accept Jesus Christ as Lord and Savior based upon new understanding with sincerity (Romans 10:13). The doubter must say no to a former religious experience in order to say yes to authentic salvation.

Read Together:
He Reads: I John 5:11–13
She Reads: Romans 10:9–13

Answer Together:
Do you possess doubt regarding salvation? Is the source of the doubt from God or Satan, and cite how you know? What role does feeling play in salvation? How might you resolve the doubt?

Pray Together:
Lord Jesus, I long at whatever the cost to have my agonizing doubt put to rest about whether I am saved or not.

124 The Bucket List

Ask your spouse about his or her dreams of things to do before death. It may surprise you. But beyond listening, where it is realistic give encouragement to the dreams' fulfillment. It is important that your mate know that you deeply believe the dreams can be turned into reality.

I read somewhere the words, "Goals without plans are merely dreams." Sadly, many fail to realize their dreams simply because of failure to have a plan for their attainment.

So give your husband/wife a positive push in the direction of seeing dreams come true, and make yourself available to assist in every way possible.

And while you are at it, jot down a *couple's* bucket list and formulate a doable plan for its realization.

Read Together:
He Reads: Ephesians 3:20
She Reads: Psalm 37:4

Answer Together:
What are the things you have dreamed for years about attaining that you desire to do before you die? Do you see a path to their reality? Are they things which would win the approval of God? What can you

do to help your spouse experience his or her dreams? As a couple, what is in your bucket list?

Pray Together:

Heavenly Father, to the extent that my dreams please You, I ask for Your help in their attainment. Ever remind me that there is absolutely nothing that I cannot do with Your strength if it is Your will.

125
Top Traits of Successful Families

According to a study of more than 500 family counselors, the following are the top traits of successful families:

*Communicating and listening
*Affirming and supporting family members
*Respecting one another
*Developing a sense of trust
*Sharing time and responsibility
*Knowing right from wrong
*Having rituals and traditions
*Sharing a religious core
*Respecting privacy.[169]

Read Together:

He Reads: Song of Solomon 8:6–7
She Reads: I Corinthians 13:4–8

Answer Together:

Which of the top traits of successful families cited in today's booster are evidenced in your marriage? Which are missing? Which traits do you need to work hard at in developing in your relationship?

Pray Together:

Heavenly Father, we desire our marriage to be counted among the successful. Help us therefore diligently and fully embrace the traits of successful families cited.

126 A Profile of a Healthy Family

Based upon a national survey of strong families, a profile of a strong healthy family includes the following things.

Appreciation. "Family members gave one another compliments and sincere demonstrations of approval. They tried to make the others feel appreciated and good about themselves."

Ability to Deal with Crises in a Positive Manner. "They were willing to take a bad situation, see something positive in it, and focus on that." Gary Collins states, "The health of our families often depends on the decisions we make, especially when difficult circumstances threaten to overwhelm us and keep us from growing together."[170]

Time Together. "In all areas of their lives—meals, work, recreation—they structured their schedules to spend time together."

High Degree of Commitment. "Families promoted each person's happiness and welfare, invested time and energy in each other, and made family their number one priority."

Good Communication Patterns. "These families spent time talking with each other. They also listened well, which shows respect."

High Degree of Religious Orientation. "Not all belonged to an organized church, but they considered themselves highly religious."[171]

Additional traits of a healthy family are shared by Dolores Curran in *Traits of a Healthy Family:* affirm and support one another, teach respect for others, develop a sense of trust, share responsibility, have a sense of right and wrong, foster family time and conversation, admit and seek help with problems, have a sense of play and humor, and respect the privacy of one another.[172]

Read Together:
He Reads: Colossians 3:18
She Reads: Colossians 3:19

Answer Together:
Based on the traits stated, how healthy is your family? In what ways do you express appreciation for your spouse? How much time in the course of a day is spent in dialogue with one another? If an

outsider was to observe your actions, would he say that family was your number one priority? Do you attend church together?

Pray Together:
Lord, our family is somewhat sick, for it fails to measure up to what constitutes a healthy family. Help us take stringent measures in adopting the traits of a healthy family that our family may be totally healthy.

127
Description of a Family

Rudyard Kipling once wrote about families, "All of us are we, and everyone else is they. A family shares things like dreams, hopes, possessions, memories, smiles, frowns, and gladness...A family is a clan held together with the glue of love and the cement of mutual respect. A family is shelter from the storm, a friendly port when the waves of life become too wild. No person is ever alone who is a member of a family."

"A family," states Chuck Swindoll "is a place where principles are hammered and honed on the anvil of everyday living."[173]

Billy Graham said, "In the home, character is formed, integrity is born, values we live by are made clear, and attitudes are formed that last a lifetime. Is your home built on a solid foundation?"[174]

Read Together:
He Reads: Proverbs 11:29
She Reads: Psalm 103:17

Answer Together:
What other traits of a family might you add to Kipling's, Swindoll's and Graham's? Does your family mirror the description portrayed by these men? What value do you place upon family?

Pray Together:
Father, thank You for the joy and blessing to be part of Your family and our family.

128

Family Boosters

Some things you can do with your spouse and family that will boost joy and deepen relationship.

1. Take a vacation together
2. Go on a dialog date night with your spouse (no movie, just conversation over dinner)
3. Build the world's biggest banana split and feed it to each other
4. Attend a family camp in the summer
5. Polish dad's shoes
6. Wash your teen's car at home
7. Fill up your teen's car with gas
8. Off-the-cuff take your wife to her favorite place (beach, mountains, etc.)
9. Bring home flowers (it's not a special occasion)
10. Prepare your husband's favorite meal and dessert
11. Give her a mom's day out, and you keep the children
12. Give your child a "Get Out of Jail Free" card (be spared restriction)
13. Write a romantic note to your spouse (place in lunchbox, suitcase or briefcase, under breakfast plate, coat pocket)
14. Visit the zoo
15. Plan a picnic at the park
16. Go on a mission trip
17. Exercise together
18. Return to the family meal time *together* for seven days
19. "Free hug" day (all the hugging children and spouse want)
20. Attend a marriage seminar
21. Family devotions
22. Attend (same) church
23. Have a weekly date night
24. Movie and pizza night
25. Play Monopoly

Read Together:

He Reads: John 10:9–10
She Reads: Psalm 118:24

Answer Together:
Which of the family boosters are you willing to try? Share some additional boosters. What boosters have you already done? Were they effective?

Pray Together:
Lord, help our family display laughter, fun, and smiles together.

129
The Forever Knot

Daniel Webster was a nineteenth-century attorney and statesman who as a young man fell in love with a minister's daughter, Grace Fletcher. Upon one occasion in his courtship of Grace at her parent's house, he held the skeins of silk so she could unknot the threads.

At last he said, "Grace, we have been engaged in untying knots. I would like to tie a knot with you that would last a lifetime." Webster then took a piece of ribbon from her sewing basket and began tying a knot; then he handed it to Grace. Without a word spoken, Grace finished tying the knot Webster had started. And with that simple proposal and acceptance they became engaged. The forever knot they tied did last a lifetime.

Daniel survived his wife by twenty-five years. Upon his death, a box marked "Precious Documents" was found which contained letters Grace and he exchanged during their courtship along with the knotted ribbon, never untied.

People who get married are said to have tied the knot. It is my earnest hope that when you tied the knot in matrimony it was done so with the same determined commitment that it would forever last as that of Daniel and Grace.

Read Together:
He Reads: Proverbs 5:18–19
She Reads: Matthew 19:6

Answer Together:
Is the knot of your marriage steadily getting tighter, or is it loosening? What are the contributing factors? How might you prevent the marital knot from ever being untied, as Daniel and Grace Webster did?

Pray Together:

Bind us together, Lord; bind us together with cords that cannot be broken.

130 Assess Marriage Health

Marriage is not like a course in school that you pass or fail but is a process of growing in intimacy, strengthening in commitment, complying and adapting to change, bonding in unity, accommodating in cooperation, and stabilizing in development.

To help you assess the progress of your marriage in the process stated above, simply enter the numerical number below (1-weakest to 10-strongest) that best describes the category's strength or weakness. The results are intended to reveal areas of the marriage that need attention.

1. Commitment to each other ___
2. Communication ___
3. Money management ___
4. Intimacy/Sexuality ___
5. Household chores ___
6. Balancing work with family ___
7. Time management ___
8. Bonding time alone ___
9. Expression of appreciation ___
10. Lordship of Christ ___
11. Accommodating each other ___
12. Activities together ___
13. Lifestyle ___
14. Private space ___
15. Common values ___

If your self-ratings on a specific topic are:

8–10: Happy and satisfied (keep up the good work)

4–7: Mediocre (be intentional on resolving these issues despite fear of conflict)

1–3: Dissatisfied (need to give these areas immediate attention by discussing them honestly with each other and developing solution)

Read Together:
He Reads: Psalm 139:23–24
She Reads: I Peter 4:8

Answer Together:
Were you surprised at the weak score your spouse entered for some of the traits of a healthy marriage? Take a moment to graciously discuss the reason for the weak score and brainstorm ways to improve any of those traits in your marriage.

Pray Together:
Lord, help us never stop at working hard to improve our relationship and the strengthening of our marriage.

131
Home Buster—Pornography

Forty million U.S. adults regularly visit Internet pornography websites

Forty-seven percent of Christians say pornography is a major problem in the home

Sixty-six percent of men in age bracket twenty to thirty are regular users of pornography[175]

What harm is pornography?

It *derails* your walk with God. "You cannot serve two masters" (Matthew 6:24). In serving pornography, intimacy with God decays, and your walk becomes cold and distant.

It *distorts* God's view of sex. Sex is intended to be shared between a husband and wife. Pornography distorts the mind into believing that any form of sex is acceptable at any time.

It *devours* peace. Pornography leads to shame and deep guilt that robs one's inner peace and joy.

It *destroys* life. Pornography fuels the heart with such lustful passion that it can lead to acts of violence to satisfy its craving.

It *depreciates* women. Pornography is primarily a man's business. It degrades women into sex objects.

It *dupes* you. It deceives you into believing that what once was thought abominable is really acceptable.

It *disrupts* marriage. Pornography leads to an unhealthy expectation regarding sex in marriage. Its pictures, movies, and magazines mar normal and healthy marital sexual expectations.

It *damages* one's reputation. Pornography injuries the believer's witness and testimony.

It *depletes* a person's time and energy. Endless hours and energy can be exhausted searching for that "right" picture on the Internet or in magazines. It robs one of time and energy that should be spent in wholesome activities with family and friends.

It *dominates* the mind. Pornography masters the will, taking you prisoner. Pornography will take you further than you want to go. It will keep you longer than you want to stay. It will cost you more than you want to pay. Freedom from the clutches of pornography takes serious action beginning with a repentant heart unto God.

Five "Must-Haves"

1. Transparency with your wife. She will be the best accountability partner. Allow her access to your computer viewing habits.

2. Focused and holy mind. Your mind must be God oriented instead of lust stimulated. Feed your mind on the Word of God, burn its truths into your heart (Psalm 119:11). We must continuously 'set our affections on things above' (Colossians 3:2) and "let this mind be in you, which was also in Christ Jesus" (Philippians 2:5). Engage in persistent and passionate prayer, for it links you to divine power needed to thwart this temptation. Pray specifically that Jesus will keep you from "the evil one" (Matthew 6:13).

Embrace the *coram Deo* life. R. C. Sproul says, "To live *coram Deo* is to live one's entire life in the presence of God, under the authority of God, to the glory of God."[176] (I Corinthians 6:19–20).

3. Zero tolerance of any visual or verbal material that arouses lust (Ephesians 4:27). Paul admonishes, "But among you there must not be even a *hint* of sexual immorality, or of any kind of impurity" (Ephesians 5:3 NIV).

4. Vigilance in battle. The soldier who sleeps or daydreams in battle is easily defeated. Maintain alertness in the battle with pornography lest you be unexpectantly drawn into its snare of defilement and infidelity. Post pornographic war notices where it is likely to attack.

"Be sober, be vigilant; because your adversary the devil, as a roaring lion, walketh about, seeking whom he may devour" (I Peter 5:8).

5. You are your brother's keeper. Give warning of the power and poison of pornography to those within and outside your home. It's the silent killer of marriages, families and lives.

Read Together:
He Reads: Psalm 101:3
She Reads: Ephesians 4:27

Answer Together:
What might be done to preserve yourself from becoming entangled in pornography? How might you be your brother's keeper with regard to pornography? If addicted to pornography, seek out a Christian pastor or licensed therapist for guidance.

Pray Together:
Lord Jesus, let there not even be a hint of sexual impurity in me as a husband. Help me live 24/7 in Your presence, under Your authority and unto Your glory.

132
Home Buster—Alcohol

If you are unwilling or unable to give up alcohol consumption for your wife's/husband's happiness and love, then it is apparent you love it more than you love her/him—and you are addicted. Denial of the problem only exacerbates it and heightens the likelihood of emotional and physical harm to yourself and all your life touches.

The Bible speaks much about alcohol's destructiveness. It is like the fangs of a rattlesnake full of venomous poison awaiting an unsuspecting passer-by (Proverbs 23:32). Once alcohol is consumed, its poison is released into the body to do its deadly, destructive work. It kills the brain cells, deadens the senses, retards the reflexes, damages glands and vital organs, and initiates the process of death.

Alcohol is like the robber who steals all one possesses, leaving him in deep poverty. "For the drunkard and the glutton shall come to poverty: and drowsiness shall clothe a man with rags" (Proverbs 23:21).

Alcohol is like Mr. Hyde taking over Dr. Jekyll's speech, leading him to say unruly and embarrassing things. "...thine heart shall utter perverse things" (Proverbs 23:33b).

A man under the control of alcohol is like a man in the ocean being tossed to and fro, unaware of what's happening. "Yea, thou shalt be as he that lieth down in the midst of the sea" (Proverbs 23:34).

Alcohol is like a mule whose blinders are removed; his eyes are free to roam the terrain (the forbidden), resulting in impure conduct. Alcohol retards mental rationality and deteriorates walls of sexual restraint. "Thine eyes shall behold strange women" (Proverbs 23:33).

Alcohol is like a man getting beat up in a fight, unaware of the harm received; he denies the hurt that alcohol produces in his life. "And you will say, 'They hit me, but I didn't feel it. I didn't even know it when they beat me up.'" (Proverbs 23:35 NLT).

Alcohol is like the tyrant that enslaves a person to serve him alone; the drunkard can't wait until he sleeps off his intoxication so he can drink again. "When will I wake up so I can look for another drink?" (Proverbs 23:35b NLT).

Alcohol is like a pretender, pretending to give a person gusto in life, only to give sorrow. "Wine is a mocker, strong drink is raging and whosoever is deceived thereby is not wise" (Proverbs 20:1).

Alcohol is the mother of sorrows and the father of trouble. "Who has anguish? Who has sorrow? Who is always fighting? Who is always complaining? Who has unnecessary bruises? Who has bloodshot eyes? It is the one who spends long hours in the taverns, trying out new drinks" (Proverbs 23:29–30 NLT).

Alcohol consumption leads to chaos in a marriage and family and is a major reason for abuse and divorce. But its deadly influence doesn't stop there, for it continues to impact spouse and children psychologically and emotionally for years.

Awaken yourself to the impact upon those you love due to alcohol and seek deliverance from it without further delay. Stop lying to your spouse and yourself that you don't have a problem with alcohol, that you can quit anytime you desire. Facing the truth about your drinking addiction and getting serious godly counseling must occur before reconciliation is possible with your spouse/children.

Read Together:

He Reads: Proverbs 23:32

She Reads: Proverbs 23:29–30

Answer Together:

What impact does alcohol have upon you, your spouse and your children? How many times have you promised to stop consuming alcohol, only to continue shortly later? Are you willing to receive godly counseling to assist you in your deliverance from it?

Pray Together:

Heavenly Father, for my wife's/husband's and child's sake I must stop drinking, but I am powerless to stop on my own. Please deliver me from this bondage to strong drink. Bring alongside me from the community of believers those that will provide counseling, help and accountability.

133 Getting the Victory over Alcohol

Don't give Satan another inch of ground in your life. Draw a line in the sand and say, "Enough is enough." Then take back all Satan took, in the authority of Jesus' name.

During football season, when the opposing team is on the one-yard line seeking to score, the great cry from fans that reverberates throughout the stadium is, "Hold that line!" You may have let them drive the ball ninety yards, played sluggishly, missed key tackles, and made senseless mistakes resulting in penalties; but at the one-yard line, you set your cleats firmly in the sod and determine enough is enough.

Life is like football in this regard. You get pushed back, knocked down, and run over by mistakes you make; and just as the enemy is about to deliver the final blow, you set your cleats in the sod at the goal line and say, "No further!"

Mel Trotter, an alcoholic, did just this on January 19, 1897. On that day, he staggered into the Pacific Garden Mission so intoxicated that he didn't even know his own name. Mel's mother was a godly woman, but his dad was an alcoholic bartender. Mel couldn't keep a job and was a hopeless alcoholic at age twenty. In an effort to overcome the craving for alcohol, he was hospitalized, but to no avail. He married in 1891. At the end of one of his ten-day drinking sprees, Trotter returned home only to discover that his two-year-old son had died. Deeply grieved, he promised his wife never to touch alcohol again—a promise short-lived, for two hours later he staggered home drunk.

In a Chicago winter, Trotter, now aged twenty-seven, decided to commit suicide by jumping into the icy waters of Lake Michigan. In walking toward Lake Michigan, he passed the Pacific Garden Mission and entered, only to hear Harry Monroe (converted alcoholic) sharing his testimony of deliverance from alcohol. That night Mel Trotter was saved.

Trotter later became the director of a new rescue mission in Grand Rapids, Michigan, where he served for forty years. By the time of his death, Trotter had established sixty-seven other rescue missions across the nation.[177]

Mel Trotter, though beaten down by Satan for ninety-nine yards, said, "No further" and had his victorious "goal-line stand."

You are not alone at the one-yard line. You have been beaten down but not defeated. There are not enough demons in Hell to drag you over the one-yard line into eternal bleakness, hopelessness, and Hell, if you cling to Jesus Christ.

You have a one-yard-line stand to make against alcohol. You have been pushed back, overrun, outplayed, and fooled by the play calls of Satan. He has beaten you hand over fist to this moment. Now your back is to the wall, and you must make the goal-line stand or else suffer utter defeat.

Don't quit. Don't despair. Don't allow what you have done, the defeats you have suffered, to break your spirit, resulting in an attitude of hopelessness. You can win. With others, you can make an unforgettable goal-line stand that will change everything.

Make a goal-line stand now. Have an enough-is-enough attitude toward how Satan has been defeating you and robbing joy, peace, and fulfillment from your life. God will stand with you as you stand against Satan; with God on your side, you "outnumber and outplay" the opponent, regardless of whom or what he throws at you. You indeed can do all things through Christ who strengthens you (Philippians 4:13). On your own you will fail, but with Jesus, you will prevail. Right now, decide to stop being beaten down by Satan, entrapped by alcohol, and robbed of what God intended.

Read Together:
He Reads: Philippians 4:13; Romans 10:9–13
She Reads: Psalm 18:2

Answer Together:
Do you identify with Mel Trotter (in what ways)? How did he make a goal–line stand against alcohol? Do you need to make a goal–line stand right now and reverse directions? [Call upon the name of the Lord, crying out for forgiveness, salvation and deliverance. Next, phone your pastor for further guidance and counseling.]

Pray Together:
"'I love You, O LORD, my strength. The LORD is my rock and my fortress and my deliverer, my God, my rock, in whom I take refuge; my shield and the horn of my salvation, my stronghold. I call upon the LORD, who is worthy to be praised, and I am saved from my enemies" (Psalm 18:1–3).

134 The Wounded Spirit

A wounded spirit (broken, damaged or crushed spirit) is the injury to the emotions by another that manifests such horrendous pain and misery that it may feel as if we have been torn open and are bleeding from every orifice of the body. It is fueled by many things, including the unrelenting focus on the injury, lack of forgiveness toward the offender, and a retaliatory spirit. It is an *inside* wound that can only be detected by conduct or confession of its presence.

Medical personnel talk of "weeping wounds," wounds which continue to fester, discharge and ooze, refusing to heal due to noxious matter. Emotionally, many people have "weeping wounds," wounds inflicted years earlier that refuse to heal due to the toxins of an unforgiving spirit, retaliatory spirit, bitterness, anger, blaming of God, fear, and pride. Doctors can close up wounds without their healing, and we are good at doing the same with emotional or spirit wounds. The wound may be closed, but it yet is unhealed deep inside the mind, bearing grievous impact.

No class of people is exempt from a broken spirit; black-tie and no-tie alike suffer from its painful stabbings. Everybody hurts. Sadly, many will live with a wounded spirit all their life and die with it when all the while help was available through Jesus Christ, Holy Scripture, church, ministers, and Christian therapists.

God cares about your broken spirit. David declared, "The Lord is nigh unto them that are of a broken heart" (Psalm 34:18). When David's spirit was wounded due to sin, he cried, "The sacrifices of God are a broken spirit; a broken and contrite heart, O God, thou wilt not despise" (Psalm 51:17). The psalmist bears testimony to God's desire for all with a broken spirit in saying, "He healeth the broken in heart, and bindeth up their wounds" (Psalm 147:3). In fact, God so longs to exhibit compassion and healing to the wounded spirit and broken heart that He sent His only Son, Jesus, into the world for that purpose (Luke 4:18).

Read Together:
He Reads: Proverbs 18:14
She Reads: Isaiah 41:10

Answer Together:
What has wounded your spirit? What keeps you from its healing? Why not cast this grievous hurt at Jesus' feet just now and be healed? Is your spouse among the walking wounded? If so, what might you do to help in his/her healing?

Pray Together:
Heavenly Father, please forgive me for bearing this wound for so long and take it from me. Your Word promises that "He whom the son sets free is free indeed." I want to walk in freedom from the bondage of old wounds.

135 Four Danger Signs of Marital Trouble

PREP (Christian Prevention and Relationship Enhancement Program) focuses on four key *Danger Signs* as a way to summarize destructive patterns of communication and conflict management. These signs drawn from research certainly overlap with scriptural principles regarding marital difficulty.[178]

Withdrawal

The unwillingness on the part of a spouse to enter into or continue in important discussions is a pattern that signifies danger in the marital union (leaving the room, "turning off" or remaining quiet during confrontations/arguments). (Ephesians 4:25–27; Matthew 5:23–24)

Escalation

This pattern involves ever increasing negative response back and forth in communication, causing conditions to continually worsen in the relationship (prompts intensified anger, frustration, threats of divorce). (Proverbs 20:3; 29:11)

Negative Interpretations

Motives of one's spouse are overplayed, seen as being more negative than is really the case (hinders reconciliation, and/or constructive conflict resolution). (I Corinthians 13:6–7)

Invalidation

This pattern belittles a spouse purposely and directly (various ways, including put-down remarks, expressions of contempt, name calling, degrading). (Proverbs 25:20; Ephesians 4:29)

For sure, as the Bible stipulates, such negative relational patterns as cited by PREP will certainly end in marital failure. (Proverbs 12:18; 15:1; 17:14; 29:22; Matthew 5:22; 7:1–5; Galatians 5:15; Ephesians 4:29; James 1:26; 4:1–3). A key factor that helps predict the failure or success of a marriage is how well the couple handles marital conflict.[179]

Dr. Timothy Faulk surmises, "Research reveals that couples can learn communication skills that overcome the danger signs described. They can retain these skills for many years, thereby significantly reducing the odds of break-up, divorce, and distress."[180]

Read Together:
He Reads: Proverbs 12:18; 15:1
She Reads: Matthew 5:22; 7:1–5

Answer Together:
Are any of the four danger signs routinely expressed by either of you? If so, may they prompt immediate resolution through biblical guidance and counsel from a trained therapist.

Heavenly Father, help us communicate kindly, lovingly, and graciously one to another and develop better communication skills.

136 Do Not Sin against the Child (Part 1)

The great London pastor C. H. Spurgeon in the sermon "Do Not Sin against the Child" states how unsaved and saved parents alike commit grievous sins against their own son or daughter. Today's subject is addressed to the non-Christian father and/or mother.

"In speaking to parents, I put the charge in the mildest terms and have said that some have done nothing to train their families for the Savior, but graver accusations may be brought. Are there not some here who have done much the other way, much to quench the motions of the Spirit in the juvenile mind, done much to harden the children's hearts and to lull their consciences to sleep? It is a disgraceful fact that many fathers educate their children for the service of Satan. They are the Devil's lackeys, introducing their sons into the courts of the evil one. When they send them to the beer shop or let them see their drunkenness, what surer school of vice can they send them to? Shame is it when from a father's lips the boy hears the first oath and learns the alphabet of blasphemy!

"There are crowds of parents upon whose head the blood of their children will certainly descend because they have launched them on the sea of life with the rudder set towards the rocks—with a false chart, a deceitful compass, and every other appliance for securing eternal shipwreck. Doubtless there are some unconverted men and women here whose example has already come home to them in the ungrateful conduct of their sons. They have seen their children grow up to be estranged from them, and if they are, therefore, blaming the providence of God, let them pause awhile and ask themselves whether they ought not rather to blame themselves—are they not reaping according to their sowing?

"What are our children, for the most part, but what we make them by our training? And if they have grown up like ourselves and our faults are mirrored in their characters, let us repent in dust and ashes before God! Never think it a hard law that our sins against our children should recoil upon ourselves. Fathers and mothers who sin against your children, I fear you will be lost yourselves, but before that doom overtakes you, I pray you remember that you will not perish alone in your iniquity—your household will suffer with you! If you have no care about your own souls, yet think, I pray you, of the little ones entrusted to you; you have some in Heaven whom sovereign mercy has caught away from the cradle and the breast that they may sing the praises of God forever.

"I cannot bear to think that you should drag the others down to the pit of Hell! For your own sake, for their sake, pause awhile—murder not your own flesh and blood! Repent of your own personal sins, and seek mercy at the hands of Jesus that you may from now on never more sin against the child!"[181]

Read Together:
He Reads: Genesis 42:22
She Reads: I Samuel 2:12, 22–34

Answer Together:
For the sake of your own flesh and blood, your child, will you right now call upon the name of the Lord Jesus Christ in repentance (godly sorrow for your sin) and faith (simple trust in Jesus to forgive and save)? Tell Jesus you never want to sin against your child again and need His power to be the best dad/mom possible.

Pray Together:
God, I have sinned against You and my child, for which I am gravely sorry. Though I cannot undo what I have done, help me henceforth live a life of godly example and instill biblical truth in my child's heart.

137
Do Not Sin against the Child (Part 2)

In yesterday's marriage booster, C. H. Spurgeon revealed how non-Christian parents sin against their own children. In this booster he will address the matter to the Christian parent.

"Do Christian parents ever sin against their children? We answer, Christian parents are not perfect; they are yet in the body and have yet to mourn over sins and shortcomings, and so, not condemning you

who fear God—for who shall condemn whom Christ has justified?—
yet let me, for the awakening of your consciences and to drive you
again to the blood of Jesus for pardon, remind you that we, alas, too
often do sin against our children!

"We are under a double responsibility, not only because they are
our children, but because God has given us salvation. We are bound,
having the light of God, to give that light to all around us, and bound
by other ties to first give the light to those who have sprung from our
loins. If we deny our most loving efforts to our own households, we
must surely be inhuman!

"Not only may we not talk of divine grace; we can scarcely boast
of fulfilling the promptings of nature itself if we have no compassion
for our children's souls. Yet what do you think—may not our incon-
sistencies be the reason why our children are not converted? Is the
boy compelled to say, 'My father hardly believes what he says, or else
he would not act as he does'?

"Do you not think that in many families where the parents are
worldly and conformed to the world, it would be a great wonder if the
sons and daughters were not ungodly? Are there not many Christians
so busy about making money that they have no time to speak about
soul concerns to their children? And if those children were to die, do
you think those parents could excuse themselves? If their children
died without hope, how would their parents quiet their consciences?

"Do we as a rule pray for our own children as we ought? Do we
wrestle with God for them night and day? Do we ever spend an hour
in pleading with the Most High that they might live in His sight? And
if we have prayed, do we use such efforts for our children as dying
beds will make us wish that we had used? Have we spoken personally
to them about their salvation? Having done it once, have we repeated
it? If we fear that we have not touched the right chord of the heart,
have we made up our minds to persevere in affectionate admonitions
and earnest entreaties until every one of them shall be saved?

"O you who have been baptized into Christ and profess to have
put on Christ! O you who claim to love your Lord and Master, what
shall we say to you if your sons shall be unchastened like those of Eli
and shall die in their sins? If your sons turn out to be Nadabs and Abi-
hus and not Samuels, how can we console you if you have not wept

over them? If they rebel like Absalom, who can wonder, if their father never poured out his heart before the Lord on their account? Do you expect to reap without sowing or to gather where you have not planted?

"Give us the Bible read from day to day and godly parents inculcating gospel truths upon their little ones' minds, and we may laugh to scorn all the powers of Satan! But once let the family altar be forsaken, and let parents forget the natural duty of ordering their households before the Lord, and you may guard the church as you will; your labor will be in vain! Christian parents...with all my heart would I say to you, do not sin against the child by your bad example or by your negligence as to his salvation, but seek of the Holy Spirit that to your own offspring you may fully discharge the solemn duties which providence and grace have thrown upon you!"[182]

Read Together:
He Reads: I Samuel 8:2–3
She Reads: 2 Chronicles 22:3

Answer Together:
In what ways have you sinned (sins of omission and commission) against your child as a Christian parent? How might you avoid such sin(s) in the future? Do you know of a parent who professes to be a Christian whose talk doesn't match his walk? If so, pray that he may come to realize his hypocrisy and its destructive impact upon his children.

Pray Together:
Father, reveal to us the sins we have committed against our child that they may be renounced, confessed and forgiven by Thy grace and mercy.

138
Restoring the Family Altar

"If therefore our houses," declares Matthew Henry, "be houses of the Lord, we shall for that reason love home, reckoning our daily devotion the sweetest of our daily delights and our family worship the most valuable of our family comforts....A church in the house will be a good legacy; nay, it will be a good inheritance to be left to your children after you."[183]

The Family Altar was part of the spiritual foundation of Christian homes of years past. Sadly, its name and meaning are all but relics of the church of yesterday. I for one believe its restoration in homes would impact the family's spiritual state, joy and harmony beyond comprehension for the better.

The Family Altar simply is a term referring to members of the family gathering daily at an appointed time for Scripture reading, prayer and worship.

It may be structured in the following manner (10–12 minutes).

1. Father or Mother opens the time in prayer.
2. Worship God through song (one verse or two).
3. Each member of age reads two verses of Scripture.
4. Discussion time (meaning and application of the Scripture). Sometimes the biblical lesson taught may be dramatized (e.g. Goliath (parent) and David (child)).
5. Memorization of a Scripture verse weekly may be included (if so, include time to repeat the verse together).
6. Father or Mother voices prayer for family members (surrender, submission, petition to God).

Keep the *Family Altar* as a time of smiles and joy, a time all family members look forward to attending. Guard against its becoming a legalistic observance. The manifold benefits and blessings of the *Family Altar* certainly compel us to erect it immediately in our home.

[See the author's book *Children's Sermons That Connect* for Family Altar texts and talks.]

Read Together:

He Reads: Genesis 33:19–20
She Reads: Genesis 26:25

Answer Together:

Did you have the *Family Altar* as a child in your home? If so, what are your fondest memories regarding it? What are the benefits of its observance? Are you willing to establish it in your home?

Pray Together:

Heavenly Father, as saints of old worshipped in their homes with family members, help us do the same.

139
Is Your Child Suicidal?

One of the leading causes of death among students ages 15–24 is suicide.

As a parent, you need to recognize the signs of suicidal tendencies. In doing so, you may just save the life of your child or grandchild.

Suicidal tendencies include expressing thoughts of despair, suicide or death; giving away prized possessions; making a will or other preparations for death; change in sleeping patterns (sleeping too much or much too little); change in eating habits, causing loss or gain of much weight; change in school performance, such as suddenly getting poor grades, cutting class, or dropping out of school activities; change in social activities like dropping friends and spending more and more time alone; personality changes like nervousness, agitation or bursts of anger, or on the other hand apathy or carelessness about health and appearance; abuse of alcohol, drugs or other self-destructive behavior such as getting into a lot of accidents or taking life-risking chances; physical symptoms often related to stress, such as chronic stomach aches, headache or fatigue; previous suicide attempt(s).[184] These signs often appear in clusters.

Second, differentiate fable from fact regarding suicide. It is fact, not fable, that people who talk about suicide are serious. *Eight out of ten who commit suicide speak of it prior to the attempt.* It is fact, not fable, that the chances of suicide are reduced by talking about it. It is fact, not fable, that there are telltale signs a person who is considering suicide exhibits, such as those cited above. It is fact, not fable, that the suicide risk remains in effect although the crisis is over. It is fact, not fable, that the suicidal are undecided about living or dying and gamble that someone will intervene to stop them. Individuals stopped in their suicide attempt rarely complain. It is fact, not fable, that parents can intervene, preventing the suicide.[185]

Third, prayerfully intervene. Hesitation to confront your suicidal child may result in taking action too late. Intervention is warranted upon evidencing any cluster of the suicidal signs previously stated. Mary Miller, suicidologist, suggests that once it is known a person intends to take his life, you should seek to ascertain the answers to four questions remembered with the acronym SLAP.

S – how Specific are the plans?

L – how Lethal is the proposed method?

A – what is its Availability?

P – what is the Proximity of helpful resources, like friends and ministers?[186]

Answers to these questions reveal the stage and seriousness of the suicidal.

Dr. Timothy Faulk, clinical psychological therapist stated, "Remember, people who are feeling suicidal isolate themselves, so reaching out to them is vital. They need you to encourage them to talk, and then they need you to listen carefully. Talk openly and directly about suicide. Use the words "suicide", "kill yourself," and "dead" in a matter-of-fact way."[187] Faulk continues, "Be nonjudgmental and accept the child's feelings, even if you disagree with them. Show your interest and support. Don't let him/her swear you to secrecy. As your child tells you that he or she is thinking about suicide, start thinking about people you can ask for help [ministers, school counselors, teachers, mental health professionals, and psychologists]. You can do a lot to help your child initially, but the situation is too dangerous to handle entirely on your own."[188] Never hesitate to call for help in dealing with the suicidal (1-800-SUICIDE or Billy Graham Ministries, 877-247-2426).

Read Together:

He Reads: Psalm 55:22

She Reads: I Peter 5:7

Answer Together:

Are we keenly observing the emotional state of our child? Are we taking too lightly some of the signs of possible suicide that our child is manifesting? When have we last face to face affirmed our unconditional love for our son/daughter?

Pray Together:

Lord, as with probably most parents, the idea that our child would take his own life has never crossed our mind, and yet it is in homes just like ours that it occurs. Help us stay involved in the life of our child so we can spot any suicidal sign and then take the necessary steps to provide the help needed.

140
Positive News about the Family

Truth for the family shared by Gary Collins in *Family Shock:*

1. Despite all the change and turmoil that disrupts family life, God is still aware of what is going on and is still in control.

2. If most people had to do it over, they would marry the same spouse.

3. While three percent of women living with men in America suffer at least one violent domestic incident during a given year, the good news is that ninety-seven percent do not.

4. The majority of families are not seriously dysfunctional. Most kids do not become "adult children of dysfunctional family backgrounds," and most of us are not in need of recovery.

5. No family is perfect and without problems and periodic crises.

6. All parents make mistakes, but most of their kids survive very well, even without therapy and twelve–step programs.

7. When families and marriages have problems, counselors can often help.

8. It is possible (but admittedly more difficult) to have good marriages, healthy families, and stable kids even when we live in bad environments or in a chaotic, immoral, God-rejecting society.

9. We can rear kids successfully even if we don't have all the answers.

10. We can rear kids successfully even if we haven't read parenting and marriage books and even if we aren't perfect.

11. Even good parents sometimes have rebellious kids.

12. Even bad parents sometimes have healthy, adjusted kids.

13. When things are not going well in your family, that does not mean that all is hopeless. Often "this too will pass."

14. God cares about each of our families.[189]

It's always good to get good news about the family, for such encourages our heart. Despite all Satan is doing to destroy the Christian family, its foundation is built upon Jesus Christ the *Solid Rock* and thus is invincible until that foundation is removed or renounced. Chins up, Christian parents, for God is still in control and has all power necessary to defeat the enemy of the home.

Read Together:
He Reads: Proverbs 15:30
She Reads: Proverbs 12:25

Answer Together:
What specifically in Dr. Collins' positive words about the family encouraged you? Surprised you?

Pray Together:
Father, amidst all the bad news about the family, help us focus upon the good regarding it and be lifted in spirit.

141 Story Behind "It Is Well with My Soul"

"Run now, I pray thee, to meet her, and say unto her, Is it well with thee? is it well with thy husband? is it well with the child? And she answered, It is well."—II Kings 4:26.

The questions that Gehazi (Elisha's servant) asked the Shunammite woman I now ask of you. Is it well with your husband/wife? Is it well with your child? Can you answer frankly that all is well spiritually with each family member including yourself, that all have experienced the new birth and are walking in harmony with the Lord Jesus Christ? Can you say with the Shunammite mother, "It is well"?

Horatio Spafford and his family decided to join the D. L. Moody team on an evangelistic crusade in Europe. Spafford's wife and four daughters departed without him; he was to join them in a week. Tragically, the ship which they were aboard collided with another vessel and sank within twenty minutes. Spafford's wife, Anna, was the family's only family survivor. Ten days later from the hospital, Anna sent her husband a message that consisted of two words: "Saved alone."

He was devastated and shook uncontrollably. Major Whittle, Spafford's friend, consoled him and traveled with him to France to see his wife. En route, the captain awoke him at the spot where his children drowned, as he had requested. Upon looking into the dark, cold water that now was their grave, he wept. He then sat down and penned the words of the hymn *It Is Well with My Soul* that has brought comfort and hope unto many in their hour of grief and grave trial.

It is most strengthening and encouraging knowing that despite what storms assail our family and its members, all will be okay because all can say with Spafford, "It is well with my soul."

Read Together:

He Reads: John 10:9
She Reads: John 3:16

Answer Together:

Is it truly well with your soul? (If not, make it well by receiving Jesus Christ into your life as Lord and Savior through repentance and faith.) With that of your spouse and child? (If not, endeavor to lead them to a personal relationship with Jesus Christ?)

Pray Together:

Lord Jesus, we sincerely long that all in our family know You as their personal Lord and Savior. Help us speak just the right words that would draw them to You.

142

A Father's and Grandfather's Squandered Influence

As Dr. George Truett preached one Sunday morning, he saw a sixty-four-year-old man who had recently been saved lay his head over on the bench in front of him and sob like a baby. Truett approached the man at the end of the service, saying, "Sir, you are troubled, aren't you?"

"Yes," he said. "My heart is broken; I need help."

Truett asked, "What's wrong? Weren't you recently saved?"

"Yes," the man replied, "I was, and baptized, and joined the church. I know I am on my way to Heaven. But I'm concerned about my family. I came by the house of two of my sons this morning. I pleaded with my sons, 'Won't you come to church with me today?' Both replied, 'Not now, Dad; maybe when we get to sixty-four.'"

The man continued, "I turned to my grandchildren and said, 'Won't you go to church with Grandpa? I want you to be Christians. I've been saved; I love Jesus, and I want you to love Him, too!'

"One of my grandchildren turned to the other, winked and said, 'Grandfather, maybe when we get to sixty-four we'll become Christians too.'"[190]

The elderly man wasted and squandered his influence until it was too late.

Father, I plead with you for your children's sake to desist in postponing salvation. The earlier in the life of your children you become a Christian, the greater the likelihood of highly influencing them to become the same. Delay to follow Christ, on the other hand, erodes your influence little by little until it is all but gone, as it was with the elderly man.

Paul and Silas told the jailer that if he would believe on Jesus, it would result in household salvation (Acts 16:31). And it did. The jailer used his influence in its best possible sense over his wife and children while it was still infectious. I beg you, father, to do the same! Don't waste and squander what influence you possess over your children and grandchildren until it is too late to win them to Christ.

Read Together:
He Reads: Acts 16:31–34
She Reads: Psalm 127:4–5

Answer Together:
Are you guilty of a wasted influence over your children? Will you determine to use what influence you have remaining to point your children and grandchildren to Christ?

Pray Together:
Father, forgive me for my wasted influence over my children/grandchildren and help me use what influence I have remaining to impact them for You.

143   Life without Father

The United States leads the world in fatherless families with twenty-four million children living in homes with an absentee dad.[191] The number of children being reared in homes by only their mother has more than tripled between 1960 and 2000.[192]

The father's being absent from his children's life is one of the greatest contributing causes to problems related to their well-being, such as juvenile violent crime, depression, eating disorders, teen suicide, and drug abuse. The largest negative consequences of the father's absence are early sexual activity, violence and juvenile delinquency.[193]

The father's role and style of parenting make a unique contribution to healthy child rearing.[194]

David Blankenhorn states that in relation to the general population individuals reared in a fatherless environment demonstrate

1. Five times the average suicide rate
2. Dramatically increased rates of depression and anxiety
3. Thirty-two times the average rate of incarceration
4. Decreased education levels and increased drop-out rates
5. Consistently lower average income levels
6. Lower job security
7. Increased rates of divorce and relationship issues
8. Substantially increased rates of substance abuse
9. Increases in social and mental behavioral issues[195]

A *Reader's Digest* article called "Life without Father" cites the lasting influence of a father upon his children. The article explained, "In the early years, more than two-thirds of all children prefer to play with their fathers. Playing with a father is very important in teaching children the importance of self-control....Children who roughhouse with their fathers quickly learn that biting, kicking, and other forms of physical violence are not acceptable....Several studies have found that a father's presence is one of the determiners of girls' proficiency in mathematics. An astonishing twenty-six-year study found that the most important childhood factor in developing empathy was the father's involvement in child care!" The father's role and style of parenting (play) facilitates normal emotional development of the children.[196]

"Though children of all ages," states Dr. James Dobson, "both male and female, have an innate need for contact with their fathers, boys suffer most from the absence or noninvolvement of fathers. According to the National Center for Children in Poverty, boys without fathers are twice as likely to drop out of school, twice as likely to go to jail, and nearly four times as likely to need treatment for emotional and behavioral problems as boys with fathers."[197]

With regard to faith, if a father does not go to church (regardless of wife's faithfulness), only one child in fifty will become a regular worshipper.[198]

Father, God has given you a specific role in the life of your children that the best of mothers can never fill. Don't desert them. Don't abandon them. Stay the course, helping them develop into the person God designed morally, spiritually and emotionally.

Read Together:
He Reads: Psalm 103:13
She Reads: Ephesians 6:4

Answer Together:
What impact does the father have in what his children do and become? Why cannot the mother fulfill that role, as well as her own, effectively? What might you do, fathers, to assist fatherless children in your family at large and/or in church?

Pray Together:
Lord Jesus, for the fatherless children's sake, please convict their father of the sin of abandonment, that he may return home to fulfill the role you assigned as husband and father. Help single moms rear their children according to Your Word and Way. Help fathers look for opportunities to mentor fatherless children.

144
Three Questions Every Child Needs Answered by Dad

Dr. Meg Meeler states there are three foundational, fundamental questions every child needs answered by his father.

1. "What do you think of me, Dad?" (Do you think I am okay? Do you think I am handsome or beautiful? Do you think I have talents?)

2. "How do you feel about me, Dad?" (Do you love me? Will you always be here for me?)

3. "What are your hopes for me, Dad?" (Do you believe in me? Do you believe I can be a teacher or a doctor? Do you believe I can become a great servant for Jesus Christ?)

Meeler says a child often reads the father's face for the answers to these questions at the kitchen table, not on the soccer field. Thus, when you as a dad come home in a bad, frustrated mood due to a bad day at the office, your child reads your face, thinking it is him with whom you are frustrated, and he will leave the room disheartened.[199]

In homes where the father is absent, the children answers the three questions for themselves. "My dad must think I am a jerk or worse, for he never calls me or sees me."

"My dad must not care much about me, or else he wouldn't be living in California while I live here in South Carolina."

"I don't have much hope beyond high school. I don't see much of a future for me in life. My dad doesn't believe in me."[200]

And such beliefs bring havoc into the child's life.

It is imperative that fathers *continuously* tell their children what they think of them, how they feel about them, and what hopes they dream for them.

Read Together:
He Reads: Proverbs 23:24
She Reads: Proverbs 20:7

Answer Together:
Dad, when have you last squatted to the eye level of your child to tell him the answers to the three questions stated above? Did you know that your children read, however wrongly, the frustration or anger you vent over a bad day at work as being directed against them? They soon will read you so well that when they see you in such a mood, they will not stay in your presence.

Pray Together:
Father, as my children's dad, help me never leave doubt in their minds as to my love and belief in them, regardless of what they do or what kind of day I am having.

145 What Changes When You Get Married?

Someone said that marriage is like getting a telephone call in the night—first you get the ring; then you wake up! Though humorous, it does contain some truth, for with marriage comes things unanticipated.

1. You handle money differently.

It is no longer yours but *ours.*

2. You fight differently.

In courtship, when a fight disrupted the relationship, you could part ways for a few days or months. In marriage, it must be worked out then and there, lovingly and compassionately.

3. You see each other differently.

In courtship, you view each other as potential mates for life, wrapping your life around him/her, seeking to make the big *catch.* In marriage, your identity is changed from boyfriend/girlfriend to husband/wife. And that makes a world of difference!

4. Your relationship with friends changes.

Instead of spending several nights a week hanging out with friends, as you did prior to marriage, you are now happy to spend nights at home with your wife/husband. You are now a family man or woman.

5. Your accountability changes.

Prior to tying the knot, you were probably accountable to your parents (where you went, what you did, when you did it, etc.). Now you are accountable to your spouse.

6. Your priorities change.

Priorities for a single adult certainly differ from those of a married person. Hopefully God was the top priority for you as a single adult, and He certainly should be as one who is married. But the other priorities (at least the order of them) do change when you say, "I do." For example, now that you are married, your spouse or family is the second priority of your life, whereas prior to marriage it may have been your career.

7. Your sexual escapades are over.

Hopefully this does not apply to you (for the Bible condemns it in I Thessalonians 4:3); but sadly for many it does apply, for prior to marriage they played the field, freely engaging in sexual activity. The married man/woman is committed to a monogamous relationship (Matthew 5:27).

8. Your love matures.

You learn that sex is not synonymous with love, just an expression of it (hopefully!). As mutual trust, appreciation, and respect for the whole person of your spouse develops, true love matures, forging a barrier against that which would destroy the relationship. This love will transcend time and all that changes "for better or for worse" (attraction, finances, health, aging).

Read Together:

He Reads: Genesis 2:22–24
She Reads: Proverbs 12:4

Answer Together:

Which of the stated changes surprised you the most once you were married? What other changes might you add to the list? Which changes are the most challenging?

Pray Together:

Heavenly Father, may our marriage continuously change more and more into that of Thy design. Help our love mature more and more as the years unfold.

146
Family Comes First

Adam LaRoche, when informed by the Chicago White Sox he could no longer bring his fourteen-year-old son, Drake, to work every day, quit his job. LaRoche, the popular first baseman for the club, is walking away from a thirteen-million-dollar contract because he believes family comes first.

The bond between a father and his son plays a crucial role in the healthy development of a boy's self-esteem, identity and emotional stability.

Read Together:

He Reads: Joshua 24:15

She Reads: Genesis 33:5

Answer Together:

Would you quit your job if your employer told you to limit the time you spend with your children? Had you been in LaRoche's shoes, would you have made the same decision? Why or why not?

Pray Together:

Lord, bless those like Adam LaRoche who put their children first with regard to their work.

147

Home Buster—Gambling

A gambling addict said, "The paradox with gambling is that if you win, you lose. If you lose, you lose. If you win, the high consumes your mind until you're back in action. If you lose, you crash and chase your losses to regain that high."[201]

Another gambling addict states, "Every night that I finished gambling, I'd say, 'That's it. I'm not going to do this anymore. It's gotta stop.' And the next day, I'd be gambling again."[202]

What is gambling? John MacArthur stated, "It's an activity in which a person risks something of value to forces of chance completely beyond his control or any rational expectation...in hope of winning something of greater value, usually more money. But it is an appeal to sheer chance."[203] As with smoking and pornography, gambling is not specifically named in the Bible but is condemned along with them through principles and precepts it sets forth (Proverbs 29:19–22; Proverbs 13:11; I Timothy 6:6–11; I Timothy 5:8; Exodus 20:17).

Impact upon Family

In a survey of nearly four hundred Gamblers Anonymous members, twenty-eight percent reported being either separated or divorced as a direct result of their gambling problems.[204] The lifetime divorce rates for problem and pathological gamblers (National Gambling Impact Study) were 39.5 percent and 53.5 percent, respectively; the rate in nongamblers was 18.2 percent.[205] Every pathological gambler affects between ten and seventeen individuals, including family members and coworkers.[206] Gambling depletes the bank and savings accounts, bringing stress and eventual poverty, among other things, to the family.

Do you or your spouse have a problem with gambling? A *yes* response to any one of the following questions reveals gambling addiction.[207]

1. Have you often gambled longer than you had planned?
2. Have you often gambled until your last dollar was gone?
3. Have thoughts of gambling caused you to lose sleep?
4. Have you used your income or savings to gamble while letting bills go unpaid?
5. Have you made repeated, unsuccessful attempts to stop gambling?
6. Have you broken the law or considered breaking the law to finance your gambling?
7. Have you borrowed money to finance your gambling?
8. Have you felt depressed or suicidal because of your gambling losses?
9. Have you been remorseful after gambling?
10. Have you gambled to get money to meet your financial obligations?

If any of these indicators reveal personal addiction to gambling, it is imperative that you admit the problem to yourself. Don't rationalize the truth away. Pretending that you don't have a gambling problem only worsens the problem. As with any wrong, injurious habit or addiction, the first step to freedom is acknowledging a problem exists.

Next, turn to God for deliverance, acknowledging the sin of gambling and pleading His intervention. God loves you and stands ready to cleanse and liberate.

Third, confide this problem to your pastor and/or Christian counselor and seek his support in remaining free from its clutches. You will need godly people to help in defeating this enslaving habit, so do not hesitate to ask for support. The National Coalition on Problem Gambling at 1-800-522-4700 also stands ready to assist. Saturate your mind with megadoses of the intake of God's Word, pray much, and daily rely upon Him for victory.

Fourth, it is expedient at the outset to let another manage your money.

Fifth, let it be a rigid rule to avoid places and people that would be a stumbling-block in your recovery. The road to recovery starts here and now. It is time to change and be free for your sake, for your spouse's sake, and for your children's sake.

Humorist Frank McKinney Hubbard stated, "The safest way to double your money is to fold it over once and put it in your pocket." Take his advice and leave the machines, race tracks, and roulette and card tables alone.

Read Together:
He Reads: I Timothy 6:9–10
She Reads: I Timothy 5:8

Answer Together:
Why is gambling a sin? Are any of the ten problem gambler indicators true of you? Are you a problem or pathological gambler? What are the consequences of gambling on your family and on you? What is the first step to being set free from gambling addiction?

Pray Together:
Lord Jesus, my problem with gambling is destroying my marriage and life. I desperately want to be delivered from its tyrannical control. I plead for Your power to set me free.

148 Benefits of Family Church Attendance

The primary focus of church attendance is the worship of Jesus Christ and growth in the faith. However, when a family attends church together, other benefits result as well because of their Christian faith.

Ten Benefits of Going to Church

1. It lessens the likelihood of divorce.

Shaunti Feldhahn states, "The rate of divorce is not the same in the church....I partnered with Barna, and we reran the numbers; and if the person was in church the prior week, their divorce rate dropped twenty-seven percent compared to those who weren't. Many studies have found that church attendance drops the divorce rate twenty-five to fifty percent compared to those who don't attend."[208] The bottom line. The Christian couple who attends church regularly together has their marriage fortified spiritually against its enemies and enjoys a greater satisfaction in marriage then those who do not.

2. Kids who attend church are less likely to experience divorce later in life.[209]

3. Kids who attend church do better in college than those who do not.[210]

4. Church attendance significantly lessens a child's use of and risk from alcohol, tobacco and drugs.[211]

Dr. Pat Fagan states, "Religious belief and practice contribute substantially to the formation of personal moral criteria and sound moral judgment," he says. "Regular religious practice generally inoculates individuals against a host of social problems, including suicide, drug abuse, out-of-wedlock births, crime, and divorce."[212]

5. Frequent church attendance reduces a student's likelihood of engaging in premarital sex.[213]

6. It anchors the family together, a cohesive effect on family members.

7. It provides family members doctrinal biblical teaching to combat skepticism.

8. It provides a code of ethics to govern life and teaches how to implement it.

9. Evangelical Christian churches, through their ministers and teachers, help family members understand the Gospel of Jesus Christ, which hopefully will lead to their conversion.

10. Through the community of believers that make up the church, encouragement, help and guidance are given to all ages.

Read Together:
He Reads: Psalm 122:1
She Reads: Hebrews 10:25

Answer Together:
Understanding the significance and value of regular family church attendance for you and your children, will you begin the practice this Sunday (if you have not already)? What benefit do you receive in going to church?

Pray Together:

Heavenly Father, we commit our family to regular church attendance to worship, adore and draw nearer to You. Thank You for the numerous spiritual, emotional, moral, and physical benefits that family worship in Your house brings.

149 Three Necessary Homes

Everybody needs three homes.

Everybody needs a *Christian home,* a home where Jesus is the head, the Bible is read and prayers are said.

Everybody needs a *Church home.* The moment one is saved, he/she becomes a part of the family of God and needs to become an integral part of the church.

Everybody needs a *Celestial home.* Jesus has prepared a home in Heaven for His children, the eternal abode of the family of God.

Read Together:

He Reads: John 14:1–4
She Reads: Psalm 127:1

Answer Together:

Which of the three homes do you possess? Many may have a Christian home but not a church home. If this is true for you, consider uniting in membership with a Bible-based church soon.

Pray Together:

Lord Jesus, thank You that based upon our faith in You we have a home in Heaven waiting. But until then, help us establish a Christian home and by membership have a church home.

150 Jesus Is "Pro-Family"

"Since when does anyone's right to live," states John Willke, "depend upon someone else's wanting them? Killing the unwanted is a monstrous evil....So, should a woman have the right to choose? I have a right to free speech but not to shout 'fire' in a theater. A person's right to anything stops when it injures or kills another living human....The pivotal question is, Should any civilized nation give to one citizen the absolute right to kill another to solve the first person's personal problem?"[214]

Life begins at the moment of conception in the womb; Baby Tom or Jen is not a mass of tissue but a living being created by God. Outside the Bible, this truth is also documented in embryology textbooks in which you may read about the developmental life of the embryo and fetus. Ultrasound images of a child in the womb also render confirmation that life begins at conception. As much as I detest the word *abortion*, it accurately describes what happens the moment the doctor terminates the life of the unborn child; the procedure (horrific as it is) aborts the wonderful life of a Tom or Jen that God created. The aborted one will never have the chance to go to school, go to the junior-senior prom, get married, and live the American dream. As for them and the millions of others who die in the womb at the "choice" of their mothers and/or fathers due to no wrong of their own, it is "Mission Aborted." God's purpose for their lives has been savagely vetoed.

In excess of ninety-five percent of the abortions performed in 2011 involved women who simply did not want to have a child.[215] The killing of a precious child because he/she would interfere with a personal agenda or due to the child's health or appearance is abhorrent.

The Bible consistently uses the same Greek word *[brephos]* to describe an unborn child, one who has been born, and a young child. In Luke 1:44 it is used to describe the unborn child; in Luke 2:12, the newborn child; and in Luke 18:15, the young child.[216] Why? It is because the God of the universe sees no biological difference between a child inside the womb or outside the womb; they are both human beings.

The Bible emphasizes the fact that the unborn child is known and valued by God. "Before I formed you in the womb I knew you, and before you were born I consecrated you" (Jeremiah 1:5). "I am fearfully and wonderfully made....My frame was not hidden from you when I was being made in secret, intricately woven in the depths of the earth. Your eyes saw my unformed substance" (Psalm 139:13–16, ESV).

There is no legitimate "pro-choice" position according to Scripture. The alternative to abortion (outside of giving birth to and rearing the child) is adoption. One and a half million Americans desire to adopt a child, so there is no such thing as an "unwanted child."

All sins are forgivable by a loving God, including that of abortion (I John 1:7–9; Isaiah 43:25–26). The Christian's response to women who have an abortion, men who encourage abortion, and the medical team who perform the abortion is disdain for what they did, yet with open arms to forgive, heal and restore in Jesus' name (Galatians 6:1; Luke 17:3).

Read Together:
He Reads: Psalm 139:13–16
She Reads: Jeremiah 1:5

Answer Together:
At what point does life begin in the womb? If a society sanctions abortion, does that make it right? What can you do to speak up for the unborn child? What is the alternative to abortion?

Pray Together:
Lord, who will speak up for the unborn child if not we? Help us wave the banner high against abortion and rescue as many of the unborn from abortion as possible.

151 Rebuilding Broken Trust

Many are the villains that may sever trust in your spouse. But the biggest are lies, deception and adultery. Rebuilding broken trust is a task almost comparable to putting Humpty Dumpty back together again. But what all the king's horses and all the king's men couldn't do for Humpty, our precious Lord can do for victims of broken trust.

As an athlete in training in high school and college, I ever remembered that "an ounce of prevention is better than a pound of cure." This is not only true with regard to athletics but also to relationships in life. Work hard at ever being transparent, telling the truth (not hedging on it), and being faithful to each other so that the trust issue will never arise.

Rebuilding broken trust doesn't happen instantly when a spouse pleads for forgiveness and restoration. Forgiveness may happen instantly, but it will take time to restore trust, depending on the offense and conduct of the offender.

Repairing broken trust involves coming clean before God and your spouse. The whole truth and nothing but the truth about the lie, deception or adulterous affair must be shared with an attitude of repentance and sincere sorrow. Upon confessing the wrong, ask for God's forgiveness and that of your spouse.

Second, it involves complete honesty from here on out in the relationship.

Third, transparency is essential. Your spouse should have free access to your computer, cell phone and calendar (you have nothing to hide, right?). Granting him/her this liberty will go a long way in rebuilding the trust that was lost.

Trust may have been lost overnight, but it will take months, if not years, to restore. So be patient in the process, trusting the Lord to enable your spouse to trust you again. And he/she will, given time and a lifestyle by you that warrants it. Always remember that the super-structure of your family and home hinges on its being built on the solid foundation of Jesus Christ, His teachings, and trust in each other.

Read Together:
He Reads: II Corinthians 7:9
She Reads: Matthew 18:21–22; Proverbs 3:3

Answer Together:
Have you abused the trust of your spouse? What are you doing to have that trust restored? As a wife/husband have you forgiven your husband/wife? What might you be doing that may be misread by your spouse as deceitful? Tell her/him and get it out in the open to protect your spouse's trust in you.

Pray Together:
Father, may we be so open and honest with each other that trust is never an issue but a foundation on which to build even a stronger and happier marriage.

152

When the Marriage Fails

"Some Christians," states Adrian Rogers, "have already failed at marriage. They've been through a divorce. But we have a God of forgiveness. We have a God of grace. If you've failed and your marriage is broken, you can't go backward. You can't unscramble the eggs. But divorce is not the unpardonable sin. If you are divorced and have repented of your sin, God forgives you. You are not a second-class citizen. 'There is therefore now no condemnation to them which are in Christ Jesus,' Paul tells us in Romans 8:1. 'Though your sins be as scarlet, they shall be as white as snow,' the prophet Isaiah says in Isaiah 1:18."[217]

"If you are divorced, ask God to forgive you. Seek to be reconciled if possible. If you or your partner is already remarried, ask God's forgiveness and share that forgiveness with your ex-partner. Even if he or she won't repent, forgive your spouse in spirit."[218]

Stages of divorce recovery

Knowledge is power in many respects, especially with regard to the divorce process. In knowing its various stages [what to expect], the pain and disruption of life will be lessened. Psychologist Thomas Whiteman, coauthor of *Starting Over*, identifies six stages of divorce recovery.[219] I took liberty to summarize or expand what he stated.

Denial. There is initially the pretending or denial of the divorce.

Anger. You perceive rightly or wrongly the injustice of the divorce, which ignites either out-of-control rage or controlled anger. The anger is directed toward the former spouse, others and/or your situation.

Bargaining. Desperate attempts are made to be reunited (promises to change, a make-over, etc.). Divorcees from experience testify that such an effort for "quick fixes" is probably too late. In fact, such may simply set you up for another fall and intensified grief. Instead of bargaining, efforts ought to be made at genuine reconciliation.

Depression. Divorce, like the death of a loved one, causes grief and despair. It's normal. However, when grief is not appropriately addressed, it leads to depression, an "empty emotional tank" (sleep

disturbances, changed eating patterns, irritability, isolation, exhaust-
tion, etc.).

Acceptance. An awareness will come when you realize the past
cannot be recalled, scrambled eggs cannot be unscrambled, and you
decide to move forward with life. Whiteman states that the acceptance
stage occurs as a "light bulb" moment, not precipitated by outside
influences.

Forgiveness. Healing of the wound of divorce will not occur until
forgiveness is extended toward your former spouse (whether or not
it is accepted) and a healthy relationship is forged (attempted, at the
least).

Read Together:
He Reads: Psalm 37:23–24
She Reads: Isaiah 1:18

Answer Together:
Have we earnestly sought to work our differences out? Will you
go with me for marital counseling to try to save our marriage and
family?

Pray Together:
Lord Jesus, forgive us and help us forgive each other for our
divorce. If possible, reconcile the marriage; but if not, give grace to
bear its severe and devastating consequences. Thank You that Your
love is unaltered for us despite our failed marriage.

153
After the Fight
"Be ye angry, and sin not: let not the sun go down upon your
wrath" (Ephesians 4:26).

You have a fight; then what happens? Do you sulk, wallow in self-
pity, and say you forgave when in reality you didn't; or do you penalize
your spouse in other ways? In Ephesians 4:26 Paul clearly states that
prior to the ending of the day our pent-up anger with one another is
to be extinguished. Don't carry today's argument into the night or
tomorrow.

Dr. James Dobson offers this advice: "After an argument with
your spouse, ask yourself these four important questions. Are there

things I've said or done that have grieved my partner? Do I need to ask forgiveness for attacking the self-worth of my spouse? Have I refused to let go of an issue even though I said it was settled? Are there substantive matters that haven't been resolved? Then move to put an end to the conflict—before the sun goes down."[220]

Read Together:
He Reads: Colossians 3:13
She Reads: James 1:19

Answer Together:
In our last fight, did we resolve the issue before the sun went down? What can we do to implement the teaching of the Apostle Paul (Ephesians 4:26) that we have failed to do?

Pray Together:
Lord Jesus, give us the grace to resolve our disagreements quickly and without damaging the spirit of the other.

154   The Materialistic Marriage

A study published in the *Journal of Couple and Relationship Therapy* revealed that couples who share the same materialistic view of life and whose values regarding money are the same consistently report having more problematic marriages.[221]

In contrast, couples who ranked low on the materialistic scale fared much better.[222]

The study is no surprise to the Christian community, for it echoes the teaching of Jesus Christ. "For the love of money is the root of all evil: which while some coveted after, they have erred from the faith, and pierced themselves through with many sorrows" (I Timothy 6:10).

Indeed, materialists pierce themselves and their marriages through with many sorrows. Solomon says, "He that loveth silver shall not be satisfied with silver; nor he that loveth abundance with increase: this is also vanity [emptiness, a bubble that bursts]" (Ecclesiastes 5:10).

The bottom line regarding materialistic goods of this world is declared by Solomon: "Better to have little, with godliness, than to be rich and dishonest" (Proverbs 16:8 NLT).

The lesson Jesus teaches in the parable of the rich fool (Luke 12:13–21) is a stern warning against materialism, being of a materialistic mind-set which is never satisfied with the new car, new home, new clothes and gadgets, but ever craving more and more ("I will tear down my barns and build bigger ones to store my surplus grain").

Marriages that drink from the well of materialism to feed their relationship with happiness and purpose will one day go to draw from it only to find it empty—the marriage sustained by money and things will then fall apart.

The sure foundation on which to build a marriage is not the shifting sands of materialism but the firm, invincible foundation of Jesus Christ. Allow Christ to control the finances and purchases in your marriage, and you will never be plagued with high credit card debt or excessive mortgage payments which are marriage killers.

Read Together:
He Reads: Luke 12:13–21
She Reads: Mark 8:36; Matthew 7:24–27

Answer Together:
Do we look to things for satisfaction in our marriage or to the Lord? What does our checkbook state about our true values? What purchase have we made on the impulse that was a miserable mistake?

Honestly, are we trying to keep up with the Joneses for vanity's sake? Are we investing money in ministries and causes that will outlast our lifetime or in fleeting things of the world?

Pray Together:
Heavenly Father, it is so easy to get caught up in the spend, spend, spend mentality of the modern culture, getting into serious debt. Protect us from that mind-set, dear Lord. Help us make changes in our lifestyle that will reflect kingdom values.

155

How a Marriage Survives When One Partner Gets Sick

The Bible does not state anywhere that the severe sickness of a spouse is cause for divorce. Pat Robertson *(700 Club)* was wrong in stating that if a spouse had Alzheimer's then divorce is okay because it is a type of death.[223]

The marital covenant made between two people in the presence of God and assembled witnesses clearly states that they will remain married "in sickness and in health." Yet the divorce rate for marriages in which one spouse is chronically ill is far greater than that of the general population.[224]

How does a marriage survive when one partner gets sick? I know it may sound too simplistic, but it survives because of love and compassion on the part of the healthy partner and God's amazing grace to cope. Obviously the marital covenant made between the two also sustains the marriage.

Couples in which one spouse is chronically ill testify that the challenges such care continuously brings actually strengthens their relationship instead of weakening it, often in ways that would benefit any marriage.[225] Love actually may flourish more strongly in such marriages.

Counsel and help are available from the community of believers and those who have experienced a relationship with a chronically ill spouse.

As the husband of my wife, Mary, for over forty-two years, the one thing I am most certain of (if there were no other) is that she would not abandon me should I be struck with Alzheimer's, cancer or some other serious illness that would make me dependent on her for care. Why? She loves me. Likewise, my response would be the same to her should she fall seriously ill.

Read Together:

He Reads: Matthew 19:6
She Reads: I Corinthians 7:10

Ask your spouse if he/she will be forever faithful, even if you become chronically ill. Why? If you have experienced a relationship with a chronically ill spouse, how might you share hope and help with others who presently are facing the same challenge?

Pray Together:
Lord Jesus, thank You for Your great love that assures us You will never abandon us regardless of what happens. We thank You for our love for each other that assures us of the same thing.

156 Infant Baptism

If baptism is an initiatory rite, it must be observed by only those who have entered into a personal relationship with Jesus Christ through faith and repentance. This is in fact the only way one enters into the family of God. Only a natural birth was necessary to become a member of the nation of Israel. Since it is a spiritual birth that is necessary in order to become a part of the family of God, only those who consciously in faith receive Christ as Savior enter into it and should be baptized.[226]

The New Testament never speaks of infant baptism but states that only those who express faith in Jesus Christ are to be baptized.

Infants are safe and secure through the grace of God until they reach the age of understanding of sin, judgment, and Calvary, at which time, based upon their profession of faith in Christ, they are to be baptized.

Read Together:
He Reads: Matthew 28:19
She Reads: Romans 10:9–13

Answer Together:
Why should you delay baptism of your infant until he/she reaches the age of spiritual understanding and receives Christ as Lord and Savior? What is the significance of baptism? Does baptism have any power to forgive sins and to save?

Pray Together:

Lord Jesus, thank You for clarifying the purpose of baptism and why our child must wait until after he receives Christ as his Lord and Savior to observe it.

157 Five Secrets of a Happy Marriage

Gary Smalley shares five secrets of a happy marriage (adapted).

1. Healthy couples know definitively the expectations for their lives and relationship.
2. Healthy couples engage in meaningful communications at five levels:
    a. The safest level of brief comments such as, "Have a good day."
    b. The fact level of sharing information such as, "The telephone bill is due."
    c. The opinion-sharing level such as, "I didn't like what you said."
    d. The level of sharing and understanding feelings such as, "I'm nervous about the doctor's appointment."
    e. The fifth and most intimate level of expressing our needs such as, "I'm really not happy with my job and really want to change."
3. Healthy couples are associated with a small support group to share friendship and give accountability.
4. Healthy couples are aware of unhealthy or offensive conduct stemming from their past.
5. Healthy couples have a vibrant relationship with Jesus Christ and depend on Him as their primary source of abundant life.[227]

Read Together:

He Reads: James 1:22
She Reads: Hebrews 13:4

Answer Together:

Based on Smalley's secrets of a healthy marriage, how healthy is yours? If there is an area of weakness in your marriage, under what secret(s) stated above would it come? What can you each do to rectify that area or those areas?

Pray Together:

Lord Jesus, help us work hard at obtaining and maintaining a healthy marriage.

158 A Child's Blame against Parents

Children blame their parents for a lot of what happens to them that is unpleasant. But thankfully there are some who blame them for how their parenting benefitted and blessed them, as with a daughter who wrote the following letter to Ann Landers.

Dear Ann Landers:

Can you stand one more letter from a daughter who blames her parents for everything?

I blame my parents for a happy childhood. They were always there when I needed them. They never missed one of my basketball games and always knew what to say when we lost.

I also blame them for my college education. They worked hard to support me and pay my way. I blame my parents for my sense of honesty and fairness. Dad never brought home from work as much as a pencil that belonged to the company.

It's my parents' fault that I'm open-minded and compassionate. They always accepted my weird friends and my off-beat opinions.

If I behave unselfishly, I blame my parents. They were always willing to help us take care of our pets, and they loaned us the car when we needed wheels. I also blame them for my ability to work hard and do a good job—they encouraged us to work hard and do our best.

Finally, I blame my parents for molding my siblings and me into people who know how to love. Every day or our lives, our parents set a fine example.

I hope that as a parent, I'll be as caring, patient, and wise as my mom and dad were to us.[228]

Read Together:

He Reads: Proverbs 23:24

She Reads: Proverbs 31:28

Answer Together:

Can your children blame you as the girl did her parents? If so, you of all parents are truly blessed. What, if any, regrets do you have with regard to rearing your children?

Pray Together:

Lord Jesus, help us rear our children so that we may be blamed for the wonderful Christians they become in life.

159 Family Abuse That Nobody Sees

Dr. Mark R. Laaser states a family can perpetuate two major forms of abuse. The first is when the safety of our minds, bodies or spirit is invaded (yelling, screaming, hitting, fighting, put-downs, sexual molestation, and judgmental talk). The second type of abuse is the withholding of love and nurture a family member needs emotionally, physically and spiritually.[229]

"Some families," writes Laaser, "simply don't ever talk about feelings; others never affirm each other; and many never touch. Such abandonment leaves a hole in a person's mind and spirit. This type of abuse is intangible but powerful."[230] Even among the most faithful church-going families there is little or no discussion of spiritual things at home.[231]

Invasive abuse and abandonment results in a person's becoming developmentally impaired, leading him to search for substitutes for the love, affirmation and approval parents/spouses failed to provide. These are sought in sex, money, work status, food, superficial relationships, nicotine, and alcohol.[232]

Though there are many victims of abuse, the most prevalent are children (mostly physical/sexual) and wives (violence).[233] "Sexual abuse," states Chuck Swindoll, "stands as one of the most devastating sins that human beings have devised, leaving deep scars and unspeakable pain. Victims of sexual abuse have had much taken from them; Jesus Christ and His church have much to offer in response."[234]

As parents, we must safeguard our family from both of these kinds of abuses by monitoring attitudes and behavior within its confines closely. To know of its actuality in your family yet fail to do anything to stop it is a great disservice and wrong to the person who is being abused. Seek out help from a Christian therapist or counselor.

Read Together:

He Reads: II Samuel 13:10–14
She Reads: Malachi 2:16

Answer Together:

Is abusive behavior occurring in your family? By whom and in what way? What preventative measures may you take with regard to abuse?

Pray Together:

Lord Jesus, protect our home from every form of abuse. Help us ever be vigilant and alert to spot abuse immediately should it ever surface in our family.

160 God Give Us Christian Homes

"God Give Us Christian Homes" was written by Baylus Benjamin McKinney (1886–1952). As I read the lyrics again, it amazed me how many details McKinney used to describe the Christian home. Perhaps you will be amazed as well. The hymn certainly serves as a checklist for every home that desires to be distinctly Christian.

God give us Christian homes,
Homes where the Bible is loved and taught,
Homes where the Master's will is sought,
Homes crowned with beauty Your love has wrought.
God give us Christian homes;
God give us Christian homes!

God give us Christian homes,
Homes where the father is true and strong,
Homes that are free from the blight of wrong,
Homes that are joyous with love and song.
God give us Christian homes;
God give us Christian homes!

God give us Christian homes,
Homes where the mother, in caring quest,
Strives to show others Your way is best,

Homes where the Lord is an honored Guest.
God give us Christian homes;
God give us Christian homes!

God give us Christian homes,
Homes where the children are led to know
Christ in His beauty who loves them so,
Homes where the altar fires burn and glow.
God give us Christian homes;
God give us Christian homes.

May God expose the hypocrisy of many who claim their home to be Christian while all the while it lacks the characteristics expressed in McKinney's hymn.

Read Together:

He Reads: Colossians 3:16
She Reads: Deuteronomy 6:7

Answer Together:

What traits cited in McKinney's hymn that constitute the Christian home exist in your home? Which are absent from your home? Is your home a Christian home in deed, not in name only?

Pray Together:

Lord Jesus, point out things in our home that are non-Christian so they may be removed, and show us the things that ought to be in our home that are absent. We want our home to be a Christian home in name and deed.

161 The Unequally–Yoked Mandate

As parents, instill in your children while they are young the Unequally–Yoked Mandate with regard to faith, friendship, dating, marriage, and business partnership. The Apostle Paul stated, "Be not unequally yoked together with unbelievers" (II Corinthians 6:14).

A yoke is a wooden bar that couples two oxen to each other and to a pulling beam so they can plow or pull a wagon. An "unequally yoked" team consisted of two different sorts oxen (e.g., a strong ox joined to a weak ox). Instead of getting the task done, unequally yoked oxen would go around in circles. One can but imagine the frustration that arose between such a team.

The biblical truth set forth in the text is clear. Christians are not to be united (coupled) to unbelievers in friendship, faith, dating, marriage, or business partnership. Why not? The two have completely different natures, values, convictions, and purposes that would cause inevitable conflict. *The Message* paraphrase of the text may enable its better comprehension. "Don't become partners with those who reject God. How can you make a partnership out of right and wrong? That's not partnership; that's war. Is light best friends with dark? Does Christ go strolling with the Devil?"

Prevention is worth a pound of cure. Following a service, a mother shared that her college-age daughter had fallen in love with an unbeliever. The relationship was moving toward possible marriage, and she was wrestling with whether or not to break up with him. It's awfully difficult to break off a relationship once the emotions are entangled with another, when the love bug bites big time. Thus, most don't.

Had the young lady ascertained whether or not the boy was a believer prior to the first date and backed off upon learning he was not, the dilemma and possible heartache she was facing would never have arisen.

Teach your child that in regard to dating and marriage, there is no exception clause for the mandate. It is not, "Don't be unequally yoked together unless you think you can win him/her to the Lord or change him/her." No. It clearly states not to be unequally yoked with an unbeliever, period. Missionary dating or marriage is forbidden.

As your child is brought to apply the principle to dating/marriage, it will be a nonissue for him to apply it likewise to faith, friends, and partnerships.

Model this principle before your children and continuously instill it in their life. By implementing it, your child will be spared much heartache and havoc now and later.

Read Together:
He Reads: II Corinthians 6:14
She Reads: Deuteronomy 7:3–6

Answer Together:

With regard to your marriage, how important was it for you to be equally yoked? Explain the meaning of being "unequally yoked." What might you do to instill in your child this principle and aid him in applying it?

Pray Together:

Lord Jesus, help us teach our child the value of not being unequally yoked, both by precept and example.

162   What Children Need from Their Divorced Mom and Dad

If divorced and remarried, you have moved on with your life, but most likely the children from the first marriage have not. They yet bear emotional wounds that will require much parental tender love and care and perhaps Christian counseling to be healed.

A child experiencing the pain of his parents' divorce says best what every child in his shoes needs from both parents for emotional healing, at least in part, to occur.

What I need from my mom and dad: A child's list of wants

~I need both of you to stay involved in my life. Please write letters, make phone calls, and ask me lots of questions. When you don't stay involved, I feel like I'm not important and that you don't really love me.

~Please stop fighting and work hard to get along with each other. Try to agree on matters related to me. When you fight about me, I think that I did something wrong, and I feel guilty.

~I want to love you both and enjoy the time that I spend with each of you. Please support me and the time that I spend with each of you. If you act jealous or upset, I feel like I need to take sides and love one parent more than the other.

~Please communicate directly with my other parent so that I don't have to send messages back and forth.

~When talking about my other parent, please say only nice things, or don't say anything at all. When you say mean, unkind things about my other parent, I feel like you are expecting me to take your side.

~Please remember that I want both of you to be a part of my life. I count on my mom and dad to raise me, to teach me what is important, and to help me when I have problems.[235]

Read Together:
He Reads: Isaiah 54:13
She Reads: Matthew 18:10

Answer Together:
From the child's viewpoint stated above, how important is it for your child to maintain contact with his dad/mother? For you to act with civility toward your child's dad/mother? Obviously there are rare cases (moral lifestyle issues) that may limit or negate such contact. In what ways can you address other emotional issues in your child's life stemming from the divorce?

Pray Together:
Lord Jesus, help us understand the emotional trauma that our child is experiencing, even though outwardly it is not visible, and take steps for its healing. Help us have grace to treat his absent *parent* with civility.

163
Home Buster—Adultery

An extramarital affair is an act to which no man or woman is immune. Many giants of virtue and integrity have been slain by this Goliath. Such giants would but testify that adultery was never intended, but due to a series of small steps (like phone calls, coffee at Starbucks, private meetings), it happened!

The counsel of the Apostle Paul is no more solemnly warranted than with regard to sexual infidelity. He cautions, "Let him that thinketh he standeth take heed lest he fall" (I Corinthians 10:12). The Message paraphrases the text, "These are all warning markers—danger!—in our history books, written down so that we don't repeat their mistakes. Our positions in the story are parallel—they at the beginning; we at the end—and we are just as capable of messing it up as they were. Don't be so naive and self-confident. You're not exempt.

You could fall flat on your face as easily as anyone else. Forget about self-confidence; it's useless. Cultivate God-confidence."

"The counterfeit pleasure of an affair," states David Boehi, "can never overcome the ways infidelity can destroy a life and marriage."[236] A king commissioned a painter and his apprentice to paint his portrait. The apprentice, fearful it would not be finished on time, sneaked into the palace and completed it. The king, viewing the painting the next morning, beheld a colossal disaster. The apprentice had ruined what was a beautiful portrait. Adultery may appear appealing, the thing to do in the short run; but it always results in colossal disaster to self, spouse, children, and one's walk with God.

If a person would ponder seriously the consequences of adultery, it would be a strong deterrent against it (infliction of pain upon spouse, self and children; horrendous guilt and shame; broken fellowship with God; possible divorce; possible that an unwanted child would be conceived in the unholy union; hurt inflicted upon the adulterous partner; injury to reputation/character; distrust it breeds in the faithful spouse for the unfaithful spouse; lengthy restoration process/counseling; children's lofty view of the adulterous parent soiled, perhaps forever; judgment and chastisement of God; loss of ministerial office/job/position). And with these, the list of adultery's devastating effects is only begun.

Now you see why I call adultery a *home buster*.

Heed the advice of Adrian Rogers: "The sin of immorality is not one we are instructed to fight. It is one we have been told to flee. Run from that compromising situation. Saturate that place with your absence"[237] (II Timothy 2:22); and that of Johnny Hunt: "When you allow your eyes to feast on the forbidden, the result will be great folly"[238] (James 1:13–15).

An added incentive to remain faithful to your spouse is the welfare of your children. Dr. William Doherty tells students and clients that he is convinced that "all things being equal, children need and deserve to grow up in a family of two parents who love them and love each other."[239] In agreement with Dr. Doherty, David Treadway calls divorce a lose-lose proposition.[240]

Read Together:
He Reads: Proverbs 6:20–29
She Reads: I Thessalonians 4:3; Deuteronomy 5:18

Answer Together:
What moral safeguards can you establish at work, social gatherings, and for Internet viewing? Discuss the consequences of adultery as cited, adding additional ones. How might you apply Dr. Rogers' advice?

Pray Together:
Heavenly Father, keep us from marital infidelity. Preserve our marital unity and purity. Help us flee the very first sign of adulterous temptation and not return to its path.

164 Accepting What Cannot Be Changed

David's baby was seriously ill, so he fasted and prayed unto God for the child's healing. The child died. Upon hearing the news, David took a bath, put on fresh garments, and went into the house of God and worshiped. Upon returning home, he broke his fast and enjoyed a good meal (II Samuel 12:20–21).

David's servants were puzzled, failing to understand how he so soon could return to some normalcy of life. David said,

"I fasted and wept while the child was alive, for I said, 'Perhaps the LORD will be gracious to me and let the child live.'

"But why should I fast when he is dead? Can I bring him back again? I will go to him one day, but he cannot return to me" (II Samuel 12:22–23).

By God's grace, David understood he had to accept that which could not be changed and not waste life away wishing that it could.

Even in the ideal marriage, devastating storms occur that sometimes result in things that just cannot be changed. Most certainly seek to restore that which has a possibility of restoration under God's guidance and power. For the other matters, accept the reality (as David did with the death of his son) that though horrendously difficult to bear, you must press on one baby step at a time, depending upon a loving and caring God and His people to sustain you. Gary Collins states, "The healthiest way to deal with some unexpected events or family shocks is to accept what cannot be changed."[241]

Though difficult to apply, the Apostle Paul instructs us in how to master the unchangeable. He states, "Brothers, I do not consider that I have made it my own. But one thing I do: forgetting what lies behind and straining forward to what lies ahead" (Philippians 3:13 ESV).

"We are to learn how to forget them," states George W. Truett. He continues, "When the sorrows come, we are to learn how to take these sorrows to the great, refining, overruling Master and ask Him to dispose, so to rule and overrule in them and with them that we may come out of them all refined and disciplined, the better educated and more useful, because of such sorrows. They tell us that when you break the oyster's shell at a certain place, it will go somewhere into the deep and find a pearl and mend that broken place in its shell with a beautiful pearl. Even so, when your sorrow in life comes, you are to learn how to take that sorrow and so have it woven into the warp and woof of your life that you shall not be weaker and worse for the sorrow, but shall be richer and stronger and better because of such sorrow."[242]

In a nutshell, Paul instructs the believer to forget past sorrows, troubles, losses, injuries, and sin consequences, changing what he can through God and burying the rest in the cemetery of eternal forgetfulness, steadfastly focusing on the future. The believer must be intentional in embracing this guidance at every juncture in marriage and parenting, ever believing that the best is yet to be.

Truett says, "Many a man goes hobbled and crippled through life and never does come to the highest and best, because he cannot forget certain things that ought to be forgotten by him."[243] Don't be such a person when help is available from God, Christians, and Christian therapists.

Read Together:

He Reads: Philippians 3:13–14
She Reads: Philippians 4:11

Answer Together:

Share an episode of life which could not be changed and how you got past it. What presently have you experienced that is unchangeable, and how are you coping? Discuss Paul's counsel with regard to dealing with the past and things that are unchangeable.

Pray Together:

"God grant me the serenity to accept the things I cannot change; courage to change the things I can; and wisdom to know the difference." (taken from the Serenity Prayer)

165 How to Stop Yelling and Start Connecting with Your Kids

Kids yelled at by parents are more likely to have depression and behavior problems, according to a new study in *Child Development Finds*. The finding but reveals what parents already know, that screaming at their kids is like thrusting a dagger in their heart. It pains them deeply.

Parents yell at their kids for two reasons.[244] The first is to endeavor to get them to listen when the gentle voice doesn't work. The ramping up of the volume is a reflection upon the parents' inability to cope with their child's behavior. Second, "many parents yell at their children because they can't control their own selves. When we are tired, irritated, and overwhelmed, yelling comes easily. We don't yell at coworkers, our boss, or even other adults. We take it out on the easiest targets: kids who know they shouldn't yell back. And that's just not fair."[245]

As parents, we ever need to remember that words hurt. Solomon tells us that "death and life [are] in the power of the tongue" (Proverbs 18:21). Choose carefully the words used and the manner in which they are spoken to your children.

Dr. Laura Markham says, "Parenting isn't about what our child does but about how we respond. Staying calm enough to respond constructively to all that childish behavior—and the stormy emotions behind it—requires that we grow too."[246]

When our buttons get pushed to the limit, we need to discipline ourselves to reflect, not just react. Doing this will signal loud and clear when there is loss of equilibrium and enable us to steer ourselves back onto a healthy response track.[247]

Read Together:

He Reads: Psalm 19:14
She Reads: James 3:5

Answer Together:

Honestly, are you a yeller? What adverse consequences will yelling at your children instead of conversing with them yield in their lives? How can you switch from being a yeller to a converser?

Pray Together:

Help our impatience, irritability or fatigue not be reflected in the tone of voice used in correcting our children, Lord. Help us control our anger instead of lashing it out upon our children.

166 Goals for the Home

You may set New Year's goals as many others do. But have you thought about setting goals for your family. Such goals obviously would evolve around the purpose of its establishment. It's good to write such goals down for periodical review to correct any drifting.

Seven Goals for the Home

* *Security.* Provision for the safety and financial welfare of the family.

* *Standards.* Implementation of a moral and spiritual compass (Bible).

* *Spirituality.* Development of an environment conducive to spiritual growth.

* *Stability.* Cultivation and preservation of a rock-firm marriage and family unit.

* *Support.* Embracing each family member's self-worth through enveloping him/her and his/her strengths or weaknesses with love and encouragement.

* *Submission.* Instruction regarding and practice of humbling oneself before Sovereign God to do as He says, when He says, where He says, and how He says.

* *Skills.* Helping your children develop foundational skills for life.

He Reads: Luke 14:28
She Reads: Proverbs 16:9

Review the seven goals cited for the home, discussing how each may be fulfilled. What additional goal(s) would you include?

Help us, Lord, establish our home upon healthy goals in keeping with Your purpose for it.

167

Relentless Teen Parenting

Teen parenting will necessitate much love, patience, fortitude, mercy, communication, understanding, and flexibility, for it is in the teen years that a child seeks to discover and manifest his own individualism, which often leads to his spending time with friends instead of parents and possibly rebelling.

Dr. Tim Sanford, in *Losing Control and Liking It,* states, "Your teenager is in the process of moving away from you. Therapists have a term for this: *developmental individuating.* It means your child is doing the following:

~disconnecting
~leaving the nest
~launching out
~becoming his own person
~growing independent
~becoming a free moral agent."[248]

Simply put, children in adolescence try their wings, which often involves tempering the close-knit ties they embraced in childhood (gradually friends will somewhat overshadow parents/grandparents). Parents/grandparents shouldn't take such a change personally or adversely. It is a healthy step toward the child's maturity emotionally and physically.

Within healthy spiritual and emotional boundaries, children must not be impeded from this "developmental individuating." Control what you can and endeavor to enable your child to control wisely what he demands is his to control. Granted, this is where parenting tension is keenly felt. Pray, pray, pray as you walk through this adolescence stage with your child.

The prodigal's father in Luke 15 loved his son enough to embrace him despite a rebellious lifestyle, keeping the door open for his return. Upon the boy's return, he granted mercy, forgiveness and complete restoration. In the event your child becomes rebellious, keep in mind this story and its happy ending. Never give up on your child's return, as exemplified by this father! The stress, heartache, and frustration experienced over a self-willed, rebellious child and the grace exhibited will be more than worth it when you come out on the other side victoriously (and you will!).

"Don't panic; stay on your child's team," states Dr. James Dobson, "even when it appears to be a losing team, and give the whole process time to work itself out."[249]

Read Together:
He Reads: Luke 15:11–24
She Reads: II Chronicles 33:9–13

Answer Together:
Hezekiah's son, Manasseh, rebelled against the Lord greatly (II Chronicles 33:2, 9). If one as rebellious as he was returned to the Lord, what hope does it offer for your child to do the same? What is developmental individuating, and what can you do to prepare for it? What attributes of the prodigal's father (Luke 15) toward his wayward son should be embraced by you toward your child?

Pray Together:
Heavenly Father, help us understand what is going on in our children's/grandchildren's lives when they seek to distance themselves from us somewhat so we won't demand to be the priority in their relationships. May we render unconditional love and acceptance as they wrestle with self-identity, values and interdependence issues.

168

Teaching Your Child the Ten Commandments

Your child needs to know and understand the Ten Commandments. Use your ten fingers to explain them simply and concisely (Exodus 20:1–17).

Hold up the index finger of the right hand to show that God is to be Number One in your life.

Hold up the second finger to show that there are not two gods; there is only One.

Hold up the third finger with the first two to form the letter *W* and show the need to watch our words.

Hold up four fingers with your thumb resting under them to show that Sunday is a day to rest.

Hold up five fingers like making a pledge to honor your parents.

Hold up the index finger of the left hand and use it as a gun shooting at the other hand to show that we shouldn't hurt others.

Hold out one hand flat and pretend it is a church floor. Place two fingers on this floor to show the need for a husband and a wife to be true to each other and keep their marriage vows.

Slightly press the four fingers of each hand together, forming a prison cell to show what happens if one steals.

Hold up five fingers on one hand and four on the other. Fold the thumb under the four fingers like it is hiding, and turn your hand around. The thumb is telling the four fingers on that hand hurtful things and lies about the five fingers on the other hand. The thumb is lying, and God tells us not to lie.

Hold out both hands, palms up, and wiggle each finger to show you have the "gimmies." They are saying, "I want what's yours, so give it to me." God wants us to be content and happy with what He chooses to give us.[250]

Read Together:

He Reads: Deuteronomy 11:19

She Reads: Deuteronomy 6:7

Answer Together:
Why is it important to instill in your child the Ten Command-ments? Practice the ten finger teaching approach with each other and then share it with your child.

Pray Together:
Lord, Your commandments are the foundation of morality that governs man's behavior toward others and Yourself. Help us do a good job in teaching these truths to our child and living them out before him.

169 Holding on Loosely to Those We Love

Shortly before her death, Corrie ten Boom gave Chuck Swindoll some loving words of admonishment about his family which he never forgot.

Swindoll states, "Following the worship service, I met briefly with her, anxious to express my wife's and my love and respect for her faithful example. She inquired about my family—how many children, their ages, that sort of thing. She detected my great love for each one and very tenderly admonished me to be careful not to hold on to them too tightly. Cupping her wrinkled hands in front of me, she passed on a statement of advice I'll never forget. I can still recall that strong Dutch accent: "Pastor Svendahl, you must learn to hold everyting loosely—everyting. Even your dear family. Why? Because da Fater may vish to take vun of tem back to Himself, und ven He does, it vill hurt you if He must pry your fingers loose." And then, having tightened her hands together while saying all that, she slowly opened them and smiled so kindly as she added, "Vemember, hold everyting loosely—everyting."[251]

Biblically sound counsel not only for Swindoll but for us. But heeding it is most difficult, especially when it comes to those we love deeply. It's hard to loosen our grip on our child, spouse or parent. "Releasing our rights to Him," Swindoll says, "includes the deliberate releasing of our grip on everything and everyone."[252]

Such is the crux of submission (surrender) to God. We hold loosely to the materialistic (temporal) and grip tightly the spiritual (eternal). Praying hands are not clinched but open. Ponder that symbolism. The believer in faith is to trust sovereign God with control of all he loves and cherishes. Forcing God to pry open your tight clutched fist which envelopes your spouse, child or grandchild only exacerbates the pain if he or she is taken home to Heaven.

Holding lightly doesn't mean we *view lightly* relationships, health or work. Not at all. We simply understand that they are transient and terminal and may be removed at any time (James 4:13–14).

Read Together:
He Reads: James 4:13–14
She Reads: Job 1:13–22

Answer Together:
Have you relinquished control of your child to the Lord, or are you yet keeping a tight closed grip about him? Holding lightly to your child involves "releasing our rights to Him." What does this statement of Swindoll mean?

Pray Together:
Lord, remind us that relationships (child, each other) and possessions are fragile and that their only security is placing them in Your loving and caring hands.

170 Second-Mile Secret of a Happy Marriage

First-century law allowed Roman soldiers to force the Jews to carry their backpacks for one mile but not a step further. Jesus urged the Jews to double the requirement set forth by the law. "And whosoever shall compel thee to go a mile, go with him twain" (Matthew 5:41). Undoubtedly many a soldier was won to Christ by a Christian going the extra mile.

E. J. Daniels states, "I can give you in one sentence one secret that will bring happiness to your marriage: GO THE SECOND MILE WITH EACH OTHER! Some wives say by their actions, 'I'm not going to do any more than I must do to stay married. If I can go around the house with my hair looking like the rats spent the night in it, I'll certainly not go to all the trouble of rolling my hair at night to make it look better. If I can serve bread or toast for breakfast, I'll certainly not cook biscuits. If I can get by with giving my husband a kiss in a coon's age, he certainly won't get more loving than that.'

"I'll tell you now, sister, you'll never make your husband a happy man. If you want to make him proud he married you and make a real go of your marriage, GO THE SECOND MILE. Make yourself just as pretty as you can and then 'pretty up the can!' Kiss him and love him when he wants you to and until he may not want you to. Then cook him biscuits, ham and eggs, and red-eye gravy for breakfast.

"I see some husbands smiling at their wives as if to say, 'He's telling you, Honey.' Let me tell you husbands something. You need to go the second mile also. Don't buy your wife just an Easter bonnet; buy her the entire outfit. Treat her with second-mile consideration, and she'll be a happy wife.

"You husbands and wives go home and do everything you can to make each other happy, and I'll guarantee you your honeymoon will be perpetuated. Now that you are married, keep on doing all of the things you did before you got married that made you want to get married, and I'll guarantee you that you will not want to get unmarried. Go the second mile with each other."[253]

Read Together:
He Reads: Matthew 5:38–40
She Reads: Matthew 5:41

Answer Together:
How does the principle of the "second mile" relate to marriage and parenting? What are some "second mile" stuff you can do for each other and your child?

Pray Together:
Help us, Lord, not be content with simply doing what is "required" in the marriage relationship but go the second mile.

171   Parent or Friend to Your Child

John Rosemond in *Because I Say So* states, "There's a time for being a parent and a time—a much later time—for being a friend. In trying to be both friend and parent, you will fail at both." Rosemond explains, "When the exercise of authority causes your child to become unhappy with you, as it often will, you will worry that you are destroying the friendship. As a consequence, you will be unable to take and maintain a firm stance on any issue."[254]

"A parent's responsibility," states Dr. Haim Ginott, "is not to his child's happiness; it's to his character."

The bottom line is that the better parent you are to your child until he becomes eighteen or nineteen, the better friends you will be later.[255]

Read Together:
He Reads: Proverbs 22:6
She Reads: Proverbs 1:8–9

Answer Together:
What is the rub when a parent tries to be both parent and friend while the child is yet young? Have you focused on being your child's friend instead of parent? Do you agree with the assessment that the better the parent you are now, "the better friends you will be later"?

Pray Together:
Heavenly Father, You have primarily given us our children to "parent." Help us not compromise that role by endeavoring foremost be their friend. Keep us mindful that the relationship of parent/child far exceeds that of parent/friend and is greatly more beneficial to the child.

172
Spankings
"Never use a cannon, when a water pistol will do."

John Rosemond suggests several things to keep in mind when spanking your child for disciplinary reasons.[256]

~The more the spankings, the less effective (child will be "immunized" by their frequency).

~They are generally more "useful" with excitable/active children.

~Use the hand only, and it to the child's "seat of knowledge."

~One or two swats are sufficient (purpose is not to beat the wrong out of the child).

~Never spank when enraged, overcome by anger.

Spankings are futile without suitable, immediate follow-through clearly expressing disapproval for their action.

Rosemond suggests

~Removal of an important privilege (like going outside remainder of day)

~Having the child apologize to offended person

~Making him go to bed early

~Sending him to a time-out zone, isolated from others for short time period

~If he is old enough, have him write the same sentence ("In the future, I will not scream when my parents tell me to something.") twenty-five or more times.[257]

The purpose of discipline is not pain but the child's correction through understanding of wrong and its disapproval.

Dr. James Dobson states, "A spanking is reserved for use in response to willful defiance, *whenever it occurs.* Period! It is much more effective to apply it early in the conflict, while the parent's emotional apparatus is still under control, than after ninety minutes of scratching and clawing."[258] (Dobson states that child abuse is more likely to occur when the child is permitted to irritate and agitate and sass and disobey and pout for hours until finally the parent reaches an explosive point.)

Read Together:
He Reads: Proverbs 29:15
She Reads: Proverbs 13:24

Answer Together:
For what time should spankings be reserved? Explain the meaning of the phrase, "Never use a cannon, when a water pistol will do." What is the purpose of punishment? Are you being effective with the *follow-through* after the spanking? If you choose to spank, when is its best time? At what point does discipline evolve into physical abuse, and how might it be avoided?

Pray Together:
Lord, help us discipline in tenderness and love, never going overboard with it.

173
Children Are Wet Cement

Dorothy Law Nolte illustrates the title of this entry in vivid terms in the poem, "Children Learn What They Live."

If children live with criticism, they learn to condemn.
If children live with hostility, they learn to fight.
If children live with fear, they learn to be apprehensive.
If children live with pity, they learn to feel sorry for themselves.
If children live with ridicule, they learn to feel shy.
If children live with jealousy, they learn to feel envy.
If children live with shame, they learn to feel guilty.
If children live with encouragement, they learn confidence.
If children live with tolerance, they learn patience.
If children live with praise, they learn appreciation.
If children live with acceptance, they learn to love.
If children live with approval, they learn to like themselves.
If children live with recognition, they learn it is good to have a goal.
If children live with sharing, they learn generosity.
If children live with honesty, they learn truthfulness.
If children live with fairness, they learn justice.
If children live with kindness and consideration, they learn respect.
If children live with security, they learn to have faith in themselves and in those about them.
If children live with friendliness, they learn the world is a nice place in which to live.[259]

Get the point? Every day we are impacting our child's character, emotional stability, servant spirit, values, relationships, self-esteem, and core beliefs by the life we live.

Harry Chapin, in the song "Cat's in the Cradle," vividly illustrates my point. Dad was always too busy for his son from infancy through college due to planes to catch and bills to pay. The final words of the song say,

"I've long since retired; my son's moved away.
I called him up just the other day.
I said, "I'd like to see you if you don't mind."
He said, "I'd love to, Dad, if I can find the time.
You see my new job's a hassle, and the kids have the flu,

But it's sure nice talking to you, Dad.
It's been sure nice talking to you."
And as I hung up the phone it occurred to me,
He'd grown up just like me.
My boy was just like me."

Read Together:
He Reads: II Timothy 2:15
She Reads: Philippians 3:17

Answer Together:
If your child turned out just like you, would such be commendable by the Lord? What negative traits in your life are molding him into someone you prefer him not to be? How may the negative traits be replaced with healthy, positive ones?

Pray Together:
Lord, help us envelop our child in the best possible environment in the home, and enable us to be worthy examples for him to imitate.

174 To Put Down or Build Up Your Child

Affirmations of your child ought to be given every day.

Sally Folger states, "Practice creative ways of affirming and uplifting [him]. This is essential. Attributing goodness by creatively visualizing [him] as achieving his goals and acting as if he is progressing ahead of his actual progress are helpful in giving [him] freedom to grow."[260]

Did you catch the technique of affirmation Folger suggests? You are to affirm your child not on actual progress but on a higher level which gives him the freedom to grow joyfully up to that level. Michael E. Kolivosky and Lawrence T. Taylor wrote, "Love them for what you are sure they will become. Blessed is the child whose parents' judgment is based on what the child will someday be."[261]

Anne Ortlund states, "Support—but don't push. Affirmations are not to make your child 'do things' faster. They are to give him emotional underpinnings for his life."[262] Ortlund continues, "Don't push—just affirm them. Give them the sense that all is well, that their rate of progress is acceptable to you, that you like them just the way they are.

That's how God loves you: 'just as you are.' And you're to 'accept one another just as Christ has accepted you' (Romans 15:7). Accept your child!"263

Read Together:
He Reads: I Thessalonians 5:11
She Reads: Proverbs 25:11

Answer Together:
Did you affirm your child today? In what way(s)? What are some possible affirmation statements which you may share with your child? How often in the course of a week do you affirm your child? (Seek to affirm once or twice daily. Don't overdo it.)

Pray Together:
Help us, Lord, be encouragers not discouragers unto our child. May our child ever see in us love and acceptance for him.

175
Nightmares and Bad Dreams Children Experience

Nightmares and bad dreams are often stimulated by insecurity (dad or mom away on business), fear of failure brought on by embarrassing experiences, or demands unachievable.264

Barbara Cook writes, "Sometimes we cause our children's bad dreams. We create insecurity and fear of failure by nagging and harsh, unloving insults. (You dumb kid! Can't you ever do anything right?) We've put too much pressure on the child or laid out too many threats of 'what's going to happen to him' if he doesn't shape up."265 Additionally, there are incidents that a child sees on television or in person in the course of a day that may trigger bad dreams or nightmares.

Bad dreams and their emotional effects may be prevented by ministering the peace of God to our child. "When mothers [dads} minister the peace of God to their children in the name of Jesus, that peace stands guard all night long; and their minds are free from disturbing influences, no matter what the source of those influences." Cook states that Philippians 4:7 cites a pattern to having the peace of God on guard continuously and that it includes learning to refuse to worry by telling God one's requests and by controlling what's put into the mind.

She continues, "A child's mind should be occupied not with negative thoughts or with ugly, repulsive things, but with those things that are true, honest, just, pure, lovely, and of good report, and with virtue and praise. If you teach a child to pray about his problems instead of worrying, and to discipline the material his mind feeds on, then you can claim the promise [and end most of the nightmares]."[266]

Betsy Brown Braun, a child development and behavior specialist and author of *Just Tell Me What to Say* and *You're Not the Boss of Me*, suggests that if your child is afraid to go to bed due to memories of the bad dream the night prior, the two of you draw a picture of the main "character" in the nightmare.

"A young child may need help to process what is real and what is not. As you draw, talk about the fact that the nightmare wasn't real. You may even want to tear the picture into little pieces, then throw it in the garbage or flush it down the toilet to reinforce the idea that the nightmare has gone away."[267]

Unshakeable security, wholesome television viewing and video gaming (applying the Philippians 4:7 principle), parental reasonable expectations and discipline, affirmations, and praying with your child at bedtime will dismiss to great measure bad dreams and nightmares. Make sure that the last moments of the day prior to bedtime are chock-full of positive impressions.

Night Terrors

Night terrors differ from nightmares in that they occur within the first few hours of sleep and without memory by the child as a rule. Nightmares occur in the second half of the night and are vividly recalled by the child.[268]

Night terrors are usually triggered by a fever, overtiredness or stress in children ages three to seven. Experts advise against awaking the child, for such generally leads to disorientation and distress. Brown Braun has this reassuring advice for parents:

"A night terror doesn't harm the child. It's the parents, not the child, who are traumatized by the experience! It's very important that the parent stays calm and uses calm, soothing tones to reassure the child. Even though your child may not seem to respond to you, your calming voice and presence will help him calm down and return to peaceful sleep."[269]

Read Together:
He Reads: Philippians 4:4–8; Proverbs 4:23
She Reads: Matthew 18:18; Psalm 34:4

Answer Together:
Does your child have repetitive nightmares/bad dreams to the point they awake crying or refuse to go to bed out of fear of them? Minister the peace of God unto them by having them share what they would like you to talk to God about in their behalf (bad dream, nightmare) and by instilling in them the principle of Philippians 4:7.

Pray Together:
Help us, Lord, identify the reasons for our child's bad dreams and nightmares and then do all possible to remove them.

176
The Shaping of Attitudes

Chuck Swindoll stated about attitudes, "We deal as severely with attitudes in our home as we do with actions. A sullen, stubborn spirit is dealt with as directly as an act of lying or stealing. The way you deal with your sons will, in great measure, determine how they will respond to the way God deals with them."[270]

How can parents shape the attitudes of their children? Attitudes are shaped by parental modeling for which there is no substitute.[271] It has been said, "The footsteps a child follows are most likely to be the ones his parents thought they covered up." If you are disrespectful to them, they learn to be disrespectful to others. If you are dishonest, they are prone to be dishonest. You can hardly expect your child to be kind, considerate of others, and appreciative if you are not. If you lie ("Tell them I'm not home"), how can you expect your child always to tell the truth. Children tend to mirror us.

Attitudes are also shaped by biblical instruction (respect, reverence, honesty, servant heart, selflessness, generosity, love, human dignity, responsibility, obedience, etc.).[272] Hear and heed the Word of the Lord as delivered to Moses for us: "These commandments that I give you today are to be upon your hearts. Impress them on your children. Talk about them when you sit at home and when you walk along the road, when you lie down and when you get up. Tie them as symbols on your hands and bind them on your foreheads. Write them on the doorframes of your houses and on your gates" (Deuteronomy 6:6–9).

"In other words," states Dr. James Dobson, "we can't instill these attitudes during a brief, two-minute bedtime prayer or during formal training sessions. We must live them from morning to night. They should be reinforced during our casual conversation, being punctuated with illustrations, demonstrations, compliments, and chastisement."[273]

Attitudes are abstractions that six- to eight-year-olds may not totally understand, so a system is needed to help clarify the target in his mind. Dobson has designed such a tool with the Attitude Chart. Daily the parent scores the child on attitude toward sibling, friends, dad, mom, work (household chores), and attitude at bedtime (the better the attitude, the lower the score). Points are tallied, and the child is rewarded (six points results in family outing; twenty points, he has to stay in room for an hour, etc.).[274]

Read Together:

He Reads: Deuteronomy 6:6–9
She Reads: Deuteronomy 4:9–10

Answer Together:

You have heard the expression, "He's a chip off the old block." What does it mean? What chips off the block of your life that are present in your child are negative and thus a deficit? What is the primary thing you must do to shape your child's attitude biblically? How can you implement the instruction of God stated in Deuteronomy 6:6–9?

Pray Together:

Lord Jesus, help us identify and rectify wrong attitudes in our life and diligently instruct our child in biblical values consistently and continuously throughout the day.

177

Are Fathers Necessary?

"Fathers are critical," states Adrian Rogers, "to both sons and daughters. Sons need fathers to learn about being a godly man: how to fear God (Proverbs 1:7), have self-control, work hard, and respect women, just to name a few. Try as she might, mom alone will be hard-pressed to teach a son these valuable lessons. For daughters, their entire self-image comes from how they are treated by their fathers. A woman's relationship with men will likely mirror her relationship with her father. The future of kids, regardless of gender, is firmly anchored in their relationship to their fathers."[275]

What a lofty responsibility we as fathers have in the spiritual and emotional formation of our children that will shape their entire life! Therefore, resolve not to be an absentee dad or workaholic dad or negligent dad. Rise up, O man of God, and firmly grasp your holy assignment with your children, doing it zealously and consistently. The hour may be late, but it's not too late to be the dad that impacts his children for the glory of God. The godly seeds sown in the soil of their heart presently will in adulthood blossom fully.

Read Together:
He Reads: Deuteronomy 11:18–21
She Reads: Proverbs 23:24

Answer Together:
Why is so much responsibility placed upon the father in the home with regard to parenting? What and who suffers when he shuns it?

Pray Together:
Lord, help me as a father diligently instruct our children in the things of God by example and precept.

178   "We're Five? No. We're Seven."

Wordsworth's poem "We Are Seven" is the story of a little girl describing to an inquirer how many were in her family.

A simple child that lightly draws its breath
And feels its life in every limb, what should it know of death?

I met a little cottage girl; she was eight years old, she said.
Her hair was thick with many a curl that clustered round her head.

She had a rustic, woodland air, and she was wildly clad.
Her eyes were fair, and very fair; her beauty made me glad.

"Sisters and brothers, little Maid, how many may you be?"
"How many? Seven in all," she said, and wondering looked at me.

"And where are they? I pray you tell." She answered, "Seven are we,
And two of us at Conway dwell, and two are gone to sea.

"And two of us in the churchyard lie, my sister and my brother;
And in the churchyard cottage, I dwell near them with my mother."

"You say that two at Conway dwell, and two are gone to sea,
Yet ye are seven! I pray you tell, sweet Maid, how this could be."

Then did the little maid reply, "Seven boys and girls are we;
Two of us in the churchyard lie, beneath the churchyard tree."

"You run about, my little Maid; your limbs they are alive.
If two are in the churchyard laid, then ye are only five."

"Their graves are green; they may be seen," the little maid replied,
"Twelve steps or more from my mother's door, and they're side by side.

"My stockings there I often knit; my kerchief there I hem;
And there upon the ground I sit and sing a song to them.

"And often after sunset, Sir, when it is light and fair,
I take my little porringer and eat my supper there.

"The first that died was sister Jane; in bed she moaning lay,
Till God released her of her pain; and then she went away.

"So in the churchyard she was laid; and when the grass was dry,
Together round her grave we played, my brother John and I.

"And when the ground was white with snow and I could run and slide,
My brother John was forced to go; and he lies by her side."

"How many are you, then," said I, "if they two are in Heaven?"
Quick was the little maid's reply, "O Master! we are seven."

"But they are dead; these two are dead! Their spirits are in Heaven!"
'Twas throwing words away, for still the little maid would have her will
And said, "Nay, we are seven!"[276]

The little girl was right. The Christian family is undivided, unbroken despite the departure of one of its members to Heaven.

W. A. Criswell says, "But oh, oh, oh—when I go to the house of sorrow and the shades are drawn and there's a hush and a quiet and there's a wreath on the door and I sit down with a beloved son or daughter or mother or father and they love God and their hearts are hid with Christ in the Lord (Colossians 3:3) and I open this Book and I read about those many mansions (John 14:2–3) and I read about that golden city (Revelation 21:10–11, 21) and I read about our raised and risen Lord and I read about the hope that we have in Him (I Corinthians 15:20–23), oh, sweet blessed comfort when I say, 'God's Book says it's better over there than it is here' (Philippians 1:23)! We have not lost. They have just entered into an inheritance that shall never pass away (I Peter 1:3–4), and we are following after, one family still—some of us there and some of us here. 'We're five? No. We're seven.'"277

Death only temporarily separates us from our deceased child; it cannot and does not dissolve the union or relationship. Sorrow indeed when a loved one dies, but sorrow not as those who have no hope.

Read Together:
He Reads: John 14:2–3
She Reads: I Corinthians 15:20–23

Answer Together:
Talk together about the biblical lesson Wordsworth presents in the poem "We're Seven."

Pray Together:
Lord, sustain and strengthen us in this horrendous hour of sorrow. Help us understand and fully believe that our child is safe in Heaven and awaits our arrival. Thank You for the irrefutable truth that despite his death, "We're five? No. We're seven."

179
A Marriage Prayer

Take your partner's hand and have someone read the following prayer or read it together. Periodically read it as a reminder of the commitment made unto each other and for marriage renewal.

Father in Heaven, thank You for this husband, _____, and wife, _____, and their commitment to Christian marriage. As we look ahead, we pray that their future will never lack the convictions that make a marriage strong.

Bless this husband, _____. Bless him as provider and protector. Sustain him in all the pressures that come with the task of stewarding a family. May he so live that his wife may find in him the haven for which the heart of a woman truly longs.

Bless this wife, _____. Give her a tenderness that makes her great, a deep sense of understanding, and a strong faith in You. Give her that inner beauty of soul that never fades, that eternal youth that is found in holding fast to the things that never age. May she so live that her husband may be pleased to reverence her in the shrine of his heart.

Teach them that marriage is not living for each other. It is two people uniting and joining hands to serve You. Give them a great spiritual purpose in life. May they seek first Your kingdom and Your righteousness, knowing that You will sustain them through all of life's challenges.

May they minimize each other's weaknesses and be swift to praise and magnify each other's strengths. Bless them and develop their characters as they walk together with You. Give them enough hurts to keep them humane, enough failures to keep their hands clenched tightly in Yours, and enough of success to make them sure they walk with You throughout all of their life.

May they never take each other's love for granted but always experience that breathless wonder that exclaims, "Out of all this world, you have chosen me." Then, when life is done and the sun is setting, may they be found then as now, still hand in hand, still very proud, still thanking You for each other.

May they travel together as friends and lovers, brother and sister, husband and wife, father and mother, and as servants of Christ until He shall return or until that day when one shall lay the other into the arms of God. This we ask through Jesus Christ, our Lord and Savior, the Great Lover of our souls. Amen.[278]

Read Together:
He Reads: Psalm 34:15
She Reads: Colossians 3:14–20

Answer Together:
What segments of the stated prayer need additional application by one or both of you?

Pray Together:
Father, may the prayer stated above be answered in each of us so our marriage will fulfill Thy heavenly design.

180

Sixty Affirmations to Make Your Child Feel Great

Most children are bombarded with far more put-downs from parents, siblings and peers than with "build-ups." As parents, monitor as you will, you can do little to control the negatives sown in your child's life by playmates. But there is much that you personally can do with the demeaning negatives you (perhaps unconsciously) hurl at him throughout the week. Understanding that demeaning comments and corrections injure the child emotionally, both presently and probably throughout life, parents need to consciously decide to use words that build up instead of tear down. Affirmations help a child internalize values, beliefs and attitudes that establish a healthy foundation for life.

Certainly affirmations may be overdone, so limit them to a couple or so a day to *each* child.

Sixty Affirmations

1. I love you.
2. I am so proud of you.
3. Just you and I are going to hang together today.
4. That's okay; I spill things too.
5. I am happy God gave you to us.
6. I forgive you and will not bring the matter up again.
7. You are so handsome/beautiful.
8. Forgive me for yelling at you. I am asking God to keep me from doing that again.
9. You are Mom's/Dad's big helper.
10. You are such a smart guy/girl.
11. I believe in you.
12. I know you can do it if you try.
13. Where did you learn to do that? You amaze me with things you do.
14. Even if you really disobey me, my love for you will remain unchanged.
15. I love your dad, and he loves me, and we both love you.
16. Thank you for being so good at the store. Others told me that you acted like a young man/woman, which made me so proud of you.
17. Pappa said you behaved excellently at his house.

18. You are growing up so fast.
19. You are the apple of God's eye.
20. You are such a great big sister to your brother. You are helping him so much to grow.
21. Tonight we are camping out in your bedroom and will "party."
22. There's no way that I ever could love your brother/sister more than you.
23. Even grown-ups break things.
24. I love you to the moon and back.
25. You matter to God.
26. Yes, you can have a snack.
27. You can spend the night with Pappa and Nanna.
28. What do you want Daddy/Mommy to do with you on Saturday?
29. We thank God so often that you are a part of our family.
30. You have some great talents/gifts that excite me.
31. That shirt/dress looks sharp on you.
32. I like your hairstyle.
33. I trust you.
34. You are so strong.
35. You are special. God says you are fearfully and wonderfully made.
36. I know it wasn't your fault.
37. Of all the children in the world, we would choose you.
38. Let's have a man-to-man talk.
39. What do you want to do on vacation?
40. You are Mommy's protector.
41. (Lay down the cell phone) You are more important than who I was talking to.
42. (Upon coming home from work, hug him first thing) I can't tell you how much I missed you.
43. Would you say the mealtime prayer?
44. God watches over you as you sleep, so there is no need to be afraid.
45. You are so brave.
46. You can do that better than I can.
47. I know you can.
48. You have friends who like you a lot.
49. God has wired you with a lot of energy.
50. You have wonderful imaginations.
51. You are full of happy thoughts.
52. You are so compassionate.

53. You brush your teeth so well.
54. You soak in knowledge.
55. You are a bright student.
56. Everything is going to work out just great.
57. You just keep growing every day.
58. You are a winner with God on your side.
59. You are safe.
60. I love you more than all the water in the ocean.

In addition to speaking words of affirmation to your child, try occasionally writing an affirmation on bright-colored posters with various crayon colors. Place the posters in the home, lunch box, car seat, overnight bag, etc.

Understand, I am not at all suggesting a child not be punished for wrong, but that even that correction should be tempered with affirmation ("Daddy loves you more than you will ever know, but he has to punish you for what you did"; "Mommy knows that most of the time you obey, but you didn't this time, so I have to punish you.").

Read Together:
He Reads: I Thessalonians 5:11
She Reads: Psalm 139:14

Answer Together:
What affirmations did you share with your child today? Why not set this book down and share one now?

Pray Together:
Lord, it is so easy in the moment of fatigue, frustration and hurriedness to snap out a demeaning comment to our child. Help us learn to get composure before we speak and be more mindful of speaking words of affirmation. Just as You share them with us in Your Word, help us share them with our child.

[1] http://www.azquotes.com/quote/726273, accessed March 26, 2016.

[2] http://www.prisontalk.com/forums/archive/index.php/t-636863.html, accessed March 26, 2016.

[3] http://fiercemarriage.com/quote-author/j-i-packer, accessed March 26, 2016.

[4] http://www.brainyquote.com/quotes/topics/topic_family.html, accessed March 27, 2016.

[5] www.whatchristianswanttoknow.com/inspirational-christian-quotes-about-raising-children/#ixzz448zWuxj2, March 27, 2016.

[6] http://tonyevans.org/tony-evans-on-the-christian-family, accessed March 17, 2016.

[7] Chapman, Gary. *Covenant Marriage*

[8] Arp, David and Claudia. *The Second Half of Marriage*

[9] Parrot, Les and Leslie. *Your Time-Starved Marriage*

[10] Morgan, R. J. (2000). Nelson's Complete Book of Stories, Illustrations, and Quotes (electronic ed.). (Nashville: Thomas Nelson Publishers), 535.

[11] http://www.whatchristianswanttoknow.com/christian-quotes-about-family-28-great-saying/#ixzz448rVaDm7, accessed March 27, 2016.

[12] Arterburn, Stephen. *The 7-Minute Marriage Solution*

[13] http://billygraham.org/story/how-to-appreciate-an-imperfect-spouse, accessed March 3, 2016.

[14] Ibid.

[15] MacArthur, John. *Truth Matters,* 172.

[16] https://www.gty.org/Resources/Print/Blog/B150427, accessed March 3, 2016.

[17] Janis Long Harris as cited in Collins, Gary. *Family Shock,* 173.

[18] Holmen, Mark. *Building Faith at Home.* (Ventura, CA: Regal Books, 2007), 173.

[18] MacArthur, John. *Truth Matters,* 172.

[18] Holmen, Mark. *Building Faith at Home.* (Ventura, CA: Regal Books, 2007).

[19] Ibid., 32.

[20] Mahan, Frederick. *God Alone Is the Truth and the Way.*

[21] https://www.insight.org/resources/daily-devotional/individual/marital-grace1, accessed March 25, 2016.

[22] Spurgeon, C. H. *The Soulwinner.* (New Kensington, PA: Whitaker House), 1995, 251–252.

[23] Havner, Vance. *Pepper 'N Salt,* 49.

[24] MacArthur, John. *The MacArthur New Testament Commentary: Romans, Vol. 1.* (Chicago: Moody Press, 1991), 473.

[25] Ibid.

[26] Rice, John R. *God in Your Family.* (Murfreesboro, TN: Sword of the Lord Publishers, 1971), 57.

[27] Ironside, H. A. "Lesson 49: Do You Really Love Your Wife? Part 1 (Ephesians 5:25-33)." https://bible.org/book/export/html/22068, accessed December 21, 2013.

[28] Lloyd-Jones, Martyn. *Life in the Spirit.* (Grand Rapids: Baker Book House), 137–138.

[29] Criswell, W. A. *Criswell Study Bible,* 1 Kings 21:25.

30 Pruneville.com, "Jokes and Quotes," http://www.pruneville.com/jokesandquotes/cleanjokes/ (accessed January 19, 2016).

31 Arterburn, Stephen. *The 7 Minute Marriage Solution.*

32 https://www.gty.org/resources/print/positions/P01, accessed February 20, 2015.

33 Barclay, W., Ed. *The Daily Study Bible Series,* Galatians and Ephesians. (Philadelphia, PA: The Westminster John Knox Press, 1976), 178.

34 McGee, J. V. *Thru the Bible Commentary* (electronic ed.) (Nashville: Thomas Nelson, 1997), Eph. 6:4.

35 Spence-Jones, H. D. M., Ed. *The Pulpit Commentary,* Ephesians. (London; New York: Funk & Wagnalls Company, 1909), 257.

36 http://www.whatchristianswanttoknow.com/21-powerful-christian-marriage-quotes/#ixzz3g5dON18f, accessed July 16, 2015.

37 http://www. .com/21-powerful-christian-marriage-quotes/#ixzz3g5h1bTut, accessed July 16, 2015.

38 http://www.whatchristianswanttoknow.com/21-powerful-christian-marriage-quotes/#ixzz3g5tUzAHg, accessed July 16, 2015.

39 Cloud, Henry and John Townsend. *Rescue Your Love Life*. (Nashville: Thomas Nelson, 2005), 161.

40 http://www.huffingtonpost.com/2013/11/20/divorce-causes-_n_4304466.html, accessed March 5, 2016.

41 http://www.psychalive.org/communication-between-couples, accessed March 5, 2016.

42 Ramsey, Dave. *The Truth About Money and Relationships.*

43 Ibid.

44 Ibid.

[45] Chapman, Gary D. from the Todayschristianwoman.com article, "Balancing Your Money Mindset."

[46] Faulk, Timothy. "Marriage: The Perfect Design," pdf., undated. Personal correspondence, April 17, 2016, 5.

[47] http://fiercemarriage.com/quote-author/billy-sunday, accessed March 26, 2016.

[48] Arterburn, Stephen. *Walking into Walls.*

[49] Piper, John. "Kill Anger Before It Kills You or Your Marriage," http://www.desiringgod.org/articles/kill-anger-before-it-kills-you-or-your-marriage, April 23, 2003. Accessed July 20, 2015.

[50] http://www.christianity.com/christian-life/christian-living-faq/how-should-i-deal-with-my-anger-11555743.html, accessed March 5, 2016.

[51] Ibid.

[52] Piper, John. "Kill Anger Before It Kills You or Your Marriage," http://www.desiringgod.org/articles/kill-anger-before-it-kills-you-or-your-marriage, April 23, 2003. Accessed July 20, 2015.

[53] David and Vera Mace, quoted in Wright, H. Norman. *The Pillars of Marriage.*

[54] Rice, John R. *God in Your Family,* 75.

[55] http://www.azquotes.com/author/20251-John_R_Rice, accessed March 26, 2016.

[56] http://fiercemarriage.com/quote-author/john-macarthur, accessed March 26, 2016.

[57] Rogers, Adrian. "Seven Secrets of Lasting Love." http://www.oneplace.com, accessed July 21, 2015.

[58] Morgan, R. J. (2004). *Nelson's Annual Preacher's Sourcebook.* (Nashville, TN: Thomas Nelson Publishers, 2004 Edition), 29.

[59] Smalley, Gary. *I Promise You Forever*. (Nashville: Thomas Nelson Publishers, 2007), 15–17; 42–45; 54–55; 62–63. (The author formulated the statements under each promise)

[60] Castillo, Stephanie. How To Get Over Rejection. http://www.prevention.com/mind-body/emotional-health/tips-handling-rejection, accessed August 16, 2014.

[61] https://en.wikipedia.org/wiki/Love_means_never_having_to_say_you%27re_sorry, accessed July 25, 2015.

[62] Rice, John R. *The Son of God*. (Murfreesboro, TN: Sword of the Lord Publishers, 1976), 233.

[63] http://nypost.com/2013/10/16/the-key-to-a-happy-marriage-is-a-shared-bank-account, accessed March 28, 2016.

[64] Dave Ramsey. "Ask Dave," www.daveramsey.com/index.cfm?event=askdave/&intContentItemId=119752, accessed August 10, 2015.

[65] Ibid.

[66] Piper, John. "Marriage Is Meant for Making Children," Disciples of Jesus, Part 1, June 10, 2007.

[67] Piper, John. *Staying Married Is Not About Staying in Love*

[68] Dr. Michelle Borba. "7 Tricks to Help Stressed Moms Chill Out." http://www.today.com/parents/7-tricks-help-stressed-moms-chill-out-1C7397996, accessed January 21, 2016.

[69] Ibid.

[70] Ibid.

[71] "Collection Captures Eddie Martin's Innovative Soul-winning Methods." www.bpnews.net/bpnews.asp?id=15248. Accessed April 9, 2010.

[72] Criswell, W. A. *The Criswell Study Bible*, Job 1: 12.

[73] Faulk, Timothy. "Marriage: The Perfect Design," pdf., undated. Personal correspondence, April 17, 2016, 8.

[74] Wheat, Ed, M.D. *Love Life.* (Pyranee Books, Zondervan Publishing House, 1980) 27–28.

[75] Faulk, Timothy. "Marriage: The Perfect Design, pdf., undated. Personal correspondence, April 17, 2016, 8.

[76] Crabb, Dr. Larry. *Men and Women.* (Grand Rapids: Zondervan, 1993), 134.

[77] Adams, Jay. *Christian Living in the Home.* (P & R Publishers, 1972), 13.

[78] Spurgeon, C. H. *Come Ye Children.* (Ross-Shire, Scotland: Christian Focus Publications, 1994), 101, 103.

[79] "Causes of Divorce," http://www.drjamesdobson.org/, accessed March 4, 2016.

[80] Criswell, W. A. *The Criswell Study Bible*, Proverbs 13: 24.

[81] Chambers, Oswald. *My Utmost for His Highest,* January 7.

[82] http://gracequotes.org/author-quote/john-macarthur/page/3/, accessed March 26, 2016.

[83] Rogers, Adrian. "Tuning Up Tired Marriages," https://www.lwf.org/articles/posts/tuning-up-tired-marriages-10556, accessed February 17, 2016.

[84] Leary, Mike. "The 20 Most Common Parenting Mistakes, According to a Family Psychologist," www. Babble.com, accessed February 20, 2016. [The author adapted six of the twenty mistakes stated.]

[85] Dobson, James. *"The New Dare to Discipline."* (Grand Rapids: Tyndale House, 1992).

[86] Fairchild, Mary. "The Healing Power of Laughter," http://christianity.about.com, accessed August 11, 2014.

[87] Ibid.

88 www.creativehealthsecrets.com/overcome-stress-part-3-laugh-often/, accessed February 20, 2016.

89 http://christianity.about.com/od/topicaldevotions/qt/laughtertherapy.htm.

90 http://www.snopes.com/music/songs/precious.asp, accessed February 20, 2016.

91 Dobson, James. http://www.drjamesdobson.org/articles/family-love/couples-devotion-february-18-22, accessed February 21, 2016.

92 Source unknown.

93 Walton, Charlie. *When There Are No Words.* (Ventura, California: Pathfinder Publishing, 1999), 50–51.

94 Ibid, 51.

95 Emery Nester. www.wordchimes.com/blog/?id=1675, accessed March 31, 2013.

96 Spurgeon, C. H. *Faith's Checkbook,* November 16.

97 Graham, Billy. *Till Armageddon.* (Waco, TX: Word, 1981), 186.

98 Laurie, Greg. "T.H.I.N.K," blog.greglaurie.com/?p=2990, January 28, 2010.

99 Stanley, Charles. *Landmines in the Path of the Believer.* (Nashville: Thomas Nelson, 2007).

100 Lewis, C. S. *Promises and Prayers,* 87.

101 Graham, Billy. *The Journey.* (Nashville: W Publishing Group, 2006), 265.

102 Dennis Rainey as cited in Collins, Garry. *The Family Shock,* 247.

103 Graham, Billy. *Breakfast with Billy Graham: 100 Daily Readings.* (Ann Arbor, MI: Servant, 1996), 72.

[104] http://billygraham.org/decision-magazine/november-2014/raising-children-in-a-godless-age/, accessed February 22, 2016.

[105] Hutson, Curtis, Ed. *Great Preaching on Fathers.* (Murfreesboro, TN: Sword of the Lord Publishers, 1989), 95–96.

[106] Gallozzi, Chuck. "Saddest Words." www.personal-development.com/chuck/saddest.htm, accessed October 16, 2011.

[107] Coleman, Joshua. "How Parents Can Start to Reconcile with Estranged Kids," August 25, 2010. http://greatergood.berkeley.edu/article/item/how_parents_can_start_to_reconcile_with_their_kids, accessed October 11, 2014.

[108] Ibid.

[109] Faulk, Timothy. "Marriage: The Perfect Design," pdf., undated. Personal correspondence, April 17, 2016, 22.

[110] Kleinfeld, Judith. "Parental Favoritism Does Long-Term Damage," *Fairbanks Daily News-Miner Community Perspective*, March 15, 2015.

[111] Ibid.

[112] Ibid.

[113] Dobson, James. "What Wives Wish Their Husbands Knew about Women," (Tyndale Momentum, October 1, 1981), http://drjamesdobson.org/blogs/dr-dobson-blog/dr-dobson-blog/2015/08/09/men-women-and-aging, accessed February 25, 2016.

[114] http://fiercemarriage.com/quote-author/zig-ziglar, accessed March 26, 2016.

[115] http://www.lightsource.com/ministry/love-worth-finding/articles/marriage-duel-or-duet-12897.html, accessed February 27, 2016.

[116] Spurgeon, C. H. "The Death of the Christian," (The New Park Street Pulpit, September 9, 1855), http://www.spurgeon.org/sermons/0043.htm, accessed April 2, 2013.

[117] MacArthur, John. *Safe in the Arms of Jesus.* (Nashville: Thomas Nelson, 2003), 133–134.

[118] Dobson, James. "Helping Children Deal with Death," http://drjamesdobson.org/blogs/dr-dobson-blog/dr-dobson-blog/2015/12/18/helping-children-deal-with-death, accessed February 28, 2016

[119] Ibid.

[120] Dobson, James. "Causes for Divorce," http://drjamesdobson.org/, accessed March 4, 2016.

[121] MacArthur, J. F. *The Freedom and Power of Forgiveness* (electronic ed.). (Wheaton, IL: Crossway Books, 1998), 97.

[122] Crockett, Kent. *The 911 Handbook.* (Peabody, MA: Hendrickson Publishers, 2003), 43.

[123] ten Boom, Corrie. *The Hiding Place.*

[124] Lewis, C. S. *A Grief Observed.* (New York: HarperOne, 2001), 15.

[125] Ibid., 65–66.

[126] Spurgeon, C. H. "No Tears in Heaven." August 6, 1865. http://www.biblebb.com, accessed April 1, 2013.

[127] Barclay, William, Ed. *The Daily Study Bible Series,* Timothy, Titus, and Philemon. (Philadelphia: Westminster John Knox Press, 1975), 248–249.

[128] MacArthur, John. *In the Footsteps of Faith: Lessons from the Lives of Great Men* (electronic ed.). (Wheaton: Crossway Books, 1998), 7.

[129] http://www.marriagementoring.com/faq, accessed March 2, 2016.

[130] http://www.focusonthefamily.com/marriage/strengthening-your-marriage/mentoring-101/marriage-mentoring, accessed March 2, 2016.

[131] Ibid.

[132] C.H. Spurgeon, "Beauty for Ashes." http://www.spurgeon.org/sermons/ 1016.htm, accessed August 11, 2014.

[133] Cohn, Andrea, and Andrea Canter, Ph.D. "Bullying: Facts for Schools and Parents." NASP Fact Sheet. Accessed February 9, 2014 http://www.nasponline. org/resources/factsheets/bullying_fs.aspx.

[134] The National Education Association. "Nation's Educators Continue Push for Safe, Bully-Free Environments." NEA. Accessed February 10, 2014, http://www.nea.org/home/53298.htm.

[135] Cohn, Andrea, and Andrea Canter, Ph.D. "Bullying: Facts for Schools and Parents." NASP Fact Sheet. Accessed February 9, 2014, http://www.nasponline. org/resources/factsheets/bullying_fs.aspx.

[136] Coughlin, Paul. "A Faith-Based Response to Adolescent Bullying." http:// www.cbn.com/family/parenting/coughlin_bully1.aspx, accessed July 29, 2014.

[137] Mayer, Bill, Gen. Ed., *Help, My Child Is Being Bullied*. (Carol Stream, Illinois: Tyndale House Publishers, 2006), 8.

[138] Ibid.

[139] Swindoll, Chuck. *Growing Strong in the Seasons of Life*. (Grand Rapids: Zondervan, 1994], 61.

[140] *Herald of His Coming*, Seelyville, IN, Vol. 75, No. 2, 8.

[141] Thompson, Lynne. "Hope for the Separated," http://www. focusonthefamily.com, accessed August 12, 2014.

[142] Ibid.

[143] http://fiercemarriage.com/quote-topic/divorce, accessed March 26, 2016.

[144] Dobson, James. "Causes of Divorce," http://www.drjamesdobson.org/, accessed March 4, 2016.

145 Rogers, Adrian. "Seven Secrets of Lasting Love," LWF.org, accessed November 23, 2011.

146 Keller, Timothy. *The Meaning of Marriage.* (Dutton Adult Publishers, 2011), 132.

147 Wright, H. Norman. *More Communication Keys for Your Marriage.* (Ventura, CA: Regal Books, 1983), 123–124.

148 Faulk, Timothy. "Marriage: The Perfect Design," pdf., undated. Personal correspondence, April 17, 2016, 44.

149 Read more at http://www.relevantmagazine.com/life/relationships/5-biggest-areas-conflict-couples#DgSy0l6O0lcY6hIF.99, accessed March 7, 2016.

150 Sproul, R. C. *The Intimate Marriage.* (Phillipsburg, New Jersey: P & R Publishing, 2004), 103–110. (Sproul gives reasoning for calling these myths in this work.)

151 Barclay, William, Ed., The Daily Study Bible Series, James and Peter. (Philadelphia: Westminster John Knox Press, 1976), 219.

152 Strobel, Lee. *The Case for the Real Jesus.* (Zondervan: Grand Rapids, 2007), 13.

153 Criswell, W. A. "Honoring God in the Home," (June 9, 1989). http://www.wacriswell.org/index.cfm/FuseAction/Search.Transcripts/sermon/566.cfm, accessed March 8, 2016.

154 Collins, Gary. *Family Shock,* 27.

155 Ibid.

156 "Prayer and Intercession Quotes," www.tentmaker.org.

157 Rice, John R. *God in Your Family.* (Murfreesboro, TN: Sword of the Lord Publishers, 1971), 23–24.

[158] http://www.whatchristianswanttoknow.com/inspirational-christian-quotes-about-raising-children/#ixzz448wFOtbz, accessed March 27, 2016.

[159] Lloyd-Jones, Martyn. *The Christian Soldier.* (Grand Rapids: Baker, 1977), 179.

[160] Young Ladies Christian Fellowship. "Overview of Spiritual Gifts." ylcf.org/you/spiritual-gift/overview/, accessed December 5, 2011.

[161] "Spiritual Gifts Chart." www.preceptaustin.org/spiritual_gifts_chart.htm, accessed December 6, 2011.

[162] "Discerning and Using Your Spiritual Gift." www.olivetbaptistokc.com/subpage18.html, accessed December 5, 2011.

[163] Piper, John. "Spiritual Gifts," March 15, 1981 (Morning), Bethlehem Baptist Church. www.soundofgrace.com/piper81/031581m.htm, accessed December 6, 2011.

[164] Rogers, Adrian. "How to Have a Meaningful Quiet Time." Lwf.org, accessed March 12, 2011.

[165] Contributed by Dr. Nina Gunter, who got it from veteran missionary, Louise Robinson Chapman (Africa: 1920–1940).

[166] Whitney, Donald. *How Can I Be Sure I'm A Christian?* Foreword.

[167] Sproul, R. C. *Essential Truths of the Christian Faith*. (Wheaton: Tyndale, 1992), 32.

[168] Rogers, Adrian. "How Do I Know If I'm Saved?" lwf.org, accessed June 16, 2011.

[169] *Focus on the Family Bulletin,* December, 1988.

[170] Collins, Gary. *Family Shock,* 21.

[171] Human Development and Family Department at the University of Nebraska-Lincoln.

172 Curran, Delores. *Traits of a Healthy Family*. (Minneapolis: Winston Press, 1983).

173 http://www.brainyquote.com/quotes/topics/topic_family.html, accessed March 28, 2016.

174 http://www.newsmax.com/FastFeatures/billy-graham-quotes-family-positive/2014/12/26/id/615146, accessed March 28, 2016.

175 "Christian Churches: Pornography Statistics Addiction & Industry," www.archomaha.org/pastoral/se/pdf/PornStats.pdf, accessed October 17, 2011

176 http://www.ligonier.org/blog/what-does-coram-deo-mean, accessed March 15, 2016.

177 "Mel Trotter Delivered from Booze." chrisfieldblog.com/2009/01/19/mel-trotter, accessed September 30, 2012.

178 Faulk, Timothy. "Marriage: The Perfect Design," pdf., undated. Personal correspondence, April 17, 2016. The author adapted the four points of PREP cited, 59–60.

179 Ibid.

180 Ibid.

181 Spurgeon, C. H. "Do Not Sin Against the Child" (sermon # 840). http://www.spurgeongems.org/vols13-15/chs840.pdf, accessed March 17, 2016.

182 Ibid.

183 www.whatchristianswanttoknow.com/christian-quotes-about-family-28-great-saying/#ixzz448tx8L00, accessed March 27, 2016.

184 Eble, Diane. "The Warning Signs of the Suicidal," Campus Life, VL (October, 1986), 18.

[185] *Suicide Awareness, Prevention, Intervention and Counseling—An Action Plan.* (Rochester, Minnesota: The National Suicide Help Center, 1987), 20.

[186] cited by Charles A. Twardy, "Suicide: The Preventable Death." (Columbia, South Carolina: The State, March 21, 1989), Section B, 4.

[187] Faulk, Timothy, personal correspondence, December 15, 2012.

[188] Ibid., (bracket content added)

[189] Collins, Gary. *Family Shock.* (Wheaton, Ill: Tyndale House Publishers, 1995), 85.

[190] Hutson, Curtis. *Great Preaching on Fathers.* (Murfreesboro, TN: Sword of the Lord Publishers, 1989), 142.

[191] Burns, Alisa and Cath Scott, *Mother-Headed Families and Why They Have Increased.* (Hillsdale, NJ: Erlbaum and Associates, 1994), p. xiii.

[192] U.S. Census Bureau, Current Population Reports, 20–537, Table CH-5. (Washington, D.C.: U.S. Census Bureau, 2001).

[193] Popenoe, David. "Life without a Father," 1997. DOCUMENT RESUME, http://files.eric.ed.gov/fulltext/ED416035.pdf, accessed March 20, 2016.

[194] Ibid.

[195] https://thefathercode.com/the-9-devastating-effects-of-the-absent-father/, accessed March 20, 2016.

[196] Ibid.

[197] Dobson, Dr. James. "Boys Need Fathers," http://www.charismamag.com/life/men/16874-dr-james-dobson-boys-need-fathers, accessed March 20, 2016.

[198] http://www.christianpost.com/news/51331/#rvgriPZjx5K0ARym.99, accessed March 20, 2016.

[199] Ibid.

200 Ibid.

201 "Quotes on Gambling Addiction," www.encognitive.com/node/24, accessed November 21, 2011.

202 Ibid.

203 MacArthur, John. "Gambling: The Seductive Fantasy, Part I," (GC 90-164), www.biblebb.com/files/MAC/90-164.HTM, accessed March 5, 2011. [This sermon depicts the biblical reasons why gambling is a sin]

204 National Gambling Impact Study Commission (NGISC) Final Report, June 1999, 7–27, http://govinfo.library.unt.edu/ngisc/reports/7.pdf (August 26, 2008).

205 National Opinion Research Center at the University of Chicago (NORC). "Gambling Impact and Behavior Study: Report to the National Gambling Impact Study Commission," (Chicago, Ill., 1999).

206 http://www.focusonthefamily.com/socialissues/family/gambling/gambling-cause-for-concern, accessed March 21, 2016. The previous two endnotes also were cited here.

207 National Council on Problem Gambling. "Ten Questions About Gambling Behavior," www.robertperkinson.com/teen_gambling.htm, accessed March 5, 2011.

208 The Sword of the Lord, June 6, 2014, 4.

209 http://www.beliefnet.com/columnists/on_the_front_lines_of_the_culture_wars/2011/08/church-kids-are-less-likely-to-divorce-or-live-in-poverty.html, accessed March 22, 2016.

210 Ibid.

211 MacQueen, Neil. http://sundaysoftware.com/site/the-life-benefits-of-church-membership, accessed March 22, 2016.

[212] http://www.beliefnet.com/columnists/on_the_front_lines_of_the_culture_ wars/2011/08/church-kids-are-less-likely-to-divorce-or-live-in-poverty.html, accessed March 22, 2016.

[213] Ibid.

[214] Willke, John C. (President, National Right to Life of Greater Cincinnati). *Abortion—Questions and Answers.* (Cincinnati, Ohio: Hayes Publishing Co., 1988).

[215] "What Does the Bible Say about Abortion?" www.gotquestions.org/ abortion-Bible.html, assessed October 15, 2011.

[216] "The Bible and Abortion," Heritage House Literature. www.abortionfacts. com/literature/literature_9410cv.asp, accessed October 15, 2011.

[217] Rogers, Adrian. "Foundation for the Family" (sermon). http://www.lwf.org/ site/News2?abbr=for_&page=NewsArticle&id=6801, accessed July 2, 2014.

[218] Ibid.

[219] Whiteman, Thomas with Randy Petersen. *Starting Over.* (NaviPress, 2001).

[220] https://www.biblegateway.com/devotionals/night-light-couples/2016/04/ 19, accessed March 23, 2016.

[221] http://www.foryourmarriage.org/how-materialism-harms-a-marriage, accessed March 23, 2016.

[222] Ibid.

[223] http://abcnews.go.com/Health/AlzheimersCommunity/pat-robertson- alzheimers-makes-divorce/story?id=14526660, accessed March 24, 2016.

[224] http://www.more.com/relationships/marriage-divorce/how-marriage- survives-when-one-partner-gets-sick?page=2, accessed March 24, 2016.

[225] Ibid.

[226] Ryrie, Charles. *A Survey of Bible Doctrine.* (Chicago: Moody Publishers, 1972).

[227] Smalley, Gary. *Five Secrets of a Happy Marriage. Seven promises of a Promise Keeper.* (Colorado Springs: Focus on the Family, 1994.) adapted.

[228] Ann Landers' column, February 11, 1994. "Blaming Mom and Dad."

[229] Mark R. Lassar as cited in Collins, Garry. *Family Shock,* 272.

[230] Ibid.

[231] Ibid.

[232] Ibid., 274.

[233] Ibid., 272-273.

[234] Chuck Swindoll. "Sexual Abuse," http://www.insight.org/resources/topics/sexual-abuse, accessed October 21, 2014.

[235] Source: University of Missouri. http://www.helpguide.org/mental/children_divorce.htm, accessed August 12, 2014.

[236] http://www.familylife.com/articles/topics/marriage/troubled-marriage/infidelity/40-consequences-of-adultery (Feb 7, 2015), accessed June 9, 2016.

[237] Rogers, Adrian. *Adrianisms: The Wit and Wisdom of Adrian Rogers,* vol. 1. (Memphis: Love Worth Finding, 2006), 114.

[238] Hunt, Johnny. "Joseph's Temptation," Sermon Search [online, cited June 9, 2016]. Available from the Internet: www.sermonsearch.com.

[239] Collins, Gary. *Family Shock,* 215.

[240] Ibid.

[241] Ibid., 370.

[242] Truett, George W. *A Quest for Souls.* (New York and London: Harper & Brothers Publishers, 1917), 49.

[243] Ibid, 47.

[244] Meeker, Meg. "Are You a Yeller?" http://drjamesdobson.org/blogs/dr-meeker-blog/dr-meeker-blog/2013/10/11/are-you-a-yeller, accessed June 18, 2016.

[245] Ibid.

[246] Markham, Dr. Laura. *Peaceful Parents, Happy Kids.* (TarcherPerigee; unknown edition, November 28, 2012), xx.

[247] Ibid.

[248] Sanford, Tim. *Losing Control and Liking It.* (Colorado Springs, CO: Focus on the Family, 2009).

[249] http://drjamesdobson.org/popupplayer?broadcastId=5403fdae-2d54-4fd1-a678-b0e3c57cc810, accessed June 21, 2016.

[250] Adapted from www.firstpresby.org/past300.htm, First Presbyterian Church in Pitman, New Jersey.

[251] http://www.insight.org/resources/article-library/individual/holding-on-loosely, accessed June 22, 2016.

[252] Ibid.

[253] Daniels, E. J. *Fervent, Soul-Stirring Sermons.* (Orlando, FL: Daniels Publishing, 1971), 65–66.

[254] Rosemond, John. *Because I Say So.* (Kansas City: Andrews and McMeel, 1996), 86.

[255] Ibid.

[256] Ibid, 81. The author adapted the first four and added the fifth.

[257] Ibid.

[258] Dobson, James. *Dr. Dobson Answers Your Questions.* (Carmel, NY: Guideposts, 1982), 157.

[259] http://www.noogenesis.com/pineapple/Kristone.html, accessed June 24, 2016.

[260] Ortlund, Anne. *Children Are Wet Cement.* (Old Tappan, NJ: Fleming H. Revell Company, 1981), 59.

[261] Ibid, 60.

[262] Ibid, 61.

[263] Ibid, 64.

[264] Cook, Barbara. *How to Raise Good Kids.* (Minneapolis, Minnesota: Bethany House Publishers, 1978), 128.

[265] Ibid.

[266] Ibid, 129.

[267] Wilson, Catherine. http://www.focusonthefamily.ca/parenting/school-age/a-cry-in-the-night-dealing-with-nightmares-night-terrors-and-more-73501304, accessed June 24, 2016.

[268] Ibid.

[269] Ibid.

[270] Lessin, Roy. *How to Be Parents of Happy and Obedient Children.* (Medford, OR: Omega Publications, 1978), 81. (quoting Charles R. Swindoll in *You and Your Child*)

[271] Dobson, James. "How to Shape Attitudes," http://drjamesdobson.org/Solid-Answers/Answers?a=63dc2a64-a70a-43f1-8d5a-cc43c8e77abc, accessed June 25, 2016.

[272] Ibid.

[273] Ibid.

[274] Ibid.

[275] Rogers, Adrian. https://thedailyhatch.org/2013/07/16/adrian-rogers-are-fathers-necessary/, accessed June 25, 2016.

[276] Wordsworth, William. "We are Seven," 1810.

[277] Criswell, W. A. "The Family of God," http://www.wacriswell.com/sermons/1957/the-family-of-god/, accessed June 25, 2016.

[278] Adapted from Dr. Louis H. Evans' "Marriage Prayer for Bride and Groom," http://proverbs31.org/devotions/devo/a-wedding-prayer-a-marriage-prayer/#sthash.qGmCGKWA.dpuf, accessed June 25, 2016.